Peter P. Ja

The Magazine Article

How to think it, plan it, write it

Indiana University Press
Bloomington • Indianapolis

The paper used in this publication meets the minimum requirements of American National Standard for Information Sciences—Permanence of Paper for Printed Library Materials, ANSI Z39.48-1984.

Manufactured in the United States of America

Library of Congress Cataloging–in–Publication Data

Jacobi, Peter.
    The magazine article: how to think it, plan it, write it / Peter P. Jacobi.
        p.   cm.
    Originally published: Cincinnati, Ohio: Writer's Digest Books, c1991.
    Includes index.
    ISBN 0-253-33265-6 (cloth: alk. paper). — ISBN 0-253-21111-5 (pbk.: alk. paper)
        1. Authorship—Marketing—Handbooks, manuals, etc. 2. Feature writing—Handbooks, manuals, etc. 3. Technical writing—Handbooks, manuals, etc. 4. Journalism—Authorship.   I. Title.
PN147.J25 1997   96-47073
808' .02—dc21

        3   4   5   02   01   00

*To all my students of writing
who through the years
have taught me so much.*

Contents

About the Author

Peter P. Jacobi is professor of journalism at Indiana University and formerly was professor and associate dean of the Medill School of Journalism, Northwestern University.

He is a consultant for magazines, a specialist in speech coaching and media training, and author of several books including *Writing with Style, the News Story and the Feature* and *The Messiah Book: The Life and Times of G.F. Handel's Greatest Hit.* He's an arts critic and freelance writer whose credits include *Folio, The Ragan Report, The Christian Science Monitor, Highlights for Children, The Chicago Daily News, The New York Times, Saturday Review,* and *World Book.*

Currently he serves also as music critic and Sunday columnist for the Bloomington (Ind.) *Herald Times* and as arts commentator for *Arts Indiana.* He is chairman of the Indiana Arts Commission.

His background also includes editing a music magazine and network news activities at ABC and NBC.

A Prefatory Note

The plan is mine. So are the propositions and bridges of instruction. This is, however, a show versus tell book. The proof of instruction comes through examples culled from dozens of different publications.

My objective has been to teach by model rather than by preaching. One can theorize, and that's basic. One can explain, and that's helpful. But when practitioners show how they have solved a problem or handled a possibility, learning becomes direct through illumination.

The Magazine Article: How to Think It, Plan It, Write It is not an anthology. But is has become, in part, a collection of bits and pieces. I gratefully acknowledge the always well-considered and sometimes brilliant manipulation of words and information by those article writers represented in the following pages. And the poets, too.

May your reading be congenial and beneficial.

Peter P. Jacobi

The Motivation — The Obligation

MY FATHER'S SHIRT

I used to joke about being my father, I
used to say I'll just give up and become my father,
but now there is no one else to be him —
a week after his death I open my suitcase
and pull out of it, slowly, as if
drawing a limp blue and white child out at birth,
his shirt his wife gave to me, and it
still smells of going to him,
opening his door and there from his chair he
rises slowly, such a big man in such
dark pants, with such a shiny face, such
dark eyes. The smell of mold is the
smell of the world under the rug and
beneath my father's skin now,
behind his eye. I put on the shirt and my
breasts look absolutely terrific in it and I
smell so wonderfully green with mold — let the
second half of my father's life begin,
let him find happiness as a woman.

— Sharon Olds

WEARING MY SON'S SHIRT

Looking for something to wear
in the garden, I put on
my son's oversized shirt. I feel
like a soul trying on a body.

This one's too large, but I like
the coolness of breezes under
my collar and cuffs. I like
believing that I can expand

in any direction. Just now
I was billowing, buoyant, a flag
flapping over the melons. I thought
birds' wings, but it was the shirt

trailing in parsley. I feel
like my son must, coming out
on the porch, seeing someone wearing
his shirt, unsure who I am.

— Patricia Hooper

Poetry can delight. Poetry can heighten and deepen. Poetry can assuage. Poetry can teach. Good poetry not only can, but does. Good poetry causes ideas to take flight and language to soar. It makes minds receptive.

So it is or can be with magazine articles. The good ones can and do delight, heighten, deepen, assuage, teach. They cause ideas to take flight and language to soar. They make minds receptive.

It is from poets and their poetry that those who seek to succeed at the art of article writing can learn valuable lessons. Eight, to be exact, including:

1. Mind opening and perspective freshening
2. Creativity
3. Willingness to experiment
4. Clarity
5. Imagery
6. Rhythm
7. Compression
8. Excitement

Let's expand:

Lesson 1. Mind opening and perspective freshening. Sharon Olds and Patricia Hooper took an ordinary object, a shirt. Olds' exploration of death makes the shirt synonymous with grief becoming continuity. Hooper's celebration of life makes it synonymous with continuity becoming joy. The sensitive reader of either poem will not think of its subject, whether death or life, quite the same way again. The reader's mind will have been opened to a new way of thinking, to a fresh perspective. What has been done with a shirt in two beautifully provocative poems can be done with the subject you, the writer of a magazine article, choose to tackle. Strive to develop your subject and use language so adeptly that, potentially at least, the reader will gain a fresh understanding. Just as the poet works for that to happen, so should you.

Lesson 2. Creativity. The two poets were not content to write of feelings about the absence of a father or the presence of a son in the all-too-familiar ways. They sought to honor father and son with creative approaches, with new meanings for long-standing relationships. Creativity isn't always make-believe. It's making the most of a subject.

Consider whether you've done so. Just as the poet works to be inventive, to be original, so should you.

Lesson 3. Willingness to experiment. Poetry thrives because of experimentation with language and method. The same old way has never been acceptable to the poet. Just as the poet seeks to experiment, so should you.

Lesson 4. Clarity. Though the approach may be individual or even strange, the poet strives to be clear. Good poetry has a clarity that extends from theme through every chosen word. Only that word is selected which serves best. To say something exactly the way it should be said: that's what the poet works toward, and so should you.

Lesson 5. Imagery. The times are visual. Our world is visual. Increasingly, we are tied together by images—on film, in video, through the environment in which we live our lives. Poets long ago became aware of the power in sight. They transmogrified that physical sight into emotions, into material for the mind. They gave words visual dimensions. They sought words that evoked images. They still do, and as they do, so should you.

Lesson 6. Rhythm. A sense of motion and of pattern and of flow that poets bring to language causes us to continue the act of reading, propels us forward while offering comfort and continuity. Despite the changes in twentieth century poetry, the element of rhythm remains a constant; it remains a poetic necessity. As the poet considers it a requirement, so should you.

Lesson 7. Compression. Poets seek to say what must be said as sparingly as possible, to waste no words lest they interrupt the movement of the language or disrupt the meaning. Good poetry says much in little space. And as the poet struggles to squeeze information and ideas, so should you.

Lesson 8. Excitement. Olds and Hooper wrote quiet poetry, but exciting poetry. The sifting of their experiences through imagination results in words that lift the spirit and exalt the reality of existence. They make ordinary objects extraordinary. They make normal relationships special. They stir reaction. They stir excitement. And so should you.

Poets look for the significance in people and objects and places and events and, of course, ideas. So should the writer of magazine articles. That attitude of the poet—to make a subject not more than it should be, but the most it can be—would be a fine beginning. Attitude.

The American teacher and poet Edward Weismiller once noted: "The artist breaks up the world of fact by making us see comparisons, analogies, meanings that we never saw before. They lead to nothing, of course, except our own deeper understanding of ourselves and of the rest of humanity." It is in the realm of the magazine article that writers and editors undertake that tricky shift from fact into meaning.

Poetry is fiction, after all. The article is nonfiction. But as the poet and, indeed, the prose writer of fiction strive to give the reader a heightened feeling of reality and actuality while handling material that is not literally, "true," so the article writer, using information that is actual and factual, should offer the reader a transcending sense of awareness about the subject at hand. Through an article the writer reveals a subject and its world, exploiting that subject so that every touch of tension or romance or excitement or intrigue, of information sharing and meaning is utilized. The subject is so thoroughly explored, so artfully verbalized, that the reader can savor it, be immersed in it, fully understand it, and remember it.

To accomplish this, you need to grasp fully the techniques of fiction and nonfiction, of poetry and journalism. And to harbor the attitude.

THE ATTITUDE

"Easy as pie," writes Sue Hubbell in *The New Yorker.* "It's easy to make good, tasty, comforting, serviceable pie. Of course, excellent pie is harder to make, and harder to find, but excellence is always rare. The Shaker Lemon Pie served at Shaker Village of Pleasant Hill, near Harrodsburg, Kentucky, is an excellent pie." And off she goes on "The Great American Pie Expedition." A subject is what you make of it. The poet knows this. The writer of the magazine article should. It's a matter of attitude. Subjects aren't boring, but bored writers can make them so. Subjects aren't small, but small-minded writers can reduce them to minuscule proportions.

There's nothing bored or small-minded about Florence de Dampierre. Her subject for *House and Garden* (August 1989) is a particular antique, a lowly one:

> As Marie Antoinette was being sped through the cobblestone streets of Paris toward the place de la Concorde and her miserable end, revolutionary guards were busy compiling an inventory of her belongings. What they discovered among the expected heaps of ball gowns, baubles, and master craftsmen furniture was a painted table composed of tin. That this humble object had fallen into such sophisticated hands testifies to the extraordinary popularity of *tole peinte*, a technique developed in the seventeenth century for finishing utilitarian metal goods.
>
> Originally a poor man's decoration, of the same ilk as today's mugs, snow globes, and other airport ephemera, tole quickly shot up in status thanks to its ornamental appeal. Trays finished with a glossy layer of varnishlike paint became a convincing and affordable knockoff of Oriental lacquer.

The writer has made her subject important, at first to herself, then to her reader. A subject is what you make of it. Need another example? "A woman we know writes," the editor of *The New Yorker's* "The Talk of the Town" (September 1984) tells us:

My house is situated on the border between the village of East Hampton and the village of Amagansett. Every day except Sundays and holidays, the East Hampton noon whistle blows, and then, after an interval that seems to vary between a few seconds and a minute, depending on the wind on any given day, the Amagansett noon whistle blows. I like to imagine that each village has its own noon, and that each part of the universe runs on its own time. In any case, the whistles have identical voices. The sound begins with a low siren, which is almost immediately joined by a deep trumpeting, like a foghorn, and which swoops up the scale until it reaches a piercing soprano blast as the bass note of the horn is dying away, and then, solo, descends the scale and fades. Quiet follows, as if a hole had been made in the day. After a while, the birds resume their chatter. The volunteer fire departments of the two villages also use the whistles as alarms, so their call has to be loud enough to penetrate everywhere. But their sound at midday is not unpleasant. It is just the noon whistle, as familiar as the day. If I have been away for a time, occasionally upon my return I am briefly surprised by the low opening note from East Hampton, and a slight feeling of urgency passes over me: It's an alarm. Then I remember that it is just the noon whistle. Like a reassuring echo, the Amagansett whistle soon follows.

At noon in August, the sun is almost at its highest point in the smooth, pale sky. At that moment, the dome enclosing the day seems to open and dilate, with the sound of the whistles rising to make its escape. The call goes out to people working in the fields and nurseries, repaving the lanes, hammering nails into shingles, hauling in the fishing nets. I don't think the noon whistle speaks to the tennis players and the golfers and the ice-cream-devouring strollers and the vacationers sunning themselves on the beaches. Rather, the noon whistle is a reminder of work and its respite. When it sounds, the reaping and the mowing and the hammering and the shovelling stop, and there is silence for about half an hour.

I think of the noon whistle, too, as a wake-up call. You, weeding your tomato patch, wake up! You, carrying the sacks of groceries into the house from the car, you are alive! The top of the day is open at the center! Sometimes when I hear the whistles, I stop whatever I am doing for a moment. Often I notice my hands then, and it is as if I had never seen them before or felt the working of their muscles. They are usually in the midst of performing a task—hefting a trowel, shifting a bicycle gear, tearing a lettuce leaf, pulling up a weed—that my attention had all but abandoned. The whistle summons me back to myself, to witness my work and the life of my hands.

Unaccountably, on some days I do not hear the whistle at all. I am sure it sounds, but it is not present to me. On other days, when I am more alert than usual, I feel what it must be like to be the noon whistle: pure sound, all sound, unmuddled, the ultimate resolution always known, a predictable blending of tones, rising from the lowest to the highest register, penetrating everywhere, entering every ear, crossing the fields and woods, passing through the hedgerows, following the direction of the wind, floating along the beaches, making all things one thing, ordering the time, framing the silence.

Here is poetry in prose. Here we find the lessons of the poet: that fresh perspective, the compression, that clarity, that imagery, that sense of excitement about an idea. Actually, that idea started as another lowly subject, a siren. The writer has enlarged that all-too-ignorable item into an essay that makes me think not only about why I haven't been paying attention to noon whistles but about such matters as where significance originates and about the perceived "down" moments of my life that shouldn't be considered so and about the power of observation when keenly used.

Attitude. If you have no enthusiasm for a subject to be undertaken, don't bother to undertake it. Chance becomes slim that you'll reach a reader. Communication becomes unlikely.

Two lessons are essential: (1) There is no captive audience, and (2) no message is a must for any audience.

Writers believe the opposite because they've worked so hard on their stories that they tend to tell readers, "Damn it, read." When by chance I happen to be around someone paging through an issue of a magazine or newspaper in which I have a piece, I watch carefully and anxiously. My hope is that this someone will perk up on discovery of my work and read it and smile and nod in comprehension or approval. If, oh life's dark moment, that someone skims the page or, worse yet, leafs past it, I want to pounce on that nonreader of my grand efforts and say, "Turn back. You've missed my article. Your life will be emptier for it. Turn back. Turn back." I don't even want to consider that maybe I just haven't done enough to entice the reader. Yes, perhaps the subject doesn't appeal, causing the reader to pass my article by. But even that could be my fault.

Unfortunately, as a writer for journalistic media I cannot try what author Anthony Burgess did when he "was teaching Shakespeare at City College . . . in New York—all of three hundred students at 8:00 a.m." He explains: "I decided to teach them something about how Shakespeare was educated. I began to write three lines of Seneca in Latin on the blackboard to show where Shakespeare learned about rhythm, and they started to walk out. Well, I wasn't going to let them get away. I rushed to the door and locked it, saying 'You're going to learn these bloody lines of Latin whether you like it or not.' "

I cannot lock my audience in a room, nor can you. Worse yet, we cannot force the audience to "listen" to us. Through our enthusiasm for facts and language we can try. The job is ours to captivate the audience by proving every moment along our shared way that what we have to offer is of interest or importance. No story has a divine right to be read.

I was reminded of this by a sign on the bedside table of my room at the Governors Inn in Research Triangle Park, North Carolina:

INSTRUCTIONS FOR GUESTS PREPARING TO

SMOKE IN BED

1 CALL THE OFFICE and notify the management where you wish your remains sent, as it is a matter of record that 42% of Hotel and Motel Fires are caused by this careless practice.

2 NOTIFY GUESTS in adjoining rooms of your intention of endangering their lives so that they may take necessary precautions to protect themselves.

3 GO TO THE CORRIDOR and locate the nearest fire escape, so that if you are fortunate enough to escape your room, you may reach safety.

4 NOW SIT DOWN and think how foolish it is for you to take this risk – you may enjoy your smoke while thinking it over.

FIRE PREVENTION is our business and we need your help. We hope you will take this with you on your trip as a reminder that this short message was heeded by you.

> Governors Inn
> P.O. Box 12168
> NC 54 & I-40 at Davis Drive
> Research Triangle Park, NC 27709

Please understand that I don't smoke. Understand also that I don't particularly care whether folks in rooms next to me or across the hall smoke. The subject of the sign, important as it is, doesn't hold much excitement for me. Nor, I would imagine, for others, including those who smoke. And that's where the sign comes in. It takes a ho-hum subject and turns it into something special, something noteworthy.

Guaranteeing Reader Satisfaction

Readers need to be enticed. They need to be understood, too. Always, before undertaking a project, consider the audience. If, for instance, the subject is some aspect of hockey, then you must determine if the readers will be sports enthusiasts or hockey professionals or mothers who might oppose their youngsters' participation in the sport or would-be coaches of little league teams or the children themselves or aging amateur athletes who seek a way to remain active or a general public. Articles must cater to readers in terms of information, angle, and language.

Ponder what your potential readers will want and not want, need and not need, expect and not expect, understand and not understand. Editors will remind you. By then, however, it may be too late. You'll have committed considerable time and energy to a project that doesn't fit its audience. Think through the character of your audience first. All that follows will not be easier, but victory—a sale, a pleased editor, satisfied readers—becomes more likely.

Help yourself also with one more thought about those people out there you're trying to reach, a lesson presented with elegant simplicity in an advertisement sponsored periodically by *Good Housekeeping*. Let the first three paragraphs of that ad suffice to make the point:

> In the year 2077, when the travel-weary passenger on the moon-shuttle has had his fill of: dinner on the anti-gravity magnetic tray, three-dimensional TV, intergalactic weather reports and conversational banter with the flight attendants as they float by—he'll then settle back in his contour couch, and return to that important, private activity each of us does alone. *Reading.* (It will be, we trust, a magazine.)
>
> The act of reading is essentially a process of thinking. It has scan and scope beyond any camera—as you have just demonstrated on the cosmic screen of your own mind. It is a concentratively individual act. An involvement. The reader makes the printed communication happen . . . releases the magic that causes words on a page to leap into living thoughts, ideas, emotions.
>
> And no matter how many millions may be on the receiving end of the message, it is addressed to, and received by *individuals*, one at a time—each in the splendid solitude of his or her own mind. There, the silent language of print can whisper, rage, implore, accuse, burst into song, explode into revelation, stab the conscience. Or work a healing faith.

Take note, please, of that third paragraph. Whether by millions or thousands or hundreds or dozens of readers, the words you write are read in solitude. The reader at that moment doesn't know about any other reader. Or care. He or she faces your words as a singular individual. One on one. *Good Housekeeping* titles its ad "Some Thoughts About a Magazine's Tremendous Audience of One." That is the size of your audience. Don't consider "readers" (plural) but "*a* reader" (singular). Keep that one reader in your mind's eye as you write. Consider the young woman seeking career advice from your article about more successful job interviewing, or the retired golf fanatic, open to your suggestions for challenging courses to play.

Penny Ward Moser had a reader in mind when she wrote "Are Cats Smart? Yes, at Being Cats" for *Discover* (1987), a publication for the layman interested in science. *Discover* readers tend to be college educated and thus bring at least a touch of sophistication to reading. So, Moser writes:

> One morning, after a round of counter bounce, refrigerator bump, food plop,

and tail slam, I took a long look at my cat. I was going off to work. He was going off to nap. I was already frantic about half a dozen things. He had been staring into the void for half an hour. "You know, Izzy," I said, "you're either very smart or very stupid."

If you ask how intelligent an animal is, those who study such matters shy away from answering. They'll beat around the bush for a while, then ask what you mean by intelligence. I didn't know what I meant by it when I began trying to find out about the goings-on in Izzy's head. I guess I just wanted to know if a housecat is really aloof and mysterious, as some would have us believe, or if it is, as I perceive, a sort of fur-covered mobile meat loaf that has become the perfect sycophant.

"How smart is a cat?" muses Randall Lockwood, animal behaviorist, cat owner, and cat expert at the Washington headquarters of the Humane Society of the U.S. "A cat is very smart at being a cat. Does it better than anybody." Animal behaviorists tend to boil it down to something like this: If you asked your cat to play chess, he would seem pretty stupid. But if your cat asked you to race up a tree, leap to a rain gutter and catch a sparrow in flight, you wouldn't seem too bright, either.

It's tough to judge cats. Here we are with our three-pound brains and one hundred billion neurons packed into our skulls, trying to figure out a critter with a one- to two-ounce brain and perhaps ten billion neurons. If Izzy were to grow to my size, his brain would be about one-third the size of mine.

Moser understood what sort of reader she would need to attract. She kept that in mind as she developed her article. Like other successful writers, she undoubtedly built the article through a four-step process.

THE FOUR-STEP PROCESS

This process, which will be amplified in the following chapters, involves: (1) idea, (2) information gathering, (3) organizing, and (4) writing. Not a word should be written until you have thoroughly taken care of the preceding three steps. Without an idea firmly in place, you're likely to wallow through all sorts of extraneous material and along misdirected paths. The idea may take a different shape once you pursue your task, but without that initial thrust of concept, you're likely to spin your wheels unnecessarily.

How much easier, for instance, to gather information if you've given yourself a sense of direction and established the boundaries of your coverage. You'll know more clearly what to look for in the library, which documents are of use, what people you should talk to as well as what questions to ask, what situations to observe.

Without unneeded information, you'll find organization easier. A structure for the presentation of your material will become evident. A plan, an order will be suggested.

And the writing, although never easy, becomes a bit less of a chore, a more bearable and possibly even somewhat pleasurable experience.

Preparation is a key to better and less painful writing. The more you accomplish during the first three steps of the writing process, the less odious that fourth step—the writing itself—turns out to be.

A Self-Editing Checklist

As you maneuver through the four steps, keep in mind a baker's dozen of words, all beginning with the letter "C" and all, if heeded, destined to make you more popular with your reader.

Be Correct. A journalist learns early the importance of accuracy. The teacher in a basic newswriting course or a boss on the first day of a new job will remind the writer that a misspelled name or an incorrect address means an F or a scolding. Those of us who write for the journalistic media must remember that readers may want to use what we tell them. One reader may want to write to the person whose name we've misspelled. Another may want to attend the meeting for which we've provided the wrong street and number. The first reader is made to look the fool and thereby perhaps ignored. The second misses an inspiring lecture that might have changed her life.

A good editor, of course, may spot the error. He'll also wonder whether to trust you again, if now.

To insure the probability of correctness, follow these suggestions:

1. *Check information against at least two sources.* If both sources agree on a fact, you're probably safe in using it. If they disagree, better go to a third and fourth source, consider which providers seem to be most authoritative, and make a reasoned decision.

2. *Find a friend or trusted family member or colleague to read your manuscript.* Don't trust yourself to be the only checker-editor of an article before you submit it. Two or three sets of eyes improve the odds that what you turn in is error free.

3. *Give your second and third readers separate, clean copies of your manuscript.* Don't let your edits influence the others. Untouched manuscripts bring closer attention from those you're counting on to find mistakes.

4. *Be your own backup.* If you can find no one to back you up, become your own backup. That requires you to complete the article several days before deadline and to leave it alone while you engage in other mind-involving activities. That way you'll distance yourself from your previous involvement with the article and come to it again with renewed vision.

Be Clear. Without clarity, does anything else matter?

Clarity depends on words, sentences and grammar, flow, and structure. The English language is huge and unwieldy. Too many word choices are available to us who would use it. Keep your audience in mind. Keep poor reading habits and limited capabilities in mind. In the May 1989 issue of *Writer's Digest*, writer Richard Lederer argues:

> Short words are as good as long ones, and short, old words—like *sun* and *grass* and *home*—are best of all. More small words than you might think can meet your needs with a strength, grace, and charm that large words don't have.
>
> Big words can bog down: one may have to read them three or four times to make out what they mean. Small words are the ones we seem to have known from the time we were born, like the hearth fire that warms the home.
>
> Short words are bright like sparks that glow in the night, moist like the sea that laps the shore, sharp like the blade of a knife, hot like salt tears that scald the cheek, quick like moths that flit from flame to flame, and terse like the dart and sting of a bee.

Lederer used only one-syllable words to make his point about simplicity. To write simply can be difficult. Try to create your own essay in short words. It takes considerable thought and discipline.

Write for your audience. Don't write down. Be careful about writing up. But always write for. Simpler words are not to be shunned.

And beware of four word problems:

1. Euphemisms. If an information source tells you the company "will lose 400 workers" during the next six months, don't let him get away with it. Workers can be dismissed, fired, laid off. Companies rarely lose workers. That's a softened word for a harder reality. It's dishonest. So is "education transport module" when "school bus" is more to the point. "Negative patient care outcome" means death of patient as well as death of clarity. Keep language honest; avoid euphemisms.

2. Jargon. If you must use jargon, make sure it really serves as a code word known to everyone in the readership. If you cannot be sure, then at least insinuate the meaning of the word in the sentence that follows it. Remember also that jargon tends to be tired language, even cliché. Use it with care, if at all.

3. "Status symbol" words and expressions. You can make your own list, but some examples would be: symbiosis, synergism, paradigm, infrastructure, *quid pro quo*, replication, explication, post-industrial society, recidivism. Too many readers don't really know what these words mean. They may have an inkling, but they don't really know. You tend to use them because they're the "in" words, the ones which suggest you have professional status. The reader, in the midst of your article, lapses into semi-understanding, maybe semiconsciousness. In this stuporous state, even were a dictionary by his side, he'd not be inclined to use it. So the message gets lost or at least fuzzed. Achieve your status through clearer writing; don't use status symbol words.

4. Thesaurusitis. This is a disease all too many writers fall prey to. Hold down on your search for synonyms. More often than not, the word already in your head is the better one.

And if simplicity of words is desirable, then so is simplicity of sentences. Most of us aren't terribly good at writing good, long sentences. If we write not-so-good long sentences for not-so-good readers, confusion sets in—fast. The reader forgets by midsentence what the root of the sentence was.

"As the day wound on," the writer wrote, "in almost record-setting late-October chill, with darkness surrounding Memorial Stadium, and with Iowa being terribly stubborn about accepting the victory most Indiana fans had considered achieved when the score reached 35-3—for all those reasons, mostly the latter, the TV timeouts ABC took met growingly louder and more negative reactions from the crowd that stood once above fifty-two thousand but somehow, curious in view of the wild activity going on in a 45-34 game, dwindled to something surely closer to thirty-five thousand by the early-evening finish." An NCAA record-setting ninety-two words, but this record would lose fans rather than gain them.

Just remember that the heart of our language is still the simple sentence. Build around it.

Good grammar is a must, like good spelling and good pronunciation. "The National Weather Bureau has issued their ninety-day forecast" is not good grammar. Savvy editors know and will lose confidence in everything else you've prepared. Should you get past an editor, the readers you most want to reach will lose confidence. They'll decide that if you can't be trusted to get the basics right, you can't be trusted with facts.

Clarity depends also on flow, on your ability to put information together so that readers know at every point where they are, where they've been, and where they seem to be going. When we read, our minds work in linear fashion. We cannot grasp jumps and jerks or even the sudden shifts of scene that we experience without problems while watching a television drama. We have to be moved carefully, smoothly through the article.

Transitional words alone will not suffice; you must be certain that the ideas behind those words of transition fit together. "But" is sometimes a splendidly useful word to slide a reader from sentence to sentence. So is "however." Phrases like "let's put that into perspective" or "the larger picture would suggest" can be helpful. They're helpful if they describe a real connection between thoughts. If linkage is weak, you'll lack transition despite the use of transitional words. There must be connective informational tissue. Words do not create transition. Ideas do. Words serve only as tools.

Finally, for clarity you must provide structure. That's part three of the writing process: structure. It's also the subject of Chapter Five. With the information gathered, with story purpose clear, with the reader in mind, you determine how best to put the material together. Call it arrangement or design or plan; an article requires one.

Be Concise. Journalists learn that early, too.

Magazine writers tend to forget. They're given more space and, if not careful, turn wordy. But as a television newswriter cuts and cuts to meet time limitations, so the magazine writer should hold on to only the words needed to make a point. Magazine articles must be packed with information and entertainment—not overpacked but packed. Editors want to give their readers the most possible in each issue. Readers want to get as much as possible from every story.

As George Bernard Shaw expressed it: "I'm sorry to have written such a long letter, but I didn't have time to write a shorter one." It's hard to be concise.

Be Cohesive. Make all parts of the article come together, hold together, stay together.

That involves transition and flow. The reader should feel a sense of continuity as the article is perused and studied, a sense of oneness, of unity. Test the relationship between the article's beginning and ending. Is there a logical progression of information from beginning to middle to conclusion?

Be Complete. Consider two kinds of completeness.

1. Informational completeness. It's good practice for you, when writing, to put yourself in the head of the reader. What questions is he or she likely to ask? Are you responding to those questions? Go through the process. Test the article against all the who, what, where, when, why, and how questions you can think of. Get a friend to do the same. If any question is not answered, do so, or at least explain why that question cannot be answered right now. Gaps in stories cause disconcerted readers.

2. Atmospheric completeness. Rare it is that we in journalism, even magazine journalism, can be informationally complete about a subject. Often we find ourselves attempting to handle, in several thousand words or fewer, material that has been expounded on in full-length books. In actuality, we rarely can be informationally complete. But we can be, and should be, atmospherically complete. We should have the instinct to select those aspects of the subject, those points, those pieces of information which will clarify the topic and satisfy the reader. That's what journalistic writing is all about. It's what editing is about, too. Our job in the preparation of articles is to be selective, to choose the most pertinent and most intriguing facts and thoughts so that the reader thinks: "No, I've not been given everything, but I like what the writer *has* given me. I'm happy. I'm satisfied."

Be Consistent. Consistency in this case involves *tone.* If you write a narrative lead, for instance, it suggests to a reader that the story which follows will include more such material. A narrative lead or a descriptive lead or an analytical lead or a fact-laden lead tells the reader what the article will be like, or, rather, it should. The reader should be able to determine what the remainder of the reading experience will be.

All too often writers begin stories fetchingly, establishing a tone, but then build the rest of the article on quite different, perhaps sludgy stuff. Don't follow an anecdotal opening with an anecdotal-less body. Don't use an atmospheric lead to introduce an article laden with statistics. Not fair. Offer your reader consistency of approach. That does not mean flexibility and variety are prohibitions. Just be careful to maintain a flavor.

Be Concrete. Abstractions can destroy your writing. Specificity, detail, particulars strengthen writing and enhance reading.

Columnist David Quammen, writing in *Outside,* first reminds, then advises: "In the fifth chapter of Matthew's Gospel, Christ is quoted as saying that the meek shall inherit the earth, but other opinion lately suggests that, no, more likely it will go to the cockroaches." He follows through: "A decidedly ugly and disheartening prospect: our entire dear planet — after the final close of all human business — ravaged and over-run by great multitudes of cockroaches, whole plagues of them, whole scudding herds shoulder to shoulder like the old herds of bison, vast cockroach legions sweeping inexorably as driver ants over the empty prairies. Unfortunately, that vision is not just the worst Kafkaesque fantasy of some fevered pessimist. There is also hard science involved."

Get the picture?

Be Constructive. T.S. Eliot once made the point that people can take only so much reality. Nowadays, the daily newspaper and the daily television or radio news program provide gloom aplenty — so much gloom, in fact, that market strategists have advised editors and news directors over the past couple of decades to lighten things up. But, of course, those dealing with hard news can lighten things just so much and so far. Current realities are current realities. The news tends to be destructive of our good feelings.

As consumers, we turn by habit to newspaper and television. We take in as much of the gloom as we can stand, then turn it off. In the process we may resist further gloom from a source of information we don't consider a habit, the magazine. Reading a magazine is an acquired taste. It is, for most readers, not the same sort of necessity as the paper or TV. So be careful in writing your article to look for the positive, hopeful, beautiful information as well as the bad news. Try to balance coverage. That's not to say hide the truth. Pollyanna serves no one. But keep additional burdens for the reader to a minimum.

Be Credible. Only then will a reader bother or believe.

Credibility depends on your ability to gauge the audience, a matter we've already explored. If you don't understand your reader, you may create the wrong kind of material which results in the loss of your credibility.

It depends also on your willingness to use credible material from credible sources. Your byline at the top of the manuscript may not convince the editor that everything which follows is wisdom and truth. The reader also may not be convinced simply by the presence of someone's name at the top of the page. Not to disillusion you, but the reader might actually not have heard of you. So bring to your story those experts, those authority figures that the reader will trust. Give yourself credibility through the credibility of others. And as you do, reinforce your efforts to be correct. Authorities can enhance factuality, accuracy, precision.

Be Conversational. When appropriate, work toward making your writing sound like you talking. The key word is *sound.* If you study the work of today's best nonfiction writers, those laboring for magazines or feature sections of newspapers, you'll discover that their writing approximates conversation. The writer seems to be in an easy chair opposite you, just chatting. The language has been cleaned of clutter, smoothed out. But it retains the informality of talk. Why? Because writers and editors have determined that people spend more time listening than they do reading and therefore feel more comfortable with the language of talk.

What you should learn to do, even if that style of language is not your aim, is to read all your copy aloud. Listen to it. The ear catches more than the eye. At the very least, you can rid your manuscript of missing steps, convolutions, and things that just don't sound right. At best, you also can over time develop that more conversational quality in your writing.

But really read out loud. Don't mumble. Listen to the words you've written. How do they sound to you? Incidentally, that's another way to improve the correctness of your article. In the editing process, the eyes can be kinder masters than the ears. You'll question more through listening. Consequently, you'll catch more.

Be Comfortable. When you're comfortable, your reader will be more comfortable.

With all that your reader could be doing besides reading your article, think comfort. Our task as writers is to ease the reader's way through information and message. Conversationality helps. So do coherence and consistency. So, surely, does clarity. Make the reader's journey through your work as pleasant, as effortless as possible.

Be Captivating. Not easy, that task, and seemingly less easy each passing year.

I receive numerous sales letters. One magazine subscription entered means thirty or forty more letters from others who'd like my business. One donation made to a charitable institution is followed by dozens of letters from others who need my help, too. With the mailbox so filled, I don't always pay close attention. But then one arrives with an opening quote: "It's like caring for a 150-pound infant who needs constant attention . . . an infant who asks you the same question fifty times a day . . . an infant who will never grow up. There's no peace. No time to rest."

Suddenly I pay attention. The words come from the husband of someone suffering from Alzheimer's disease. The letter comes from the Alzheimer's Family Relief Program. Suddenly I'm inclined to give. The quote captivates me.

When *New Yorker* cartoonist Charles Saxon has a seizure in his home, knocks down a lamp, and is heard telling medical technicians carrying him out, "I guess I'd better die; I just broke our best lamp," that again is the quote that matters, the captivating detail in his obituary, his final joke.

This book is devoted to showing you how to make your articles more captivating. The possibility begins with your falling in love with the subject, in your being convinced that at a particular moment in your life a particular subject is the most important matter for your attention and involvement. We mentioned *The New Yorker.* Another writer for its "Talk of the Town" section noted that at midday in midtown Manhattan "most color tends to disappear, and you get a bone-colored clutter: a clutter bustling, bleached, and dirty — dust-smeared glass, streaked aluminum, discolored brick, dirty concrete, potholed asphalt." The writer continues:

Of course, if you look closely, you can see that the city is not entirely a colorless mess, but the order and the colors don't stand out. Take midday midtown reds—they are everywhere: in the signs on the sides of buses, in the folksy script announcing Bojangles', in the chunky letters spelling out "Burger King," in the "Express" of "Federal Express" (on white trucks), in the signs taped to the *Times*-dispensing machines which say, in white letters on a red ground, "Find Your World in Ours." But these advertising reds, like the reds of the stoplights and tail-lights, do not operate strenuously in the large white glare. Part of the reason is the way colors behave in bright light: diffusion and suffusion are limited, and so colors drown in the spectrum's imperialist, or total, white.

This writer's love for the subject indicates something close to compulsion, thoughts that need to be verbalized and shared.

That's attitude again. Such an attitude communicates itself to a reader whose enthusiasm is likely to be enhanced. A writer's involvement is catching.

A FORMULA FOR SUCCESS

Consider the following formula as a guide in your magazine article writing:

$$E/A + I + I^2 + I = S$$

You won't find it in a math or science book, but it works. The E stands for Entertainment and the A for Artistry. The first of the three I's represents Information, the second Intelligence, and the third Insight. The S on the other side of the equation means Success.

The given in the equation is that first I, information you have as a writer. Information you want to pass along to a reader who might be able to use it. That's a start. In most news stories that's more than a start; it's sum and substance. But in a magazine article, providing information is but a part of what you must accomplish.

The E for Entertainment is vital. Even if your article is basically educational in purpose, you must consider what can be done through language, use of facts, and method of attack to cause that ho-hum-prone reader to perk. Just as the university professor most remembered blended entertainment with education, so must you—without even the hold of tests and grades—work for a blend. Should you find the idea of entertainment beneath you and your subject, emphasize in your mind the letter A. Artistry may seem to you a higher class word. Think artistry, again something in the way you handle your subject that makes the article stand out. To quote Shaw again: ". . . art is the only teacher except torture." Readers won't permit themselves to be tortured for too long. Act accordingly.

That I^2 represents Intelligence in two ways. One: language that makes sense to the reader; use it. Two: the sort of information on your subject that a Central Intelligence Agency would want to keep secret; give your reader the kind and depth of information that make the reader feel like an insider, that causes him or her to say, "I couldn't have found this material anywhere else, but this writer, because of his knowledge and sources and grasp, has enriched me."

The *I* for Insight completes the equation. If your readers are like me, and I suspect they are, they'll ask themselves, "Why am I reading this story right now?" You must tell them why. Give them reason. Offer an understanding of why this subject is important to them. Don't simply imply; come right out and say.

Test what you do against the formula.

It may help for you to read this passage from Charles Monaghan's article on New Guinea for *Travel and Leisure* called "A South Seas Adventure." He says:

> Somewhere there is a place that will change my life." Its physical beauty will shock me into seeing my own world in a wholly new way. The lives of the people there will be so sharply different from mine that they will be a mirror to me, and in that mirror I will see all my faults and fears, and gather the courage to eradicate them. This place will be so untouched by my civilization that I will be renewed just by coming to know it. To visit it will be a once-in-a-lifetime adventure, a necessary adventure of the soul . . .
>
> The longing for such a place is buried deep in our psyches. It is an idea that surfaces again and again in our literature and myth. And it surely is a part—a small part, sometimes a great part—of the impetus that drives us to travel, that makes travel such a poignant and important part of our lives.

That longing is part of the impetus that drives us to read.

To read is to travel.

Writers thus become travel guides.

So what starts as your journey through immersion in a subject becomes a reader's journey to a place that may change his life, that will shock that individual into seeing the world in a wholly new way, that becomes "a once-in-a-lifetime adventure, a necessary adventure of the soul."

2
Where Ideas Come From

The first one lasted thirteen years
And helped them get two children;
It sagged and angled gravity
And rolled the two of them together,
Peacefully fallen in their sleep
Where curling the same way every night
They shared his snoring, her chilly feet.
Now at forty, they buy another
and figure one more after that.
Two more rounds of breaking in and down,
At first the favored sag and then
the deep canal of their linked sleep
Deepening farther every year they keep
to the same old wager, he from his side,
She from hers, the mattress not so wide
Now but serviceable, as they reckon
Under the current spread, three score and ten.

—Wyatt Prunty

The bed is a terrific subject for an article. So is the bookcase. So is the kitchen table.

Objects distill into memories and realities. They have utilities and histories. Find the right object, collect the right information, find the right market, and you're in the money.

Is it that easy? Well, yes and no. Sometimes the natural notion presents itself, you grab hold, and an article ensues. At other times, you search and think, study and think, agonize over the absence of ideas and think some more. And more.

For an editor, good ideas mean the continued life and prosperity of the magazine. For a staff writer, good ideas mean kudos from the boss, job security, and perhaps some cherished writing assignments during which several of those ideas become flesh and words. For a free-lancer, good ideas mean sales which mean publication which mean credits which mean more sales—but only if the ideas keep coming.

What to print, the editor is always asking, and not merely for the issue currently in preparation but for issues months into the future. What to write, the writer is constantly fretting. After all, ideas are dollars. Ideas in hand are nerves eased and fingernails saved.

So where do they come from?

"Everywhere" is the obvious answer.

"From hanging out," one writer said to me.

From walking. From talking. From listening. From observing. From doing. From reading. From believing. From disagreeing. From dreaming. From scheming. From asking. From having an open mind.

A student of mine, Chris Moeller, listened in as second and third graders talked to their teacher and each other about the world we live in, or really the world *they* live in. He created a composite statement and used it as introduction to a class assigned article about teaching science. An idea did not lead him to the children. The children, and what they said, led him to the idea.

There are nine planets in our solar system, ten if you count the sun. But the sun's not a planet, is it? People live on each of these planets, with the Pluto people being the shortest since Pluto's the smallest planet. The Earth is the middle planet in the universe. It has one moon which is a million trillion billion zillion feet wide and made up of mayonnaise and granola. The Earth itself is trillions of feet long and made up of lots of different stuff. There's water. Fifteen thousand gallons of it on the planet's surface. This is where the fish and sea monsters and water people live.

Surrounding the Earth's water is land. Lots of land. This land is home to the world's ten million inhabitants. The land is divided into three continents and 153 countries. This is so the people know where to send their mail. Out of these countries, the United States is the greatest, Alaska is the biggest, Japan is the smallest, and California is the closest country to America.

The painter Grant Wood once claimed, "All the really good ideas I ever had came to me while I was milking a cow." Well, why not? Or walking the dog. Or running. Or pumping iron. Or eating lunch alone. Or relaxing in bed during those moments just before sleep or just after awakening. Or riding the train to and from work. Or listening to music. Or getting your teeth cleaned. Or having your hair trimmed and styled. Or shopping for groceries.

While at the hair stylist, listen to what people are talking about. Do that in the checkout line at the supermarket. Do it at the neighborhood saloon. Do it wherever people congregate and talk. What seems to be concerning them? What's the meat of their gossip? What about their jokes and their stories? What are they buying? Has the news of the day had an impact? Are they excited about anything or anyone?

Those everyday activities and everyday thoughts from Everyman and Everywoman could turn into story ideas.

But that's so ordinary, you might argue. Well, most everything is ordinary, unless you refuse to believe it so. Lightning and a kite were ordinary, but Benjamin Franklin discovered the extraordinary through them. "The idea must constantly be seen in some new aspect," said philosopher Alfred North Whitehead. "Some element of novelty must be brought into it freshly from time to time."

The bulk of the September 1988 issue of *Good Housekeeping* was devoted to the subject of child care. The editors' thoroughness resulted in a National Magazine Award. Every aspect of child care seems to have been explored, from the perspectives of home and school, of physicians and psychological counselors, of play and responsibility. A freelance writer, Paddy Yost, contributed a single-page charmer, "What Every Child Should Know by Age Five." She didn't talk to adult experts. She talked to those who would know best, the children. They provided the element of novelty within coverage of a subject that's been done before and will be done again. Enjoy it.

These days, parents of children under five worry about what youngsters should know before starting school. The endless amount of expert advice doesn't make things any easier. However, the one authority seldom heard from is the *child*. So we decided to ask kids what *they* thought they should know by age five.

We talked to several savvy youngsters who agreed to open up only if we promised to describe them as "unnamed sources." We met in out-of-the-way places — candy stores, ice cream parlors, donut shops. The kids talked (between bites), and we took notes. Here is what they said. As you might guess, it doesn't match up with what the experts have been telling us!

Hygiene
How to wet a toothbrush to look as if she just brushed her teeth.
. . . wash his hands and face without using any soap.
. . . stay grubby after spending forty-five minutes in the bathtub.
. . . find a mud puddle during a month-long drought.

Safety
How to walk with both her shoelaces untied.
. . . get down from the top of a bunk bed without using the ladder.
. . . climb the stairs on the *outside* of the railings.
. . . play with the dog (or cat) while it's eating.

Nutrition
How to pick the mushrooms out of the casserole and feed them to the dog without attracting a mother's attention.
. . . swap a roast-beef sandwich for peanut-butter-and-jelly.
. . . persuade Dad that chocolate donuts are more nutritious than whole-wheat toast.
. . . conceal a helping of spinach under a baked-potato skin.

Justice
How to leave the room before the lamp hits the floor.
. . . be sure her younger brother gets blamed.
. . . lose all important communications from school before he gets home.

. . . insist his civil rights are being violated when sent to bed earlier than his older sister.

. . . invent a "very, very bad" pal who leads good kids astray.

. . . think of eleven good reasons for not picking up her toys.

Business

How to trade three marbles and Dad's video camera for a friend's new bicycle.

. . . negotiate for a cookie *before* picking up his toys.

. . . keep the change from the money Mom gives her for bubble gum.

. . . get money from his Grandpa without actually *asking*.

Attire

How to lose a glove each week in the months of January and February.

. . . look as if his new clothes came from a flea market.

. . . choose the right T-shirt to wear during a snowstorm.

. . . angle her foot so it won't go into her boot.

Entertainment

How to beat the rest of the family to the telephone.

. . . turn a trip to the rest room into a tour of the restaurant.

. . . hear "just one more" story before turning out the lights.

. . . get the dog to eat crayons (to see what happens when he does).

. . . make his little sister cry by making horrible faces at her behind Mom's back.

Politics

How to get privileges because she is the littlest.

. . . get privileges because she is the biggest.

. . . persuade grandparents that Mom is too strict.

. . . persuade grandparents that Dad is too strict.

And last, but certainly not least:

. . . *How to* sneak into Mom and Dad's bed in the middle of the night without waking them!

IDEAS ARE EVERYWHERE

A lecture is a lecture, but after one lecture another philosopher, William James, was confronted by a lady of advanced years. "We don't live on a ball rotating around the sun," she theorized. "We live on a crust of earth on the back of a giant turtle."

James was silent for a moment, then answered, "If your theory is correct, madam, what does this turtle stand on?"

"The first turtle stands on the back of a second, far larger, turtle, of course, " she said.

"But what does this second turtle stand on?"

"It's no use, Mr. James," she said with finality. "It's turtle all the way down."

As long as there are people, there'll be ideas. As long as there are people, we can write about them and their ideas. Consider, for instance, the head of the American Society for the Conservation of Gravity, who tells us in a press release: "Americans, with only six percent of the world's population, use 68 percent of the gravity. What goes up requires gravity to come down. Our countless skyscrapers with elevators whizzing, our huge jet freighters, our incessant rocket launchings bear witness to our shameful national don't-give-a-damn attitude. Gravity is our most precious terrestrial resource. It is a vital resource. And it is a nonrenewable resource. When we run out, everything will float off the earth's surface into space. Women and children will go first."

He's worth writing about. So is his society. So are other eccentrics. We may find them funny or sad or strangely meaningful, but they bring us ideas and can become our ideas for articles.

We need not always go so far. Those who fill the emotional niches of our own lives can turn into subjects or prompt thoughts that turn into subjects. Two essays from *Harper's* come to mind.

In the November 1989 issue, essayist-novelist-teacher Scott Russell Sanders reveals:

My father drank. He drank as a gut-punched boxer gasps for breath, as a starving dog gobbles food—compulsively, secretly, in pain and trembling. I use the past tense not because he ever quit drinking but because he quit living. That is how the story ends for my father, age sixty-four, heart bursting, body cooling, slumped and forsaken on the linoleum of my brother's trailer. The story continues for my brother, my sister, my mother, and me, and will continue as long as memory holds.

In the perennial present of memory, I slip into the garage or barn to see my father tipping back the flat green bottles of wine, the brown cylinders of whiskey, the cans of beer disguised in paper bags. His Adam's apple bobs, the liquid gurgles, he wipes the sandy-haired back of a hand over his lips, and then, his bloodshot gaze bumping into me, he stashes the bottle or can inside his jacket, under the workbench, between two bales of hay, and we both pretend the moment has not occurred.

"What's up, buddy?" he says, thick-tongued and edgy.

"Sky's up," I answer, playing along.

"And don't forget prices," he grumbles. "Prices are always up. And taxes."

The memoir becomes a lesson. Sanders writes of his father for himself and for a growing son who now watches *his* father, not a drinker but a being burdened by guilts and fears. Father-son. The price of drinking. Ordinary subjects only for ordinary writers. Extraordinary in depth and dimension when Sanders explores the subject. It becomes a modern tragedy and sociological study and love poem.

In the March 1989 issue of *Harper's*, Edward Hoagland writes about feelings.

A friend of mine, a peaceable soul who has been riding the New York subways for thirty years, finds himself stepping back from the tracks once in a while and closing his eyes as the train rolls in. This, he says, is not only to suppress an urge to throw himself in front of it but because every couple of weeks an impulse rises in him to push a stranger onto the tracks, any stranger, thus ending his own life too. He blames this partly on apartment living—"pigeonholes without being able to fly."

It is profoundly startling not to trust oneself after decades of doing so. I don't dare keep ammunition in my country house for a small rifle I bought secondhand two decades ago. The gun sat in a cupboard in the back room with the original box of .22 bullets under the muzzle all that time, seldom fired except at a few apples hanging in a tree every fall to remind me of my army training near the era of the Korean War, when I'd been considered quite a marksman. When I bought the gun I didn't trust either my professional competence as a writer or my competence as a father as much as I came to do, but certainly believed I could keep myself alive. I bought it for protection, and the idea that someday I might be afraid of shooting myself with the gun would have seemed inconceivable—laughable.

One's fifties can be giddy years, as anybody fifty knows. Chest pains, back pains, cancer scares, menopausal or prostate complications are not the least of it, the fidelities of a lifetime, both personal and professional, may be called into question. Was it a mistake to have stuck so long with one's marriage, and to have stayed with a lackluster well-paying job? (Or not to have stayed and stuck?) People not only lose faith in their talents and their dreams or values; some simply tire of them.

Hoagland writes only of thoughts, of fleeting reflections. They are not unusual thoughts, but words have made them so.

Ideas also come from speeches, from meetings, from brochures, from publicity releases, from annual reports, from sales letters.

They come from reading. A writer must read: to learn from the good and bad techniques of other writers, but also to gain ideas. Since there is nothing new, as they say, you can transform material used in one magazine for another.

A Case Study

Let's take an issue of *Harper's*, a magazine from which you can easily quote, as I just did, and from which you can glean ideas, spin-offs, variations for a different reader of a different magazine. Each issue of *Harper's*, for instance, contains a page labeled "Harper's Index." It's a collection of statistics.

The particular issue I'm looking through tells me that airfare for a corpse on an American Airlines flight from New York City to Los Angeles, one way, is $630 but for a live person, round trip, is $398. The estimated total value of candy distributed on Halloween was one billion dollars. The estimated amount of glucose used by an adult human brain each day, expressed in M&M's, is 250. The estimated number of seconds that humans perceive "the present" to last is three.

   In other issues of the magazine, one can discover that 70 percent of the American people have visited Disneyland or Disney World, that an ant can survive underwater for fourteen days, that the estimated number of calories a person consumes during Thanksgiving dinner is 2,250, and that the estimated number of calories a Thanksgiving turkey consumes in its lifetime is 110,000. Three percent of Americans say Monday is their favorite day of the week; 70 percent of us who own running shoes don't run. The average number of years that an American spends looking for misplaced objects, in the course of a lifetime, is one, and the percentage of us who say "a good car mechanic is worth as much as a member of Congress" comes to 40.

   You get the idea, and if you read with an open mind, you should realize there are article ideas in such statistics: The most popular places to visit. How to survive Disneyland if you bring your children. How to talk your family out of going to Disney World. The might of the tiny ant. My antfarm and I. Taking the calories out of holiday dinners. Fifty ways to prepare turkey leftovers. The turkey. How to face the new work week. Wishing our lives away. The sneaker in America. How to avoid runners and bikers, or how to make them get out of the way, or how to make them feel guilty that they're taking up space that should be reserved for my automobile. How long we wait during our lives for traffic lights to change and other necessary but useless activities. Where all those socks disappear to. Our love-hate affair with the government. How to make our legislators listen. Whether good auto mechanics still exist, or plumbers or carpenters or others of that sort.

   The ideas are out there. We simply need the antennae to tune in to them.

   Back to that issue of *Harper's*. It includes excerpts from a 292-page transcript of the police interrogation of a Florida murder suspect. The trial judge later threw out the confession, "ruling that the detectives' interrogation methods—which included sleep deprivation, leading questions, and inadequate *Miranda* warnings—had deprived the suspect of his right against self-incrimination." What does that suggest about police methods or about trials? Can you think of other kinds of transcripts which might lend themselves to an article?

   This issue of *Harper's* also reprints an Editor's Note from *The New York Times*. It says in part: "A review of Patsy's restaurant in Manhattan on March 24 gave it a rating of 'Satisfactory' and discussed both the food and the decor, including celebrity photographs. The review said . . . 'Where do all these black-and-white glossies come from? Are they actually tokens of gratitude from stage and screen stars, or does some photo lab simply churn them out and peddle them by mail?' In a letter dated May 11, the owners of Patsy's complained that the passage implied that their photos were inauthentic. No such suggestion was intended; the comments, which should have been phrased specifically rather than ironically, were intended only to remark on the sameness of such restaurant decor."

What about newspaper corrections? Are they ever adequate? Do they undo the initial damage brought about by the initial error? That could become an article. What about restaurant reviews? What should they cover? Are they to be believed? That could become an article. What about restaurant decor? How have eating environments changed? What are restaurateurs doing to woo clientele? That could become an article.

Further on in *Harper's* we discover three poems by Marine Lt. Col. Oliver North, a political celebrity. The poems were based, North explains, on his testimony before a Congressional committee. Might such a discovery lead a writer to other poems by non-poets and to an article about why they write and how experts interpret what the poems signify about the celebrity's personality?

The magazine reprints the index to Paul Slansky's *The Clothes Have No Emperor, A Chronicle of the Reagan Years.* One can find the page numbers for "chops wood," "confusion admitted by," "Democrats embraced posthumously by," "detachment from reality imputed to," "doodles of," "incessant pop-culture references by," "on invasion from space," "and jellybeans," "macho bluster of," "oversized props of," "photo opportunities of," "vetoes of," and "on the waking or non-waking of." How a book is indexed: that would make a subject. So would how people remember their Presidents. So would the fine art of writing biography about public figures.

Illinois Representative Richard Durbin is quoted in a short boxed item. He rose before his colleagues "to condemn the desecration of a great American symbol. No, I am not referring to flag burning; I am referring to the baseball bat." Experts say, he continues, "that the wooden baseball bat is doomed to extinction, that major league baseball players will soon be standing at home plate with aluminum bats in their hands." He expresses anger: "Baseball fans have been forced to endure countless indignities by those who just cannot leave well enough alone: designated hitters, plastic grass, uniforms that look like pajamas, chicken clowns dancing on the baselines, and, of course, the most heinous sacrilege, lights in Wrigley Field. Are we willing to hear the crack of a bat replaced by a dinky ping? Are we ready to see the Louisville Slugger replaced by the aluminum ping dinger? Is nothing sacred?"

Traditions and breaks from tradition always make story possibilities.

"A Pre-Game Prayer" from the *Blue Book of PONY Baseball* is reprinted in the magazine: "May each swing be powerful, may each throw be straight and true, may each decision be accurate. May feet be swift, hands be agile, minds alert, and hearts determined. Give us Thy blessing that injury may be avoided and sportsmanship exhibited in its finest form." Etcetera. I think an article on prayers for special occasions, from political conventions to testimonial dinners, would be fascinating. What special messages do we ask God to hear? There is considerably more in this issue of *Harper's*: an interview with an anti-Stalinist historian about changes in the Soviet Union, an essay on "Lives of the Body," a forum by "four masters of horror" asked to update "the edgy killer of Poe's masterpiece, *The Tell-Tale Heart*." They were to consider what he would look like, what would goad him to murder, and on what victims he would prey. A report on Cambodia and another on the state of Washington, D.C., also were featured. From each the alert writer might fashion variations.

And the Ideas Flow On . . .

Read your newspapers carefully. Listen to the radio talk shows. Watch television, from the Sunday morning public service programs through the nationally syndicated forums of opinion to the daily news shows.

Art in America runs "Renoir: A Symposium." The editors have gathered the experts "to reflect on this most loved—and damned—of the Impressionists." You can gather experts. You can create a symposium on any topic you deem appropriate for a market (but better get a go-ahead from the editor first; experts generally want the publicity if they're going to give you the time).

Connoisseur investigates the art of the concierge via nine of the world's top practitioners "Performing the Impossible." *ARTnews* poses: "What Would You Ask Michelangelo?" Here's the editor's explanation: "Art history is riddled with mysteries, the questions on which, as Giacometti's biographer James Lord puts it, 'every biographer or art historian stubs his toe.' Why did Cézanne paint so many portraits of his father, whom he claimed to despise? Did Rembrandt sign any paintings executed by his students? How did the years in therapy affect Jackson Pollock's art? These are the puzzles that cause sleepless nights for art scholars. But what if these artists were magically reincarnated for just one hour? What if a scholar could get the answer from the single person who knows the truth? It was this bit of fantasy that *ARTnews* asked thirteen art historians to indulge: What would you ask the subject of your study if given this impossible opportunity?"

What a profusion of take-offs you might dream up. Ask scientists what they'd most like to know. Or doctors. Or theologians. Or teachers.

The calendar and promoters of all persuasions proclaim Fred MacMurray Day, White Cane Safety Day, Women Veterans Recognition Day, Community Economic Development Day, Firefighter Appreciation Day, Water Awareness Week, CPR Awareness Week, Mental Illness Awareness Week, Doll House and Miniatures Week, Black History Month, Disability Awareness Month, Correct Posture Month, and Professional Social Workers Month. Ideas.

"The 100 Greatest Albums of the 80s" *Rolling Stone* presents its readers. *Discover* writes of "The Eight Big Ideas of the Eighties." "One Day in the Life of Louisiana" *Louisina Life* covers. *Time* lays before us: "A Day in the Life of China"; "A Letter to the Year 2086" also comes courtesy of *Time.* "The Unofficial Census, Incredible answers to credible questions—What Difference Does True Make?" *Chicago* offers. *People* lists "The Year's 25 Most Interesting People." *U.S. News and World Report* introduces us to "Ten Forces Reshaping America."

Idea prompters all.

Esquire asks thirty-nine Americans to choose a book for the President's night table. *Roper Reports* queries a scientific sample to determine what we daydream about.

The *Spy* Poll tells us how "A Nation of Nobodies Speaks Out About the Somebodies." The editors "wanted to find out what the public thought celebrity life was like. We asked respondents to agree or disagree with certain statements about celebrityhood." Those statements included "a celebrity can't make it without the little people" (to which 85 percent agreed), "money changes everything" (71 percent said yes), and "it's lonely at the top" (65 percent agreed). Height, hair, build, talents, hobbies were asked about, as was this question: "The perfect celebrity would actively support which of the following causes?" The answers ranged from being antidrug and antihunger to recycling and doing a telethon. Oh, and when readers were asked whether they "would . . . sacrifice a finger for a big part in a successful movie," 5 percent said yes.

Surveys and polls take special skills, scientific sampling, construction of questions, and evaluation of responses among them. They're not easy to do. But they can result in salable articles.

Ben Bova writes in *Omni*: "It is growing. Like a living, sentient creature, its tendrils hide in our walls, snake out to the streets, run from pole to pole, tunnel beneath the pavement, and arc across space on microwaves. Like an extraterrestrial invader with superhuman powers, it has become so ubiquitous that we barely notice its presence among us. Yet its instruments have penetrated virtually every home in the United States and every office of business and government in the world." He has begun to describe the phone system, giving it mystery, paying attention to its complexity.

System of our everyday. And what of television? And what of our electricity?

"The steps are the same everywhere, steep and worn, scarred, gummy and sometimes running with the clouded rivulets of the city's squeezed-out poisons. It is a descent into the never ending twilight, into the cave where the blurred phantoms of the commuters still shoulder past." Eugene Kennedy then takes the reader of the *Chicago Tribune Magazine* on a journey via rapid transit. "Life and Death in the City," the article is titled. "A View from the L" is what it shows. How about spending a day with your city's bus system? How about a trip from the beginning to the end of a line?

Or how about a visit to the Museum of the Thousand and One Curiosities in Guadalest, Spain? You'll find there a collection of miniature art including the Statue of Liberty re-created in the eye of a needle, Picasso's *Guernica* painted on a bean, Leonardo's *Mona Lisa* painted on a lentil, a sculpture of an elephant modeled from the eye of a mosquito, and more.

Books are sources of ideas, too. How about looking through *The First Really Important Survey of American Habits* by Mel Poretz and Barry Sinrod? You'll discover that only 7 percent of us admit looking behind a closed shower curtain when visiting a friend's home; that 38 percent of us clean our belly button every day; that 53 percent eat spaghetti by winding it on a fork and 47 percent cut it; that 80 percent eat corn on the cob by going around the ear in a circle while the rest nibble from side-to-side like a typewriter.

We just need to appreciate the magic in people and what they do. The ideas are endless. Observe keenly. Think expansively. They'll occur to you. And when they do, record them. Keep them close. The occasions for using them will arise, never fear.

3
Matter and Manner Count, But First Think Focus

THE PURPLE COW

I never saw a purple cow,
    I never hope to see one.
But this I will say anyhow
    I'd rather see than be one.

—Gelett Burgess

Two cats were sitting in a tree,
kritte vitte vit bom bom,
a cat called Lew,
a cat called Lee,
kritte vitte vit bom bom.
"Now follow me,"
said Lew to Lee,
kritte vitte vitte vitte vit bom bom,
"for I no longer like this tree,"
kritte vitte vit bom bom!

—Danish Nursery Rhyme

Two little rhymes, each designed for a specific reader and a specific purpose.

Two little rhymes, the first with information intended to interest its reader, the second with sounds to attract its reader.

"The Purple Cow" manifests *focus*. It also features *matter* likely to allure. The Danish nursery rhyme is focused too, designed for a specific reader, but it tantalizes through *manner*.

The article writer, immersed in a project, must consider those who ultimately will read the finished version and, with that in mind, make inclusions and exclusions, select angle and language. That's what focus is all about.

In deciding what to include, you must be able to select the appropriate material (or matter for your specific audience.) In choosing the angle and language you must write in a style or manner that's right for the article.

Call them interrelated imperatives: focus, matter, manner.

For us in the article writing business, focus and marketing are nearly synonymous. Focus is what separates one magazine from another. It's that set of journalistic traits, that personality which distinguishes a publication. Good editors keep focus in mind with each decision they make about content as well as with every word they write or evaluate. They understand the mental and environmental makeup of their readership. They know if the audience comes from the halls of government, or from academia, or from party zealots, or historians, or people from all over who just happen to be interested in politics and government. A magazine on political affairs can be very practical or theoretical or polemical or historical or general. The editor obviously has to know the market. The writer had better understand, too.

Focus is angle. Sense of direction. Slant. Material sharply, clearly defined. Coverage planned for a certain kind of reader and only that reader. Editorial decisions about which articles fit and which do not become central to the process of putting out a magazine. A writer is faced with such decisions also.

Through appropriateness of idea, approach, and language, you convince an editor that your work fits the purpose and personality of the magazine. Thus, understanding the market can save you grief, loss of time, loss of temper, and loss of sale.

Differences can be subtle. *Time, U.S. News,* and *Travel & Leisure* each marked the 50th anniversary of a beginning, that of World War II. From the August 28, 1989 issue, here is *Time's* opening, the work of senior writer and essayist Otto Friedrich:

> World War II began last . . . Friday, September 1, when a German bombing plane dropped a projectile on Puck, fishing village and air base in the armpit of the Hel Peninsula.

> That sentence, appearing in *Time* magazine fifty years ago, reported the start of a cataclysm that would ultimately sweep across five continents and change the world forever.

> By the time the slaughter ended, nearly six years later, more than fifty million people, two-thirds of them civilians, had been killed — shot, drowned, bombed, frozen, starved, gassed. A number of ideas and institutions, too, had been killed or gravely wounded: the Third Reich, the British Empire, isolationism, appeasement, peace in our time.

> But out of all that suffering, new ideas had been born, from the technologies of radar, sulfa drugs, jet aircraft and nuclear energy to the concepts of collective security, the Atlantic alliance and the United Nations. New horrors, almost beyond description, now had to be given names: fire storm, radiation, holocaust. But other terms suggested rays of hope: jeep, airlift, and the symbol of three dots and dash: V for victory.

This is how it all began, a half-century ago.

The reader is reminded that *Time* was there. To the editors, that's not a small point; authority and continuity are implied.

U.S. News & World Report, lacking such a reporting history, turned to John Keegan, a contributing editor who at the time of the 50th anniversary commemoration was completing a book on the war. He reports in the August 28, 1989 magazine without a lead from the past, but with a fuller suggestion that he's amassed facts:

> This year is the 50th anniversary of the outbreak of World War II. The war was the largest event in history. It killed fifty million human beings, wounded in body or mind tens of millions more, laid waste the heartland of Western civilization and spread death and destruction across six of the world's seven continents and all of its oceans.
>
> It was a war that sent Brazilians of African descent to fight Germans in Italy, Australians to attack Frenchmen in Lebanon, Americans from the oil towns of Texas to bomb the oil fields of Romania, Gurkhas from the mountain kingdom of Nepal to battle Japanese soldiers in the malarial plains of Burma, Cossacks wearing German uniforms to defend the beaches of Normandy against French Canadians, Spaniards to perish from exposure in the snowbound wastes of the Russian steppe, German submarines to torpedo Norwegian seamen in the Indian Ocean.
>
> It is a war vividly remembered by those who fought it, never to be forgotten by the families of those who perished in it. It is also a war that generations too young to recall it continue to find of deep and compelling interest. They know that the world they inhabit was changed and shaped by World War II. But how the war was fought and, to an even greater degree, why it was fought are questions that tantalize and mystify.

The business of *Travel & Leisure* is what the magazine's name says. So its editors were sold on freelancer John McDonough's travel-oriented "Radio Days," subtitled "A Shortwave tour of World War II." Appearing in the April 1989 issue of *T & L*, it begins:

> Not long ago, while traveling around Europe, I had the extraordinary sensation of walking through a war that began fifty years ago this September, a war that was half over before I was born. Yet I heard it and felt it firsthand.
>
> There was nothing mystical about the experience. It had to do with the fact that World War II was Radio War I, that it produced a new breed of war correspondents whose voices conquered time and distance. Murrow, Collingwood, Sevareid, Shirer—they and their colleagues laid the cornerstone of modern broadcast news. They turned journalism into literature. They brought remote capitals and faraway battles to the nation's living rooms. They were America's eyes and ears.
>
> It also had to do with the fact that there's a peculiar jolt that comes from standing in a place where history happened. With hindsight and a little imagination, you can leap back in time to conjure the mood of a vanished moment. The Second World War turned on many moments, and some were

reported as they happened by this fraternity of broadcasters. When I visited some of those places, I felt that jolt. But I took more than my imagination with me; I carried cassettes of the correspondents' original shortwave transmissions.

I stood where they stood, let their words walk me through the events they witnessed, saw the landscapes and buildings they saw. I heard the sirens and guns that were in the air as they spoke, and the tension in their voices as the world shook before their eyes. I felt the mounting drama of a righteous war as it passed through the airwaves in a series of lightning bolts to America.

I started with the overture: Vienna, 1938.

ONE TOPIC, SEVEN WAYS

Global warming has been, and most assuredly will continue to be, a subject of vital interest to readers of all persuasions and, therefore, to editors. How different editors handle the subject will depend on what their readers seek or comprehend. A report in the July 11, 1988 issue of *Newsweek* begins:

> We were born under the yellow sun of the African plains, and we grew up in the ice age, and went on to declare our independence of nature. Inside our glass-walled cities we decreed perpetual springtime for us and our computers. Only now it appears that we may have been too hasty; watching thirteen million acres crumble to dust, we are reminded that none of us is ever really any farther from nature than his next meal.

> There was, for the first time in living memory, a note of panic in the weather reports last week. The farmers sensed it as the sun climbed each day through a cloudless blue hemisphere. The Drought of 1988 was barely two months old before it began to earn comparisons to the dust-bowl droughts of the 1930s. More sinister was the possibility that this year's weather was merely the foretaste of a warming trend that will by the next century cause unprecedented disruption in the environment, not just of the United States, but the world.

> That such a disruption will occur eventually seems all but certain; whether it has already begun is very much an open question. The first five months of 1988 are the warmest on record, but the record extends back only about one hundred years, and the most salient characteristic of weather is that it changes over time. Once it happens, though, we will know it. Global mean temperatures may rise as much as eight degrees in half a century, especially in the temperate and polar regions. The deserts of the Southwest will creep up on the Great Plains; sea levels will rise, threatening low-lying coasts.

> And all of it unintended, an oversight resulting from the addition, since the start of the Industrial Revolution, of a trifling seventy or so parts per million in the atmospheric content of carbon dioxide. Of all things, carbon dioxide — a principal byproduct of the combustion of anything containing carbon. Who could have guessed that this innocuous gas might in effect turn the globe into a giant greenhouse?

Who could have imagined man himself rendering the earth uninhabitable? We drew the wrong lesson from the Copernican Revolution. In the Middle Ages, global warming — of several thousand degrees — was considered a very real threat, although mostly to sinners. The demonstration that the solar system was governed by natural laws undermined the belief that God might at any time smite it with fire. Since then, we have tended to assume the contrary: that the earth and its complex machinery would continue into the indefinite future as they have for the billions of years leading up to this moment.

We forgot the one force capable of upsetting the balance that it took those billions of years to create. Ourselves.

The ifs and possibilities are built into the story, but the mood is gloomy. A general and geographically scattered readership interested in current affairs and issues is asked to pay attention and to worry. Focus.

Over at *Not Man Apart*, the newsmagazine published by Friends of the Earth, the prominent environmental group, all "ifs" have been removed. In an article in its July/August 1986 issue, the theme is urgency:

For years scientists have argued over the reality of the "greenhouse effect," the warming of the earth's climate caused by the buildup of carbon dioxide from fossil fuel combustion and other industrial gases. Now the argument is not over whether or not it will happen, but over when and where it will happen, and what to do about it. The world is already guaranteed to be substantially warmer because of present accumulations of "greenhouse" gases and because of the momentum of current investments in fossil fuels production and consumption. The world will be far warmer if we do not act promptly.

The economic costs and political consequences will be staggering. Agronomists predict that U.S. corn production could be cut by 10 percent, causing social dislocation and political conflict. Oceanographers and coastal hydrologists warn that virtually all U.S. coasts will be inundated, and billions will have to be spent to continually rebuild beaches by dredging.

To moderate the greenhouse effect some have proposed stiff taxes on the use of fossil fuels. But taxes don't go far enough. In 1983 the Environmental Protection Agency found that even a 300 percent tax would only delay the warming now in progess by five years. Only a ban, said EPA, would change long-term temperature increases.

Different reader. Different purpose. Different approach.

Pessimism suffuses *Discover's* report, too. In "Endless Summer: Living with the Greenhouse Effect" (October 1988), author Andrew Revkin spews facts for a reader already convinced that science is an important topic and prepared to assimilate a heavy dose of information:

On June 23 the United States sizzled as thermometers topped 100 degrees in forty-five cities from coast to coast: 102 in Sacramento; 103 in Lincoln, Nebraska; 101 in Richmond, Virginia. In the nation's heartland, the searing heat was accompanied by a ruinous drought that ravaged crops and prompted talk of a dust bowl to rival that of the 1930s. Heat waves and droughts are nothing new, of course. But on that stifling June day a top atmospheric scientist testifying on Capitol Hill had a disturbing message for his senatorial audience: Get used to it.

This wasn't just a bad year, James Hansen of the NASA Goddard Institute for Space Studies told the Senate committee, or even the start of a bad decade. Rather, he could state with "99 percent confidence" that a recent, persistent rise in global temperature was a climatic signal he and his colleagues had long been expecting. Others were still hedging their bets, arguing there was room for doubt. But Hansen was willing to say what no one had dared say before. "The greenhouse effect," he claimed, "has been detected and is changing our climate now."

Until this year, despite dire warnings from climatologists, the greenhouse effect has seemed somehow academic and far off. The idea behind it is simple: gases accumulating in the atmosphere as by-products of human industry and agriculture—carbon dioxide, mostly, but also methane, nitrous oxide, ozone, and chlorofluorocarbons—let in the sun's warming rays but don't let excess heat escape. As a result, mean global temperature has probably been rising for decades. But the rise has been so gradual that it has been masked by the much greater, and ordinary, year-to-year swings in world temperature.

Not anymore, said Hansen.

U.S. News & World Report (October 31, 1988) chooses to take a less heated view. "Rediscovering Planet Earth" seems to supply thoughtful background, again a particular aim of that particular publication. It's the same subject, though it doesn't appear to be:

The world's worst ecological disaster made human life possible. Two billion years ago, the tiny organisms that dominated Earth's primordial oceans dumped huge amounts of toxic waste into their environment. Eventually it killed them, along with much of the other life on the planet. That deadly substance was oxygen.

The ability of simple bacteria to remake the entire atmosphere is a striking illustration of a new view of the planet Earth that has emerged in just the last decade. Using satellites to monitor ocean currents, examining tree rings and fossilized pollen for evidence of past climates and simulating the world's future climate on computers, researchers are beginning to see Earth as a much more complex, interdependent system, in which oceans, atmosphere and life all affect one another and all help shape the face of the planet. Among the new discoveries:

- Plant and animal life have saved Earth from a fate similar to Venus's "runaway" greenhouse effect.
- Ocean plankton may play a crucial role in regulating global climate.
- Sudden shifts in currents such as the Gulf Stream can trigger mini ice ages that last for centuries.
- Tiny fluctuations in the Earth's orbit, augmented by changes in the proportions of atmospheric gases, control the advance and retreat of glaciers.

"Save the Planet," the editors of *Omni* plead in their September 1989 issue, calling on six journalists to seek answers to the earth's problems. This article begins:

> From the vantage point of Earth we look up to see the heavens. At night we gaze at the stars, new moon, full moon, or no moon at all; during the day the sun blasts or browns us, while nimbus or cirrus clouds ease on by. But if we're not careful, if we're not thoughtful, if we're not, yes, committed, we may lose our vantage point — this Earth — for millions of years home to us and our fellow species. It's time to stop gazing upward and to look around at the planet itself, to look at our fellow human beings, at some of their problems and their suffering.
>
> The earth's in serious trouble. We've polluted the very water we drink and bathe in with human sewage and an endless amount of toxic chemicals. We've chopped down forests all over the world — we've even got a name for it, deforestation — without any sense of what we're losing. And worse, we're becoming nearly illiterate, unable to read technical manuals, high-school textbooks, or billboards on buses, to say nothing about *Don Quixote* or *A Midsummer Night's Dream*.

The view is broader, spatial, futuristic. Editors have made a conscious decision on focus.

Anthony DeCurtis at *Rolling Stone* focused on the destruction of the rain forests. In "The Scorched Earth" (February 23, 1989) he offers warning:

> For most Americans, so unwilling to confront problems in their own country, much less halfway around the world, few environmental crises could seem of less significance than the destruction of the tropical rain forests. But these forests, which are being burned and chopped down at a perilous rate, are essential for regulating the temperature of our world and maintaining its ecological diversity. Forty percent of the rain forests has been lost — most of it over the past three decades — and incalculable and irreversible damage could be done to plant, animal and human life if this destruction persists.
>
> Rain forests cover approximately 7 percent of the surface of the earth in a belt that stretches along the equator. Scientists believe that within this relatively small area reside millions of as yet undiscovered biological species — an astonishing fact, considering that only 1.7 million species are currently known. Some of these life-forms are disappearing before they can even be discovered.

The earth is still in trouble. The subject really hasn't changed. Aspect has. The *Rolling Stone* piece is short, punctuated by dramatic photos in dramatic layout. A different audience requires a different focus.

Forbes called on syndicated columnist Warren Brookes to remind readers that "Apocalypse sells well in the media and even better on Capitol Hill. And that is why fears of the greenhouse effect threaten to push the U.S. into a costly environmental mistake." Such is the focus of "The Global Warming Panic," published in the December 25, 1989 edition, which begins:

> On November 7 the U.S. and Japan shocked environmentalists around the world by refusing to sign a draft resolution at a Netherlands international conference on global climate change calling for the "stabilization" of emissions of carbon dioxide (CO_2) and other "greenhouse gases" by the year 2000. Instead, they made the conference drop all reference to a specific year, and to a specific CO_2 reduction target. The Bush Administration view was set forth by D. Allan Bromley, the presidential science adviser, in testimony to Senator Albert Gore's subcommittee on Science, Technology & Space: "My belief is that we should not move forward on major programs until we have a reasonable understanding of the scientific and economic consequences of those programs."
>
> President Bush was immediately savaged by environmentalists, and by politicians like Senator Gore (D-Tenn.). The Bush viewpoint does not sit too well with most of the media, either. Last January *Time* published a cover story on environmental catastrophes, declaring that greenhouse gases could create a climatic calamity. The *New York Times* weighed in a month ago with a story about how melting polar ice would flood the nations that can least afford to defend themselves, Third World countries like Bangladesh and India. Or perhaps you have seen the ads for Stephen Schneider's *Global Warming*, accompanied by a blurb from Senator Tim Wirth (D-Colo.). In his book this well-known climatologist paints a future of seas surging across the land, famine on an epidemic scale and ecosystem collapse.
>
> Is the earth really on the verge of environmental collapse? Should wrenching changes be made in the world's industry to contain CO_2 buildup? Or could we be witnessing the 1990s version of earlier scares: nuclear winter, cancer-causing cranberries and $100 oil? The calamitarians always have something to worry us about.

Brookes, writing for this hard-headed publication, will have none of it.

Mind Over Matter

You, having read these excerpts, will react in conversion or with aversion. Or you may remain emotionally untouched. It depends on how closely you fit the profile of a magazine's readership. Editors must consider focus. Writers should strive for focus, too.

Think carefully about how you want to handle your chosen topic. Magazine editors don't purchase subjects. They purchase subjects that have been angled, made exclusive for their readers like tailored clothing. As a writer, you shouldn't depend on an editor to do the tailoring.

The editor will be looking for material likely to interest as many of his readers as possible. That adds to your responsibility as preparer of the article. You need to look for material within the assigned topic that will perk reader attention. Build your article around informational interest factors. Here are fourteen:

1. Problem. If your readers agree that your subject unfolds a problem, one they share or may face, then they'll pore through your words without hesitation.

2. Wants and needs. Whatever your reader wants or needs, he'll want to read about. All you have to do is remind him that he'll want or need whatever you are asking him to want or need. That depends heavily, of course, on your understanding of what the reader wants or needs.

3. Celebrity. People are interested in people. They are even more interested in well-known people. If someone famous can be used as the source or the object of an anecdote, include that someone.

4. Heart strings. The child saved from death through the gift of an organ. Good neighbors taking in a homeless family. The reunion of mother and daughter after years of separation. Human interest stories which tug at the heart captivate the reader.

5. Fear. What we fear intrigues us.

6. Competition. In politics or sports, in contests or business, the element of competition may be present. If it is, use it. Readers are fascinated by competition. Sports pages are proof; they wouldn't exist without our enthusiasm for competitors in action.

7. Conflict. This more dangerous, potentially damaging form of competition is what the news of most days is about. Whether individuals or groups of nations are in conflict, their heated arguments, their struggles involve us.

8. Controversy. Disagreements, whether in political campaigns or in the halls of academe, interest other people, particularly if these debates about positions and rights and wrongs have impact on them.

9. The unknown. Inner and outer space intrigue us. What you can tell me about what I don't know or understand but should or would like to will satisfy a longing. From the safety of my living room I can explore dangerous physical or mind-numbing mental vistas with you.

10. The unusual. "Departure from the norm" is what my first journalism teacher termed it. Readers are drawn to the different: embryos in divorce cases, fusion in a jar, wingless airplanes, designer vegetables, mink duffle backpacks, a museum for atheists, lazy lawns, a vampire census.

11. Progress. We all love progress. Killer diseases, environmental crises, poverty, conflicts: Bring readers the latest on progress and improvements, and again, your article will be gobbled up.

12. Solution or success. When in the generally discouraging course of human events a victory occurs, people are generally elated. They want to know the good that has taken place. We all need encouragement. If your article can supply some, the readership is loyally yours.

13. Consequence. Every magazine readership considers certain matters consequential. Perhaps family, perhaps health, perhaps economic well-being, perhaps faith, perhaps the beauty of art, perhaps weather, perhaps good and usable recipes, perhaps education. Think about what subjects and what aspects within these subjects are consequential to the readers. Fold those in.

14. Humor. Read Russell Baker's delightful blend of whimsy and reality. The handling of a less than important topic compels reading and brings pleasure.

In the December 25, 1983 issue of *The New York Times Magazine* Baker argues that "Fruitcake Is Forever."

Thirty-four years ago, I inherited the family fruitcake. Fruitcake is the only food durable enough to become a family heirloom. It had been in my grandmother's possession since 1880, and she passed it to a niece in 1933.

Surprisingly, the niece, who had always seemed to detest me, left it to me in her will. There was the usual family backbiting when the will was read. Relatives grumbled that I had no right to the family fruitcake. Some whispered that I had "got to" the dying woman when she was *in extremis* and guided her hand while she altered her will.

Nothing could be more absurd, since my dislike of fruitcake is notorious throughout the family. This distaste dates from a Christmas dinner when, at the age of fifteen, I dropped a small piece of fruitcake and shattered every bone in my right foot.

I would have renounced my inheritance except for the sentiment of the thing, for the family fruitcake was the symbol of our family's roots. When my grandmother inherited it, it was already eighty-six years old, having been baked by her great-grandfather in 1794 as a Christmas gift for President George Washington.

Washington, with his high-flown view of ethical standards for Government workers, sent it back with thanks, explaining that he thought it unseemly for Presidents to accept gifts weighing more than eighty pounds, even though they were only eight inches in diameter. This, at any rate, is the family story, and you can take it for what it's worth, which probably isn't much.

There is no doubt, though, about the fruitcake's great age. Sawing into it six Christmases ago, I came across a fragment of a 1794 newspaper with an account of the lynching of a real-estate speculator in New York City.

Thinking the thing was a valuable antique, I rented bank storage space and hired Brink's guards every Christmas to bring it out, carry it to the table and return it to the vault after dinner. The whole family, of course, now felt entitled to come for Christmas dinner.

People who have never eaten fruitcake may think that after thirty-four years of being gnawed at by assemblages of twenty-five to thirty diners my inheritance would have vanished. People who have eaten fruitcake will realize that it was still almost as intact as on the day George Washington first saw it. While an eon, as someone has observed, may be two people and a ham, a fruitcake is forever.

It was an antique dealer who revealed this truth to me. The children had reached college age, the age of parental bankruptcy, and I decided to put the family fruitcake on the antique market.

"Over two hundred years old?" The dealer sneered. "I've got one at home that's over three hundred," he said. "If you come across a fruitcake that Julius Caesar brought back from Gaul, look me up; I'll give you ten dollars for it."

To cut expenses, I took it out of the bank. Still, there was that backbreaking cost of feeding twenty-five to thirty relatives each Christmas when they felt entitled to visit the family fruitcake. An idea was born.

Before leaving town for a weekend, I placed it on the television set. When burglars came for the TV, they were bound to think the antique fruitcake worth a fortune and have it in some faraway pawnshop before discovering the truth.

By Monday morning the television set was gone, all right, but the fruitcake was still with us. "I should have wired it," I told Uncle Jimmy. "Burglars won't take anything that isn't electronic these days."

Uncle Jimmy was not amused. "You're a lucky man," he said.

Lucky? Bankrupted by an idiotic faith in higher education was what I was.

"Lucky!" he shouted. "Don't you know there's a curse on the family fruitcake? It is said that a dreadful fate will fall upon anyone who lets the family fruitcake pass out of the possession of the family."

That really didn't scare me. Still, it couldn't hurt to play safe. After that, I kept the fruitcake locked in the crawl space under the kitchen. This afternoon, I shall bring it out again when twenty-five to thirty relatives come to dinner, and afterward we will all groan as people always groan when their interiors feel clogged with cement.

I now suspect Uncle Jimmy of lying about the curse. I suspect the dreadful fate carried by the family fruitcake is visited upon the one who inherits it. I wish I had a relative in the higher-education business so I could will it to him.

Make sure, as you develop your article, that it holds in ample measure one or more of these interest factors. Editors will be looking for them, by instinct. Readers will be searching for them subconsciously. From such matter comes writer-reading bonding.

TO THE MANNER BORN

"What if a much of a which of a wind gives the truth to summer's lies; bloodies with dizzying leaves the sun and yanks immortal stars awry?"

e.e. cummings had a manner, a style, a voice. It was his. His alone. You, too, must offer that voice which not only separates you from other writers but over time identifies you.

These are vague terms, abstractions. What is a manner? How is voice achieved? Can style be defined? Well, I'd ask you to consider clarity and vitality and visuality and personality as part of a definition. I'd ask of you as stylist to always know the right word. "To be or not to be," Shakespeare has Hamlet say. He doesn't call on the word "live." He doesn't open the soliloquy with "To exist or not to." It's "To be or not to be," and no other way should it be.

I encountered style one February day as I sat to read an article labeled "Bats" in *The New Yorker* (February 29, 1988). The writer tells us:

> In old wives' tales bats were thought to tangle in women's hair and drive them insane.
> "Want to tangle?" I offer, as if inviting him to perform an Argentine dance. We lift him onto my hair, which is thick and curly, and at first he slides off. Finally, he hooks his five-toed feet on and hangs down one side of my head as if he were on a motel curtain. Travelling with Tuttle, he's had to put his feet up in some pretty odd places, but human hair is clearly not one of his favorites. At last, he creeps around my head a little, and I hear him sneeze gently again—from my cologne, it seems. Then he wraps his wings around my neck, his tiny claws search my skin for a foothold, and he looks up at me with his liquid eyes.
> "What's the best way to show affection to a bat?" I ask Tuttle.
> He carefully considers the question, then says, "I'm not even sure I know the *best* way to show affection to a person."

The author's name was new to me at the time, but Diane Ackerman had style. She turned her attention a few months later to "Crocodilians," in *The New Yorker*, October 10, 1988.

> Nothing looks more contented than a resting alligator. The mouth falls naturally into a crumpled smile, the eyes half close in a sleepy sort of way, the puckered back looks as harmless as the papier-mache maps of the Alps that children make in elementary school. The thick toes hug the mud like tree roots. Alligators, because their massive jaws curve upward, appear to be laughing even when they're in repose. They seem caught in a great big private chuckle.
> Sitting on an alligator is an ideal way to learn about its anatomy. Some people think that "alligators wear a built-in ugly job," as one writer put it. If so, they haven't studied an alligator closely. Alligators have beautiful undulating skin, which feels dense, spongy, and solid, like a good eraser . . .
> When you look down on an alligator, if you let your sense of perspective go you'd swear you were flying over the Rockies at thirty thousand feet. Its back is covered with miniature mountain ranges—horny plates that pucker and interfold and are geometrically arranged. Only the top of the alligator has these spiky ridges.

What style. For the writer of an article, the how of presentation is nearly as important as the what. Diane Ackerman fills her articles with a feast of informational enlightenment. But she truly makes the reading a feast because of how she puts the ingredients together. She let a bat roam about her hair and head. She sat on an alligator. Style seems with her to be a way of life. She needs to get close to her subject, thereby bringing her reader close.

You cannot copy someone else's style; it comes from within. But you can learn from stylists, which is why writers must read. By reading the verbal stylists — of fiction as well as nonfiction — you'll come to understand what writers do to win their readers. And you'll gain the courage to experiment with your own gift and personality. You begin to add art, the personal, to science, the craft.

Novelist and travel writer Paul Theroux took a "subway Odyssey" for the January 31, 1982 issue of *The New York Times Magazine*. His article attracts less for its matter (a subject much written of) than its manner:

> New Yorkers say some terrible things about the subway — that they hate it, or are scared stiff of it, or that it deserves to go broke. "I haven't been down there in years," is a common enough remark from a city dweller. Even people who ride it seem to agree that there is more original sin among subway passengers. And more desperation, too, making you think of choruses of "O dark dark dark. They all go into the dark . . . ."
>
> "Subway" is not its name, because, strictly speaking, about half of it is elevated. But which person who has ridden it lately is going to call it by its right name, "the Rapid Transit"?
>
> You can wait a long time for some trains and, as in T.S. Eliot's "East Coker," often
>
> *. . . an underground train, in the tube, stops too*
> *long between stations*
> *And the conversation rises and slowly fades into*
> *silence*
> *And you see behind every face the mental*
> *emptiness deepen*
> *Leaving only the growing terror of nothing to*
> *think about . . . .*
>
> The subway is frightful looking. It has paint and signatures all over its aged face. It has been vandalized from end to end. It smells so hideous you want to put a clothespin on your nose, and it is so noisy the sound actually hurts. Is it dangerous? Ask anyone, and, without thinking, he will tell you there must be about two murders a day on the subway.
>
> You have to ride it for a while to find out what it is and who takes it and who gets killed on it.
>
> I spent a freezing week in December doing little else except riding the subway.

Theroux, like a poet, makes the subject fresh through his manner.

Manner. Matter. Focus. Three vital concepts for you as you plunge into the labor of creating an article.

James Gorman's essay, "Amphibian Rights," gave distinction to the May/June 1988 issue of *The Sciences* that earned for the publication a National Magazine "General Excellence" Award. Gorman designed a focused piece for an educated readership. His selection of material is appropriate. He provides controversy and the unusual and heart strings and humor as his interest factors. His style is impeccable and appropriate. There's no lack of clarity or vitality. The words evoke images. And *he* can be found in every word.

Savor it.

Amphibian Rights
— The Frog That Insisted on Being a Frog

Sometimes its hard to take frogs seriously. From Aristophanes' chorus to Jim Henson's Kermit, frogs have been universally regarded as comic figures. If Aristophanes had wanted to write a tragedy, I'm sure he would have called it something else — *The Snakes*, perhaps, or *Oedipus Rex*, or if he had been following the animal rights movement, *The Chimpanzees*. True, chimpanzees once were comic creatures themselves, but that was some time ago. These days, neither Bonzo nor Ronald Reagan seems as funny as he once did.

Unlike the President, chimpanzees have not effected their own transformation. We have changed the way we view them by studying their behavior, teaching them language, and using them in medical research. We now know that they share our genetic makeup to an astonishing degree. We've learned, largely through Jane Goodall's work in Tanzania, that they're intelligent, and have rich individual personalities. We also know that their existence in the wild is in jeopardy. So when Goodall makes an impassioned plea for (at the least) more humane treatment of chimpanzees, as she did not long ago — when she describes animals caged in isolation, deprived of company, comfort, and stimulation, and finally driven insane — few of us can fail to be moved.

But what if the plea were made in behalf of frogs? Would we be moved? Or perhaps the question is, Are we moved? — for such a plea has, in fact, been made. In the spring of 1987, a high school student named Jenifer Graham, of Victorville, California, refused to dissect a frog in biology class. Her contention was that there were other ways of learning about frogs and biology. She is a vegetarian and is opposed to raising and killing animals for human enlightenment. Her grade was reduced from an A to a C, so she went to court, with the help of the Humane Society of the United States. She contends that her position on frogs is a moral belief protected under the First Amendment.

The case, scheduled to be heard in federal court in August, is of the sort that attracts attention. Because of it, Jenifer Graham has found herself featured in *People* magazine. She has also made it into commercials, starring in a television ad for Apple Computer. Apple has a computer program called Operation Frog, which allows students to learn about the insides of frogs without wielding an actual knife. The commercial outraged certain groups of scientists and educators, who complained that it would fan opposition to experimentation on animals. Apple, which knows which side its double-density disks are buttered on, withdrew the ad.

I'd rather Jenifer Graham reap the benefits of publicity than, say, Oliver North. But neither of these turns of event is going to help the public—the lay, omnivorous, American public—take the whole frog conflict with a straight face. I suspect that the mythical educated layman is going to think the stakes just aren't that high, on either side. We're not going to cure any dread diseases by chopping frogs up in high schools. Nor can one imagine that the suffering of a pithed frog is in the same league as that of a caged chimpanzee. But the stakes are not as small as they might seem. Apart from the questions of results and suffering, there is an issue common to the plight of both chimpanzees and frogs. It has to do with how we think of these animals, what we imagine them to be. You might say that the plight of chimpanzees embodies this question in tragic form, while in the case of frogs—lower, more vulgar animals (much like the characters Aristotle recommended to comic playwrights in his *Poetics*)—the drama takes the form of comedy.

I admit to bias on this issue. I take both comedy and frogs seriously. It never pays to dissect a love of comedy, but the roots of my profrog stance are easily traced. At nine or ten years of age, my best friend and I decided to dissect a frog. We had been slaughtering them for years, killing them with rocks and spears, and I suppose we had decided to stop playing at hunter-gatherer and to start playing at scientist. We caught a big bullfrog in a swamp, brought it to my friend's backyard, and hypnotized it by flipping it on its back and rubbing its stomach.

I don't know what the physiological reality of this so-called hypnosis is, but the frog ended up apparently anesthetized. The next step was to skin it. Our plan was to dissect the animal while it was still alive. After all, we had seen plenty of frog innards in other contexts, dead contexts. Now we wanted to see the inside of a living frog, to watch heart and lungs in action. This was no offhand cruelty; we acted in the spirit of scientific inquiry. We wanted to lift the veil on the workings of nature. And we did. We removed all the skin except that around the feet, forefeet, and head, which was too hard to remove without causing excessive damage. The frog, thus neatly exposed, was off-white, the bundled fibers of its muscles clearly delineated. It looked just like a biological illustration, except for the green boots and mask.

My memory goes hazy at this point. I don't recall whether we got any further, whether we breached the abdominal wall. What I do remember is that the frog woke up. It began to hop around. Without its skin. We were horrified, giddy with panic and shame. We shrieked. I believe we laughed. And we ran around in a kind of frenzy looking for some way to kill the creature. We finally found a big enough stone and crushed it.

My purpose in telling this gruesome story is not to drum up sympathy for frogs. Who knows precisely what pain the frog felt? Amphibians are not mammals, and I don't remember the frog's giving any sign of suffering. And whatever its pain, however grim the dissection, this was still no tragedy. It could even be argued, though it might seem heartless, that a skinless hopping frog captures the essence of comedy, which can be every bit as brutal as dissection. The frog's awakening was a kind of comic reversal. It turned things upside down, or perhaps inside out. It caused a startling juxtaposition of two ideas that could not rest comfortably side by side—frog as frog, and frog as thing to be dissected. The scientific object (or intended object) had played a prank on its investigators and literally leaped away from their idea of it. The joke was on us.

Until that dissection, we had thought of frogs in one way, as quick and slimy, prey to our predator. Then we had tried to view one particular frog in a new way, as a collection of enlightening parts. The two views came into violent conflict, just as Jane Goodall's vision of chimpanzees is in conflict with that of scientists whose goal is, through research on chimpanzees, to find a vaccine for hepatitis B. She sees the animals as wonderful, worthy, individual beings, ends in themselves, whereas medical researchers use them, and must inevitably come to conceive of them, as means to another end.

There probably is no other way to get a vaccine for hepatitis B. And I don't doubt that we need to cut up at least a few frogs to keep up with Soviet science education. But it wouldn't hurt to remember that Goodall's work is science, too, that her view of chimpanzees is the result not of sentiment but of research. And, though it may not be a matter of national importance, there is the question of how we want to think of frogs. For all the knowledge gained from a dissection, there is something lost as well. It's very tempting to view a dissected frog as the sum of its parts, but the temptation should be resisted. There's more to even such a lowly, comic creature as a frog—as frogs themselves, on rare occasions, may remind us.

4

Information Gathering

SIX HONEST SERVING MEN

I keep six honest serving men
  (They taught me all I knew);
Their names are What and Why and When
  And How and Where and Who.

—Rudyard Kipling

You're only as good as your material.

Your words may have plenty of swing and sway. Your nickname may be Style. But if you haven't anything to say, if you haven't enough to work with, your article will be stillborn, informationally stale, and intellectually sterile.

Facts and viewpoints must be gathered in profusion.

More than you want to collect and far more than you'll use.

You'll recall the old iceberg theory, attributed to Ernest Hemingway. The tip we see above the waterline represents the article. That's only one seventh of the mass hidden beneath. The unseen bulk is the rest of your research, important because the gathering and the studying of that material have given you a fuller understanding of the subject and because they permit you to choose the best stuff for the edification of your reader.

Therefore, don't skimp on information gathering time.

Think first. Think carefully what sort of information you're going to require. Then consider where and how to get it. Will research help, in libraries, in files, in documents? That sort of gathering should be done early, first if possible. From records comes the background which makes what follows in the collection process more rewarding. During this step also peruse the existing literature. What other articles have been written about the subject? What books? You can determine how previous writers have perceived the subject, how completely it has been covered, whether that coverage is dated, what you need to add or can add with an article at this time. Sources available and sources important to contact will become clear to you. Not only does such research provide important information, some of which you will end up using, but it gives you the foundation. It supplies the education that begins to make you the expert, that changes you from the generalist to a quick-study specialist. This initial research should not make you believe, however, that now there's little more anyone can contribute to your knowledge. It should prompt, tempt, tease, force you away from the books and papers to the world of people where the action is and where developments will be found. Research will get you ready for that world.

BUILDING A SOLID FOUNDATION

Robin Wright won a National Magazine Award for excellence in reporting as a result of his September 5, 1988 *New Yorker* piece, "Teheran Summer." He could not have written these two trenchant paragraphs without research.

> Teheran this summer had the appearance and the feeling of an embattled city. It has never been a pleasant place. Because it was chosen as the capital in the late eighteenth century, by the Qajar dynasty, it has no history comparable to that of Damascus or Cairo, and it lacks the scenery of prewar Beirut. With the exception of the mosques and some of the newer villas, the architecture is mostly block functional, and most buildings are dirtied by some of the worst pollution in the world; beginning at dawn, the air is thick with exhaust from aging motorcycles and carbon-belching bus mufflers. Angry traffic is more aggressive than that in Rome and Mexico City combined; stoplights, lane dividers, and street signs such as "Stop" and "One Way" are largely ignored, as are, often, ambulance sirens. An Asian envoy told me that the police reported an average of five hundred accidents every day in Teheran, and on some days I felt as if I had witnessed most of them. Like any other capital, Teheran is not totally representative of the entire nation, but, with an estimated twelve million of the nation's fifty-million population now crammed into it — the figure was about five and a half million at the time of the 1979 revolution — it has become a fair reflection of Iran's travails, especially since it was drawn into the war this spring.
>
> In July, the windows of high-rise office buildings and shop fronts downtown, of clinics and mud-brick shanties in the arid south, and even of splendid villas in the wealthy northern suburbs, were still crisscrossed with thick strips of tape, and the entrances and entire first floors of many government offices and all banks were protected by layers of burlap bags filled with sand.

Granted, Wright observed carefully. But before he observed, he searched for history and statistics that, carefully and sparingly used, gave depth to his observation. Yes, he proves also the effectiveness of skilled observation:

> On the busy highway to Behesht-e Zahra, we passed two funeral corteges. The first was led by a green hatchback. Two men sitting in the open rear were running a large tape recorder, from which a man's chanting of Koranic verses was amplified on two loudspeakers strapped to the car roof. On the hood of the car, a garland of flowers surrounded a picture of the deceased, a young man who had died at the front. A beige ambulance van carrying the

body was next; its back doors were open, and I could see young men — probably family members or fellow-soldiers — crowded on both sides of the body. Buses packed with relatives and friends followed. On the rear of one bus was another enlarged picture of the victim; a banner on one side read "Congratulations on Your Martyrdom." Traffic was so congested at the entrance to Behesht-e Zahra that a policeman was frantically whistling directions to converging funeral convoys. "Fridays are always like this," my friend said.

Our senses can, if used, supply us with wonderful material. Wright could not and probably would not have attempted his story without on-site reporting. He watched and listened and sniffed. What he observed became much of the article's substance. What Wright experienced as onlooker enriched the writing and led a panel of judges to consider the article award-worthy.

Seeing Is Believing

The best of articles, even just marketably good ones, are rarely created from library work. You have to be willing to get out in the field. Where the grape harvesters work or the children learn to read or senior citizens retire to or strikers carry their picket signs or bankers determine mortgage qualifications or emergency medical teams operate or soldiers man an Arctic outpost or cruise ship passengers bask in the sun or a priest administers Communion or a troupe of actors rehearses for a play opening.

It was the observational work of writers like Alex Shoumatoff that helped the editors of *Vanity Fair* win a general excellence category National Magazine Award. He went "In Search of the Source of AIDS." For its July 1988 issue, *Vanity Fair* sent him "on a journey of exploration along the equator, where he met the fatalistic bar girls of Kinshasa, the exhausted doctors of war-shattered Uganda, the folk healers of Guinea-Bissau" and others. He must have immersed himself in research before his trip and more after he returned. But the guts of the article come from what he saw on the scene. In Uganda, according to Shoumatoff, people refer to the disease as Slim. He wrote:

> The road leads on and on through marsh and pasture. We are dead on the equator, and the sun is incredibly hot. I imagine myself a latter-day Ponce de Leon, searching for the Fountain of Death. Or as Captain John Speke, about to discover Lake Victoria, the source of the White Nile. How curious it would be, I think, if the source of the Nile and the source of AIDS prove to be one and the same, that huge teeming lake deep in the dangerous heart of darkest Africa.
>
> We pick up a couple and give them a lift to the next village, Kyotera. Baker tells me that "they burned one [a Slim victim] yesterday in their village, and where they are going so many have died" that *bazungu*, whites, have come to study the situation. I ask how many are so many, and Baker says very

many. Having been through this several times before in the Third World, I know it is futile to expect reliable figures. Numbers are a Temperate Zone precision trip. Here they are flourishes, thrown out for effect. The figures are figurative. I ask how the couple think Slim is transmitted. "Mainly by sex, but sometimes by witchcraft against debt welshers," they say.

Further on we are told:

In the village of Kyebe we stop and walk uphill to a small, tidy clinic. A dozen women are seated on benches. A stench of diarrhea hovers over the scene. There are drumbeats in the adjacent banana grove. Who's in charge? I ask. He's in there, I am told. I look into the dark dispensary. The doctor comes out, coughing. He sees me, pulls himself together, and flashes a winsome, white-toothed smile. He is in his late twenties, with large shiny eyes, a good-looking chap, except that he is very weak and wasted. There is no flesh on his arms. He cannot stand alone, and props himself up against the door as we talk. His assistant tells me that there are 1,800 people in Kyebe and that "we bury every day about six. This month we treated about twenty, and more than thirty died." The number problem again.

I give the doctor a letter of introduction from a clinic I visited the day before. He reads it and says apologetically, "I'm afraid I can't take you around. There are only two of us here and many patients."

"You don't look so good yourself," I say.

"Just a cough," he replies cheerily.

Obviously he can't go anywhere. He's got it. Shit, I realize, even the doctor's got it. He's a goner. He has maybe two months to live.

Shoumatoff's observation borders on participation. He isn't merely watching. He is interacting with those who can supply the insights, and yet he remains on the sidelines. He is not a key player. That would be not only inappropriate for the story but, in this case, dangerous for the writer. John Heminway, on the other hand, took a safari to do "On the Wild Side" for *Condé Nast TRAVELER* (November 1988) and help that publication win a National Magazine Award, again for general excellence. His information gathering involved participation. The author's involvement made the story possible and exciting. Here's how he gets the action underway:

The three of us light our campfire at nightfall near a mountain range of volcanic rock in the southern Masai Steppe of Tanzania just before the evening rain and eat ugali, cornmeal dipped in a mix of onions, tomatoes, and bits of wildebeest. Peter Jones, archaeologist turned safari guide, is talking about the Pleistocene lives of the wa-Ndorobo, traditional hunter-gatherers, that we are on our way to visit—another hundred miles to go—when a quiet cough comes from the oily darkness. I stare but hear only the clinking of metal. Then, gradually, I see our firelight reflecting off two spears. A pair of near-naked Masai *morani*—warriors—appear at the edge of the light.

"*Hodi*," they intone.

They are asking to be welcomed.

"*Karibu,*" Jones replies. ("Welcome.")
They prop spears against a thornbush, remove shields from their arms, and collapse next to us by the fire. We give them the remains of the *ugali.* I listen to the soft plainsong of their conversation and reflect on the fitness of the encounter. When we wake, only embers of the fire are left. The *morani* are gone.
 We have driven south all day from Arusha on mud-wallow roads with the photographer Robert Freson, not pausing at all to view the scattered clusters of wildebeest and zebra. "Everybody who comes to Africa," says Peter Jones, "thinks the continent is populated only by animals. They're missing half the story." Jones spends much of his time on the Serengeti in a luxurious tented camp, introducing visitors to the world's largest terrestrial animal migration. His ultimate aim, however, is to create safaris that focus on both animals and man to show how some traditional people survive in an alien modern world.
 I have joined Jones for a three-day walk back in time with the wa-Ndorobo. I want to taste the experience for travelers, and as chairman of the African Wildlife Foundation, I want to see how hunters like the wa-Ndorobo fit the "enemy" stereotype other conservationists and I have developed over the years.

Not only are we there, but we've found out why author Heminway chose to be there.

Ways and Means of Research

It's your decision as to how best gather your information. Sometimes the subject dictates method. More often, however, you have a choice. Base that choice on where and how the information is most readily attainable but also on your instinct about what sort of information will best serve subject, magazine, and reader.

 Surveys and analysis may be your most useful approach. The views of a multitude may be what you need. How do CEOs feel about the economy in the year ahead? What high ticket items are consumers most likely to purchase? Is the nation turning more liberal or conservative and what goups of people seem to be shifting? How do children view the future? What do viewers of a television news show tend to remember, what not, and how should these tendencies be reflected in the structuring of more effective news programs? Get your polling expertise honed.

 Always be alert to the possibility of simply assembling statements from selected sources. Simply assembling, mind you, is not necessarily a simple task; it requires research on whom to ask and exactly what, writing for cooperation, obtaining that cooperation, and then shepherding the chosen flock so that statements asked for become statements received. Editing (smoothing, cutting, bridging) probably comes next, followed by requests for approval of those edits.

American Heritage, another National Magazine Award general-excellence winner, published the work of Bill McCloud in their May/June 1988 issue. McCloud is an Oklahoma high school teacher who asked prominent figures via handwritten notes "What Should We Tell Our Children About Vietnam?" According to the editor's subtitle: "Politicians and journalists and generals and combat veterans answered him. Secretaries of Defense answered him. Presidents answered him. Taken together, the answers form a powerful and moving record of the national conscience."

Indeed so.

For instance, television critic Michael Arlen says (in part):

> My own opinion about television and Vietnam is that its effects were contradictory. To some extent television showed us war (though not its horrors) and turned the audience against it. To some extent, in the safe banality of its coverage (especially in the early years), television banalized war and made it seem okay, manageable, winnable.

And chief Indochina correspondent for the Associated Press, Malcolm Browne, says:

> Maybe the lesson of Vietnam was this: If you really want to win a war, you're best off fighting it on your own, with as little help from outside as possible. I watched South Vietnamese fighting spirit evaporate in direct proportion to increases in the level of U.S. aid, combat assistance, and advice that was poured in. It's just possible that Saigon would have waged a better war if we had simply stayed out. In the early 1960s it cost one of the Trung Lap rangers about thirteen cents to kill a Communist guerrilla. When we began using Guam-based B-52s for that job, the cost rose to about $137,000 for every guerrilla killed. The Saigon troops stood back and laughed at us, until they realized they were laughing at their own doom, and then it was too late. Fed up, the United States pulled out, and the roof caved in.

Secretary of Defense Robert McNamara responds succinctly:

> The United States must be careful not to interpret events occurring in a different land in terms of its own history, politics, culture, and morals.

The array is impressive; the lesson, at times, profound. For Bill McCloud, information gathering was by far the most important task, once he had the idea. The writing took care of itself or, rather, others took care of it for him.

But for nearly all articles — whether or not statement solicitation or surveying or participation or observation or record research is involved — interviewing remains a necessity.

THE ART OF INTERVIEWING

Interviewing is a complex skill made more difficult by imponderables ranging from availability problems to human eccentricities, and even by the mood of the participants, the how-I-feel-about-how-you-feel-I-feel-and-how-you-feel-about-how-I-feel-you-feel factor. The same two participants can end up with quite different results on any one day. How does the interviewee feel? What's on his mind? What has she just experienced? How comfortable is the environment selected? How busy has the interviewer been today? How pressured does he feel? How improved is her flu-ridden child?

Joy has an impact. So does lack of it. So do the assurance of an interviewer, the fear in an interviewee (or the reverse), the care for or dislike of one person for the other, the enthusiasm over the assignment or the lack thereof. As an interviewer, you need to be a psychologist, to be sensitive to personalities and nuances.

Playboy has made an art of the form. Its interviews are almost psychoanalytical, autobiographies in quotes. You may not have anything so complex in mind. But even a seemingly simple interview requires more of the writer than the surface result would indicate. An absorbing interview is difficult to achieve. The good interview is shaped all along the way. First the interviewer (possibly in collaboration with the editor) decides what the reason for the interview is and what sort of material to seek. He bases his questions on research, so the questions come from knowledge rather than guesswork and the answers become the desired package of information. Later he shapes the answers so that they're true in spirit to the speaker's words and intent but smoother, more comprehensible for the reader, and reordered for sense.

G. Barry Golson, *Playboy's* executive editor and for years responsible for the magazine's distinguished series of interviews, once explained some of the difficulties to me this way: "The interview isn't an article *about* someone. To an extent, it is *by* that person. The interviewer has to prod and challenge and draw out, but ultimately the subject of the interview must have enough to say—and the ability to say it well." He noted that not all journalists are good interviewers, likening "the interviewer's craft to the playwright's art, only in reverse. As a playwright must know instinctively how the dialogue he writes will sound when spoken aloud, so must an interviewer listen for, and elicit, responses which will read authentically in print."

He spoke also of specific skills. "First, a willingness to prepare exhaustively. He or she will have researched the subject so thoroughly that, like a lawyer, there should be virtually no answers, or topics, that come as a complete surprise. Next, the journalist's personal traits— aggressiveness, persistence, patience, diplomacy, to say nothing of the ability to lead a conversation rather than be led by the subject: these are vital. And finally, the interviewer needs the skill to shape verbal dialogue, with all its twists and pauses and repetitions, into something which is terse and seamless on paper."

Golson called on Larry Grobel to interview entertainer Dolly Parton for the October 1978 issue. Grobel called his preparatory efforts exhausting. "I try to make myself fully aware of the people I interview. I'll see their films, read their books, go to their concerts, listen to their records, read what has been written about them, talk to people who know them. I try to feed my mind so that when I'm with that person, I don't have to rely on my written questions (although I usually prepare more than five hundred) but know enough about them to be genuinely interested in how they do what they do, where they come from, and where they think they're going."

It took knowledge of the subject on Grobel's part to make Parton come alive through words on paper. He had done enough footwork to know that she wouldn't be offended by a question that other people might consider rude, as illustrated in this exchange:

Playboy: OK. Now, why *do* you choose to look so outrageous?

Parton: People have thought I'd be a lot farther along in this business if I dressed more stylish and didn't wear all this gaudy getup. Record companies have tried to change me. I just refused. If I am going to look like this, I must have had a reason. It's this: If I can't make it on my talent, then I don't want to do it. I *have* to look the way I choose to look and this is what I've chose. It makes me different a little bit, and ain't that what we all want to do: be a little different?

It's fun for me. It's like a little kid playing with her paints and colors. I like to sit and tease my hair. If there's something new on the market in make-up, I like to try it. You've got to have a gimmick. You've got to have something that will catch the eye and hold the attention of the public. But the funny thing is, no matter how much I try new stuff, I wind up looking just the same.

Playboy: Do you think you'll become a fashion trend setter? Isn't there already a Dolly Parton look?

Parton: [Laughing] Can you imagine anybody wanting to look this way for *real*? When people first get to know me, they say, "Why do you wear all of this?" Then, after a week of knowing me, they totally understand. They know it's just a bunch of baloney. But why not? Life's boring enough, it makes you try to spice it up. I guess I just throw on a little too much spice.

Playboy: Why are there so many Dolly Parton look-alike contests?

Parton: Because they're fun. Who would be better to impersonate than Dolly Parton? All you gotta do is get a big blonde wig, make-up, and if you're pretty well proportioned . . . or you can even fake it. The best parts of Dolly Parton look-alike contests are guys dressed up like girls. It's so *easy* to do me.

Playboy: Have you ever met any of the winners?

Parton: I sure have. They were the biggest bunch of pigs I ever saw, most of them. I thought to myself, Is that how people think I look? I thought, Oh, Lord, some of them were in worse shape than I even thought I was. I've only seen two that would even be classified as a human being.

Playboy: So you don't think they've ever been able to imitate the real, sexy you?

Parton: Listen, I never thought of myself as being a sex symbol. It never crossed my mind that anybody might think I was sexy . . .

Playboy: But surely, after all the media exposure you've received, you have to be conscious of what people say and think about you.

Parton: I didn't say what *you*-all thought. I said that it never once crossed *my* mind, even now. I still can't get it through my head that people think I'm supposed to be sexy or somethin'. I don't want that responsibility. I don't want to have to keep up an image like that. I don't want to have to be like a beautiful woman, like a Raquel Welch—which is no trouble, I never would anyway. I'm just sayin' I wouldn't want people to look at me and if I gained ten pounds, they'd say, "Oh, God, she's ruined her looks," I'm made up of many things. I'm very complex. I have much more depth than just my looks, which to me are not all that hot, anyway. I've always looked a certain way and had an image. I like the big hairdo, the gaudy clothes. There's not much sexy about that. Men are not usually turned on by artificial looks and I've always been like that.

Playboy: If that's true, why do you suppose there's such a huge cosmetic industry in this country?

Parton: I'm talking about *my* kind—the big wigs, the total artificial look. I don't try to dress in style or to be really classy. I've got my work to do and I *like* to look good, but I don't try to keep an image other than just this gimmick appearance that I have. If I was trying to really impress men or be totally sexy, then I would dress differently.

Playboy: How would you look?

Parton: I would wear low-cut things. Try to keep my weight down. Try to really work on my body. I would find a new, softer, sexier hair style—it would be my own hair, some way. But why bother, I'm already married and *he* don't mind how I look. He likes me gaudy or ungaudy.

The editors of *Meetings & Conventions* had a more specific agenda when, as part of a section devoted to "Tomorrow's Meetings—What's Next," (September 1988) they asked futurist Alvin Toffler to predict "The Shape of Future Meetings." Their questions were limited to that particular. Still, the questions had to be selected, based on editorial needs. And a published answer such as this from Toffler undoubtedly required compilation and compression:

I think that we will see smaller, more intimate meetings. Or maybe a very large number of people coming to the same city but broken into discrete groups. I've been saying this for many years, and it hasn't happened, so maybe the timing is wrong. But I think there is an upper limit. There's a point beyond which the value is lost.

As a speaker I go to many meetings, and there are some that I enjoy. I've spoken to groups as small as ten and to groups as large as thirty thousand. You can guess which of these are more fun.

There are three things I guess that people get out of meetings. One is the formal information that comes off the platform and out of the meetings. The second, and by far more important, is the networking that goes on. The flesh markets, the recruiting, the exchange of job information and so forth.

The third is recreation and simply a change from the daily routine. There comes a point at which the delivery of information is less effective when it is more "massified." There comes a point at which the networking is simply uncomfortable because of too many bodies around. You can't network with ten thousand delegates. You can only network with fifty, or one hundred if you're lucky.

And there comes a point at which even the recreation is no fun because it's cookie cutter. It's the same for everyone. Everyone gets crowded into a bus and dragged over to the side of the pool. There is, I believe, a scale of diminishing returns.

Interviewing: A Basic Guide

The following list outlines the basics of interviewing. Just the basics because of space limitations, but it should get you started. We'll touch briefly on the interview format again in Chapter Five. You might, however, look up a book devoted exclusively to interviewing. My personal favorite is *Creative Interviewing* by Ken Metzler (Prentice-Hall).

1. *Ask intelligent questions.* Playwright of the absurd Eugene Ionesco once noted: "Why do people always expect authors to answer questions? I am an author because I want to *ask* questions. If I had the answers, I'd be a politician."

Questions must be asked. You must want to ask questions. You must want to be with the person who can answer the questions. Prepare the list of questions to be asked; the greater the preparation, the more flexible you become. Be specific in the wording of your questions, but make them open ended whenever possible. Avoid asking questions that can be answered simply "yes" or "no."

Magazine writer Laurence Gonzales, whose specialties include *Playboy* interviews of notable personages, advises: "Your questions have to be as creative as any piece of writing you will do — bold, probing, yet tactful. You must stay with the interview, persevering until the questions are answered fully and until they honestly illuminate major issues and personality traits. You need to recognize and deal promptly with side-stepping responses, half-truths, braggadocio, and even outright prevarication."

2. *Consider the interview a performance.* Play your part with respect for the other participant. Show your respect through a friendly attitude and a zest for the moment. Give the impression that you know a lot and yet know nothing. Make it clear that you've taken the trouble to find out as much as you can about the subject and person being interviewed but that now you're there to learn from an expert. Evince curiosity, an eagerness to be enlightened.

When asked how she prepares for an interview, journalist Nora Ephron said: "One of the first things I do is try to find everything that has been written about the person or subject. I use the public library. If I'm doing a piece about someone in the theater, for example, I look up every production the person has been in and find others who have been in the same production and call them all." As for personal stories, she added, "I usually see all secondary people before interviewing the person I'm writing about. What other people tell you is often useful in making up questions for the main interview."

3. Know why you are talking to a source. Is it for information, for clarification, for justification, for argumentation, for a combination of some or all? Ask questions accordingly.

4. Engage in preliminary discussion. Make clear what it is you want from the interviewee. Also make sure it's clear to you what the interviewee wants the interview to accomplish. Help the answerer be better. That makes your story better.

5. Listen. Questions prompt. Answers impart. Give the source a chance to talk. Encourage him to talk. Don't interrupt. Remember that the person you're talking to is your source. Be open to what that source can impart. Listen for information you never even thought about and threads you never even considered. Listen for prompters that lead you into new directions.

6. Work to establish an atmosphere of trust. The interview is a collaboration far more often than it is combat. Consider it as two people working together to provide information for a third person, the reader. As interviewer, let your colleague understand that a good reporter probes until the source supplies a satisfactory answer, but that, in turn, a good interviewee gets the reporter to ask questions so that the interviewee can say what she wants to say.

7. Use a tape recorder. Openly. You can ask permission, and probably should. Most sources feel reassured by the presence of a recorder. They know at least that you're more likely to get things right. Take notes as well, in case the recorder didn't operate properly.

8. Take it easy, but take it. Build toward the more difficult or sensitive questions. Gain the source's confidence first.

9. Ask and ask again. Make sure you've heard correctly. Give the respondent a chance to correct or elaborate. Probe. Ask for more detail.

10. Use eye contact. Eye contact is important but less so than notetaking. Don't think you have to look at the other person all the time. He or she would rather see you take notes than stare.

11. Be humble. Make the other person feel more important than you.

12. Be empathetic. Understand the interviewee's problems. Express through your manner an interest in what's being told you.

13. Wrap it up. At the conclusion say, "Is there anything else you want to tell me? Have you any final thought?"

THE REWARDS OF RESEARCH

Articles are only as good as the information they contain. Bad writing can ruin good information, but without a backbone of solid information, even the best writing tends to become an empty exercise.

The following excerpt from an article in the November 1988 issue of *American Heritage* illustrates what happens when good information is handled well. Think how much research and observational consideration the editors put into just one page of an extended section about New York City, circa 1928.

On the Town

(Where do you stay? What will it cost? How do you get a drink? Where to eat? What will *that* cost? What's playing? Is it a talkie? How many people live here, anyway? What kind of place *is* this? All the answers are here.)

To begin at the beginning, a baby is born in New York every four minutes and six seconds — a total of 126,332 in 1928.

Using a twelve-hour day as a basis of computation, couples are getting married in New York at the rate of fourteen every hour — a total of 62,424 getting married in 1928. Everybody can't get married, however, and stay within the law, because in the population of 6,065,000 it is estimated there are fifteen thousand more females than males.

Food Consumption

These 6,065,000 people are consuming food at the rate of approximately 3,500,000 tons a year, an average of more than one thousand pounds of food being consumed or wasted by every man, woman and child.

These people use 2,659,632 quarts of milk a day, almost a pint a piece.

The Health Department estimates that they use seven million eggs a day.

Fifteen hundred freight cars are needed daily to bring the food that New York eats.

If placed together they would form a train twelve miles long.

35 Telephone Lines to Moon

More than 190 people in New York pick up the telephone receiver every second, on the average.

There are approximately 8,233,000 intra-City telephone calls every twenty-four hours.

In addition, the people make 508,000 commuting calls — calls within a fifty-mile radius — and 34,383 long distance calls every day.

The city has 1,700,000 telephones in operation, almost one-fifth as many telphones as are in all of Europe. The 8,367,000 miles of wire in the City would string thirty-five lines between the earth and the moon.

681,818 Buildings

To house the activities of New York's residents and visitors, there were, on October 1, 1928, 681,818 buildings, including 277,118 one-family houses, 143,534 two-family houses, 121,557 non-elevator apartment buildings, and 3,970 hotels and elevator apartments.

There are 89,263 garages and stables to accommodate their automobiles and horses. There are still fifty thousand horses in New York City.

New York's largest building (the Equitable) houses twelve thousand people every day.

5

Structure, the Blueprint
of an Article

MUSHROOMS

they are found in Moss,
   Under bark,
    on Stumps,
 on the sides of patHs in the woods,
   near stReams,
    arOund trees,
 in the spring in Old orchards,
  in the autuMn
among fallen leaveS,

   at any tiMe,
even while eating a picnic lUnch,
    or croSsing a bridge,
 or driving along a Highway,
 or going to the supeRmarket,
    Or
    lOoking out the window,
   or coMing home,
   or viSiting friends (providing you
      live in the
      country).

   soMe are edible:
  the matsUtake,
   ruSsula virescens,
  some Hydnums,
  the moRel, the chantarelle,
and the lepiOtas:
    prOcera,
    aMericana,
 and rachodeS, the honey, and lots of others.

—John Cage

Poet/composer John Cage wrote an additional thirteen stanzas. In each
he positions words and thoughts around the word "MUSHROOMS."

That becomes the poem's structure. The word might be considered the trunk of a tree of words or the vertical foundation of a building of purport. On it and around it Cage builds his poem.

He makes of the effort a game much as he has done in a lifetime of writing both music and words. For him, art is play, format is experiment, problem solution is surprise.

For you, the structure of an article may be far less a matter of game playing than required utilitarianism. But just as Cage selects a method to tie his materials together, so must you.

The tie is structure.

You must consider it carefully.

Call it a blueprint. Call it the design. Call it architecture.

When you have collected all the materials for your projected article, when you have more than enough to write, when you're poised to begin your wordsmithery, hold off. Decide first how all that information should be put together, what sort of plan or order would best convey the data and their essence to the reader. You must make sense of all this stuff, bring the reader into and then through the subject, provide a logical arrangement.

An imposed logic probably won't work. You can't tell yourself, "The magazine seems to feature dramatic article structures, so I better make this story turn somersaults. It has to supply a series of bursts. So maybe on this story I'll try the parallel structure."

If that particular format doesn't suit the information you've gathered to work with, then you could destroy your entire project by forcing the facts into a structural strait jacket. Content and purpose will help you determine the appropriate plan.

Good editors spot improper structuring. They may be able to fix the problem or offer you guidance in fixing it yourself. Poor structure may not necessarily lose you a sale. If the subject of your story holds so much potential and the substance you've come up with is so solid that your editor remains loyal to the assignment he gave you, then he may also remain loyal to you by either letting you improve the flawed article or doing it himself. But add a sensible design to idea and information, and you assure yourself of publication.

Come up with the right structure within that four-part process we call writing, and you also make the final, painful step much less troublesome. That alone is a significant benefit. It makes your writing life more pleasant.

A SMORGASBORD OF STRUCTURE POSSIBILITIES

The following list represents thirteen possible approaches to structure. Although there are undoubtedly other structural techniques, these are the most common, and the most useful.

1. Chronology
2. Inverted pyramid or spiral
3. Hourglass
4. Building block
5. Cause and effect
6. Classification
7. Compare and contrast
8. List
9. Question and answer
10. Parallelism
11. Motivated sequence
12. Reinforcement
13. Compartmentalization

The remainder of this chapter will examine these thirteen structural techniques in more detail. Content and purpose may lead you to select not one but two or three of these approaches for one article, which only means that out of these thirteen ways you can create more through combinations.

Chronology

A narrative is chronological. It happens in time. Even if you employ flashbacks, you offer a series of events or happenings that become consecutive. If you have a story to tell, an event to relate, chronology becomes your means from a beginning to an ending.

How-to articles also lend themselves to chronological treatment. They involve sequential activities. Therefore, think chronology, the technique of the storyteller.

US magazine asked rock musician Jon Bon Jovi to keep a diary when he and his band traveled to the Soviet Union for a Moscow Music Peace Festival. The diary entries (October 30, 1989) became an article allowing the reader to accompany Bon Jovi. Each entry is the chronological story of a day. Here's a sampling from that article:

From Day One:
We all assemble for a press conference, the first of many. Afterwards, we attempt to board *The Magic Bus* — a chartered 757, complete with a Peter Max painted on the side. But we're told that there's a problem, and that we have to wait. The problem turns out to be a bomb scare! They pull luggage off the plane and dogs are brought in to sniff out explosives. Never a dull moment! It's very low-key, and of course there isn't a bomb or anything, just some cheap threat. Unfortunately in this business it happens a lot, so I never think they're real.

We finally board the plane at 9:30 p.m., an hour behind schedule. On board, everyone is excited, talking and joking and comparing junk food. When we were in Moscow last November to do press and introduce ourselves to the public, we discovered that food there is not like we're used to. Russian food includes dried meats and very, very salty cheeses. Even the water is very salty. I've never been one to moan about food, but this stuff really pushed me to the limit. So this time everyone's come prepared. We've brought stuff like Tastykakes, M&M's, Oreos and Twinkies. Twelve hours to go and already they're digging into their supplies!

As the plane takes off, everyone applauds and whistles. We're on our way. I never really believed this day would come.

From Day Three:

I wake up this morning and understand why the Russians have such a great weight-lifting team: My pillow must weigh 110 pounds. The weather is cold and rainy. As I pull on my jeans, I can't help thinking, "Nice day for a murder."

I turn on my TV, searching for MTV, and lo and behold, they have it: Military TV! Six of the seven channels have the same news program, and the seventh is a test pattern.

Interview is the word of the day. The first, at 10:00 a.m., is with Sky One, which broadcasts throughout England and Ireland. I'm interviewed by Mick Wall, an old friend, while we drive around Moscow—a great idea, since I'll be able to see more of the city while I work. We cram in the Soviet equivalent of a 1969 Valiant: Mick, his cameraman (who's carrying full sound and light gear), the director, the soundman and the driver (who doesn't speak English). The windows immediately steam up as we take off. This sums up how most of my interviews go today.

Finally, around 7:00 p.m., I get some dinner at the stadium, which is our base. It's my first real meal of the day, served up by an English caterer we use when we're in Europe.

From Day Five:

I go to see the festival's opening ceremonies at 1:00 p.m., and after some short speeches, the most amazing thing I've ever seen happens. The Olympic torch is relit for the first time since the 1980 Games—in the name of rock & roll. It blows my mind to realize that we, as musicians, did what politicians couldn't or wouldn't do.

At 1:30, the Soviets get their first taste of New Jersey. Skid Row comes onstage and opens the show with more energy than a power plant, rocking the more than seventy-five thousand people in attendance.

After the Skids finish, I go back to the hotel to try to sleep. I feel more like Mike Tyson readying for a fight. I am pumped up, and all I can do is pace around my room.

From Day Six:

The band and I hit the stage in full stride, knowing that tonight's show will go out via satellite to millions of people around the world. As I'm walking through the crowd in a Soviet coat, I can see my band onstage and feel the electricity of the audience. I spot a girl sitting on top of a guy's shoulders, waving the largest Amerian flag I've ever seen. It's been a hell of a day.

After the show, the mayor of Moscow has a party for the bands. There is much toasting, of course, plus Soviet food and dancing.

Chronology works. It shows us here what happened and how.

Inverted Pyramid or Spiral

The traditional news story structure puts an article's most important material up front. What follows is supporting information in descending order of importance. Some practitioners of the art form object to the "pyramid" tag because the word suggests blocks. And whether one refers to blocks of stone in Egypt or blocks of words in a story, blocks upon blocks do not bring flow to mind. Today's newswriter wants the inversion principle to include the smooth movement of information from one sentence to the next, from one aspect of the story to the next. Thus, the substitution of the word "spiral" for "pyramid." A spiral is formed out of continuity of line.

Magazine editors tend to relegate the inverted pyramid to news pages, but if your article fits the mold—if, for instance, your story covers a conference and means to single out major elements in order of importance—go ahead and use it. The news story design hasn't lost its effectiveness:

"It's the highest high we've ever experienced." That's how rock musician Jon Bon Jovi described last month's appearance by his band before seventy-five thousand screaming fans at Moscow's Lenin Stadium.

The group was one of nine that journeyed to the Soviet Union for the first Moscow Music Peace Festival, held to break down barriers between east and west as well as to raise funds for the Make a Difference Foundation, a not-for-profit organization based in Raleigh, North Carolina, and devoted to cultural and social interchange.

Bon Jovi told reporters on return to the United States that during his group's hour-long performance, he could "feel the electricity of the audience." Such events, he added, "bring the world together. We were no longer Americans and Britishers and Australians and Irishmen and Russians. We were all citizens of the world, a brother and sisterhood."

Other bands participating included Motley Crue, Cinderella, Gorky Park. . . .

If as writer you want to make of that trip a news story, then do as I just have. The inverted pyramid or spiral is your method.

Hourglass

An article which begins as an inverted pyramid or spiral and then turns into a chronology or story is called an hourglass.

The Moscow Music Peace Festival story above could start as news. With the most essential information taken care of, the writer could move on to say: "Bon Jovi recounted the seven-day trip during the news conference. 'We're ending this journey much the way it began. We arrived at Newark Airport on August 8. My car was greeted by an army of reporters advancing like storm troopers.' " And then through a series of direct and indirect quotes, the information introduced in the spiral first section is enlarged, but this time as chronology, ending with: "As I'm thinking about the doors that we've helped open this week, the doors of the plane shut. During takeoff, I think of the Who song, 'Long Live Rock.' Sounds good to me."

The hourglass enriches the news structure by giving you the flexibility of moving through information in two complementary ways.

Building Block

If the article you're writing is meant for instruction, here's your approach. You begin with the simplest elements of the subject, then move through progressively more complex material. In a way this book is designed on the building block model. I take you from the basics to more specialized and formidable responsibilities and techniques.

Call it a lesson plan; it's the way a teacher might instruct a class of novices. A trip through Existentialism might begin with a definition, then examine its roots and the environment in which it originated and bloomed, then re-evaluate the definition, this time with greater depth and application, then move to how its various practitioners explored and expanded and twisted the principles to individualize this philosophic system, and finally into criticisms and further analyses.

Your purpose in such articles is to teach. You become the teacher. An article on the Federal Reserve system or the problems of nuclear waste or the quark as the heart of matter might be developed in this fashion.

Cause and Effect

If your article involves the elements of cause and effect, then a natural development is a cause-to-effect or effect-to-cause structure. A history of the 1929 stock market collapse might begin with the various contributing factors: lax control procedures, unreasonable credit margins, a volatile economic decade, a soft employment picture, inflation. These combined to become the cause. The fall was the effect, the result. Cause to effect.

On a stock market plunge just happening, you—as writer—might choose to start with the drama of the moment, the effect. You then present whatever you've been able to find out from authorities/experts about the apparent causes, the background. Effect to cause.

It's a logical unfolding for such topics. Try it on a sports story. The effect: a team championship. The causes: what brought it about.

Classification

If your material divides itself into classes or types or kinds—whether classes of frogs or types of undergraduate students in private universities or kinds of Christmas trees a family can choose from—the article you plan to write neatly divides itself: class by class by class or type by type by type or kind by kind by kind.

In their September/October 1989 issue, *HYATT Magazine* published as travel advice, "Kick that Jet Lag" by a frequent-traveling scientist, Charles Ehret, and his collaborating writer, Lynne Waller Scanlon. They suggested as jet lag remedies "The Henry Kissinger Approach," "The Dwight D. Eisenhower Approach," "The Lyndon Johnson Approach," and "The Three-Step Jet Lag Approach." The article is divided into four sections, one for each approach.

The Kissinger solution, for instance, reads in part:

> When former Secretary of State Henry Kissinger knew he had to attend an important meeting in a foreign country, in the hope that he could systematically shift his body clock to foreign time before he actually boarded the airplane, he would try to retire one hour earlier each night and rise one hour later.
>
> Did it work? The problem with the Kissinger approach to "shuttle diplomacy" is . . .

The two presidents practiced other techniques:

> Former President Eisenhower, in 1955, flew into Geneva on a Friday for a summit meeting with Nikita Krushchev the following Monday. Eisenhower had arrived early in order to try to reduce his jet lag symptoms in time for the meeting.
>
> Was Eisenhower successful in reducing his jet lag symptoms? Partially, but not totally . . .
>
> Former President Johnson rarely, if ever, reset his wristwatch when Air Force One landed in a foreign country. When he flew to Guam to confer with President Nguyen Van Thieu of South Vietnam, Johnson remained on his usual time schedule, eating when he would have at the White House, sleeping when it was dark in Washington, D.C., and arranging meetings at his convenience during what were reasonable hours in the United States.
>
> Was Johnson's technique effective? To a degree, yes, but his approach required an iron will and total denial of events transpiring around him. . . .

Easy to structure. Easy to read.

Compare and Contrast

If your aim is to compare (show how two or more things are alike) or contrast (show how they differ), then that goal can be aided by structuring with one or the other or both as your means. An altered benefits package, a new tax program, the educational results from a previous curriculum and the new, the relationships between Dostoyevsky and Kafka, the similarities in the work of two contemporary photographers, change and circularity in fashion: any of these could be built on elements of alikeness and difference.

List

This chapter is a list. I have structured it by listing thirteen ways to design an article. If you're writing about ten "must" items for a traveler to take to Europe, then create a list, explaining the what and why of each item. It's the easiest structure of all. Don't overuse or abuse it. List when you firmly believe it's the clearest, cleanest way to present your subject, when a series of points is the point of your article.

Question and Answer

The Q and A approach works well (1) as background, (2) as sidebar, (3) as a way to answer the reader's questions about a problem or situation or reality or what, in the writer's view, the reader should be asking and learning.

Addressing the outburst of violence in the long struggle between blacks and whites in South Africa, is this concise backgrounder in question and answer format:

> Apartheid. Too many South Africans, mostly blacks, are losing their lives to it.
> **What is it?**
> Apartheid is the South African government's system of racial segregation. *Government* means Afrikaners, whites of Dutch descent. *Apartheid* is a word from their language, and it means separateness.
> **How does it work?**
> It makes sure that whites rule the country. Whites make up only one-seventh of South Africa's population, while blacks make up almost five-sevenths. The remaining seventh is composed of coloreds (their term for people of mixed races) and Asians.
> **How does apartheid affect blacks?**
> Blacks cannot vote, or own property. They must live in separate districts, and need passes to enter urban areas. Denied citizenship, they are people without a country in the middle of their own birth land.

What better way to push essential information at a reader?

The words of an authority can also be presented as Q and A; in interview format. (Refer to Chapter Four for a thorough discussion of interviewing.)

A variation of the interview is the monologue, based on a journalist's session with someone but with all the questions removed and the answers shaped into one, running statement. *TWA Ambassador* published "Andy Rooney, 24 Hours in the Life of an Essayist." The byline read "Interviewed by John Grossmann." The article sounds like it's all Rooney, although it isn't, of course.

I get up at 5:40. I catch a 6:13 train from Connecticut and read *The New York Times* on the way in. I get into New York City about ten after seven and catch a cab over here to CBS. Yesterday morning I got in at about 7:25. I promised somebody I would do a half-hour radio show on the subject of laughter and I wanted to collect my thoughts and make some notes. I played tennis with Cronkite at 11:00. Kurt Vonnegut's wife was there from *Life* magazine taking some pictures of Cronkite, and it threw my game off badly and he won. Because I played tennis, I ate in yesterday. After lunch I worked on the first piece of the season for *60 Minutes.* We had shot the day before and we were short of pictures of some silly things, some words we had shot on the blackboard and we didn't have enough pictures of them on tape. Then I thought I had better get a column started. I had a column due this morning. In addition to my *60 Minutes* pieces I write three columns a week for syndication to newspapers.

I do whatever strikes me at the moment. I was thinking yesterday of doing something on handwriting. My handwriting is bad. I was thinking it would make a good column — maybe we ought to go back to school every five years and learn how to write.

If an idea has potential visual merit, I try to save it for *60 Minutes.* I have no formula, though, for what goes on television and what goes in print. Obviously, I have more ideas than *60 Minutes* can use, but it's not that I save the best ones for television, because I don't often think one idea is better than another. It depends more on how you treat an idea than what the idea is in the first place.

The Q & A method focuses reader attention on specific information or accentuates the language of a story source.

Parallelism

This technique probably originated with oratory. An example comes in President Franklin D. Roosevelt's second inaugural address:

Here is the challenge to our democracy: In this nation I see tens of millions of its citizens — a substantial part of its whole population — who at this very moment are denied the greater part of what the very lowest standards of today call the necessities of life.

I see millions of families trying to live on incomes so meager that the pall of family disaster hangs over them day by day.

I see millions whose daily lives in city and on farm continue under conditions labeled indecent by a so-called polite society half a century ago.

I see millions denied education, recreation, and the opportunity to better their lot and the lot of their children.

I see millions lacking the means to buy the products of farm and factory and by their poverty denying work and productiveness to many other millions.

I see one-third of a nation ill-housed, ill-clad, ill-nourished.

It is not in despair that I paint you that picture. I paint it for you in hope — because the Nation, seeing and understanding the injustice in it, proposes to paint it out. We are determined to make every American citizen the subject of his country's interest and concern; and we will never regard any faithful, law-abiding group within our borders as superfluous. The test of our progress is not whether we add more to the abundance of those who have much; it is whether we provide enough for those who have too little.

Roosevelt, a brilliant orator, used a rhetorical device. He knew how language could enhance the drama of his message. "I see millions . . . " he says again and again. He has created parallelism, in this case a phrase repeated for emphasis.

Articles lend themselves to this approach occasionally. Economic cycles, repetitions of events, similarities in detail, recurrence of views or situations lend themselves to such treatment if your intent is to highlight the drama of such replays.

Here's part of an article on Johann Sebastian Bach I planned for *Highlights for Children*:

Picture a lovely June day, a garden bordered by linden trees and a river flowing nearby. The garden is filled with guests to a wedding. A long table almost groans from the weight of food: roast ox, pigs with apples stuck in their mouths, cheeses and sausages and fruit. There's music, too, for listening and for dancing.

But the bride is captivated by a voice, so much so that she orders the dancing stopped to hear more of it. The voice belongs to a six-year-old boy with curly hair and a cheerful smile. His is a beautifully clear soprano, and as he sings one folk song after another, the bride, her husband, and the guests listen with smiles on their faces.

Such a singer he is with such a command of the music. And such a performer.

But then, that six-year-old was Johann Sebastian Bach.

*   *   *

Picture a moonlit room and a shadow gliding toward a locked cabinet, the shadow of a boy eleven years old. He steps on a chair and reaches toward a top shelf. His slim fingers manage to grasp a manuscript behind the grillwork and to free it from its imprisonment. By moonlight he copies the music, as much as he can in the few minutes he dares to be in that room. Then he replaces the manuscript and tiptoes out.

The boy does this as often as moonlight permits, until one evening he completes his task.

But just as he's about to leave the room, he's discovered by his older brother, the very person who had forbidden him to study that music, the very person who now demands that the boy tear up what he has copied so diligently.

No matter, because in the act of copying the youngster had memorized the music.

That eleven-year-old was Johann Sebastian Bach.

*   *   *

Picture a young man, age nineteen, walking fifty miles to hear a famous organist perform, then forgetting his weariness as he listens for hours to the organist's magnificent music filling the church. And afterwards, without a penny to his name, he sits down to rest on a bench just outside an inn. He wonders how he's going to eat and how he's going to get home.

Suddenly he hears a thud. And then another. Something has fallen. And something else. His eyes discover two fish heads. Fish heads? Well, that little voice within him prompts him to pick them up. And when he does so, he spots in each a silver coin.

Those coins provide him not only with dinner but with the courage to stay in the town for a while to hear more music.

That nineteen-year-old was Johann Sebastian Bach.

*   *   *

He was just one of several hundred musical Bachs. Everyone who was born a Bach for generation after generation was expected to become a musician. So it wasn't too much of a surprise that Johann Sebastian, born in 1685 — the same year as two other great masters of music, Georg Fridric Handel and Domenico Scarlatti — would prove to be a musical child.

But, Oh, how musical.

I use the parallelism to highlight precociousness and commitment. What follows in the article does not hew to the format, but I felt the beginning deserved special treatment. Parallelism is what I chose.

Motivated Sequence

Should you be writing an editorial or commentary, something with which you want to guide reader belief or action, this structure might be your solution. It's a five-step format designed to motivate:

1. Attention step, your lead or attention getter, the anti ho-hum beginning.

2. Need or problem step, during which through assertion, illustration, ramification you identify the need for the course you're about to propose.

3. Satisfaction or solution step, in which you enunciate your plan to solve the problem.

4. Visualization step, your sales pitch, the section reserved for proof; it's where you say to the reader, "If this is done, here's what will happen."

5. Action step ("So, let's do it, and here's how.").

It works beautifully. The following are examples of how you might use these steps to structure an article on the Arts in Education program.

Attention. Anecdote of third graders acting out the story of a jelly bean thief as part of a reading program. The teacher points out to the writer that the youngster reading the narration could not have done so three months earlier and that the drama technique gave him the motivation to improve his reading. Anecdote of teachers bringing busloads of inner city children to see the Franco Zeffirelli film of Shakespeare's *Romeo and Juliet* and how during its showing even the rowdiest became enthralled.

Need or Problem. Arts in education programs are needed because they work, you tell the reader. They're not fluff. They shouldn't be tangents in the schools but at the heart of the curriculum. The problem is to convince school boards and administrators and teachers of that and to find funds to support such programs.

Satisfaction or Solution. Curricula must be revised. Federal-state-local partnerships must be forged. Industry must be enlisted. Even taxpayers must be enticed through carefully constructed and modulated marketing programs.

Visualization. Verbal pictures of reduced illiteracy, improved job performance, enhanced quality of life, larger and more sensitive audiences.

Action. Let's ask for starter grants from the U.S. Department of Education and the National Endowment for the Arts. Let's call for volunteers from the private sector including marketing and advertising experts to initiate a sales plan. Let's urge the fifty governors to call a national conference of educators and artists to establish curricular goals.

Using the motivated sequence model, your position unfolds step by step.

Reinforcement

Advertisers develop their messages around the principle of reinforcement: (1) Tell them what you're going to tell them; (2) tell them; (3) tell them what you've told them. The principle has become the structural basis for numerous articles. Consider this piece by Sharon Begley and Patricia King from the November 27, 1989 issue of *Newsweek*:

The Supply-Side Theory of Garbage

Another day, another 3.5 pounds of garbage to generate. Sound like a challenge? It's a snap to fulfill your quota. Brush your teeth, rinse, toss the paper cup. Shave with a disposable razor. Comb your hair — oops, a couple of comb teeth snapped off; out it goes. For breakfast, a single-serving cereal box and a juice-in-a-box. There's no time to do dishes, so use a paper bowl and plastic spoon. Off to work, buying a cup of coffee and newspaper on the way. And on through the day . . .

Every American seems to be doing his part; we're producing twice the solid waste per person as the Europeans. This dubious achievement, says Steve Romalewski of the New York Public Interest Research Group (NYPIRG), means that cutting down on trash is "a primary component in a safe and sensible solution to the garbage crisis." The less there is, the less that must be recycled, burned or buried. Known by the unglamorous name source reduction, its potential is huge. Packaging accounts for about one third of solid waste and throwaway items such as plastic utensils account for still more: 1.6 billion disposable pens, two billion disposable razors and sixteen billion disposable diapers a year. "We have been a throwaway society," says Norman H. Nosenchuck, director of the New York State Division of Solid Waste. "We simply have to change our ways."

Thin Diapers

Some changes are already here. In the last twenty years, the soft-drink industry has cut the plastic used in two-liter bottles by 21 percent, the aluminum in cans by 35 percent and the glass in nonrefillable bottles by 43 percent. Each cut saved money for the manufacturer. McDonald's now pumps syrup for soft drinks directly from delivery trucks into tanks in the restaurants, rather than shipping it in disposable cardboard containers. That saves sixty-eight million pounds of packaging a year. Last week Procter & Gamble announced that it is test-marketing fabric-softener concentrate that the shopper purchases in small paper cartons, pours into a dispenser at home, adds water to and shakes. Those steps replace the plastic jugs of ready-made softener, reducing packaging by 75 percent. P&G's disposable Pampers diapers now come in a thin variety that does the job with half as much material. Aveda, a cosmetics firm in Minneapolis, is designing a metal makeup bottle that the consumer can take back to the store for a refill.

Further reductions will require more radical changes. All packaging exists for a reason. Concerns about tampering led to the plastic collars around products from aspirin to yogurt. Waxed-paper inner bags keep cereals in cardboard boxes fresh. But many products owe their existence to the quest for convenience and to marketing ploys. Today we use microwavable, throwaway trays of frozen foods rather than casserole dishes and buy microwave cake mix complete with a throwaway baking pan. Our kids tote juice boxes to the playground and play miniature Helmut Newtons with their Kodak Flings or Fuji disposable cameras. Toothpaste tubes come in boxes so stores can stack them easily; cereal boxes are bigger than needed so they make an impressive display on the store shelf. Cookies come neatly arranged in plastic trays inside paper bags. This list is as long as a supermarket aisle.

Americans won't give up their disposable lifestyle easily, but a little old-fashioned Yankee ingenuity can help. Office workers might make photocopies on both sides of the paper, halving the amount intended for the memo tray as well as, eventually, the circular file. But short of having the state set wages, there is little hope of making it cheaper to repair a radio than buy a new one.

White-Cloth Gentility

What if consumers had to pay up front for their wastrel tastes? The Environmental Defense Fund, an environmental research and lobbying group, has proposed a sales or user tax based on the quantity of packaging in a product, and a national sales tax on disposable items like diapers, razors and plates. NYPIRG prefers a deposit on packages, to induce consumers to opt for minimal packaging or to at least return the containers for recycling. Rhode Island taxes fast-food packages already; the revenue is earmarked for a litter-cleanup program. None of the changes will be easy. Politicians like taxes even less than they do garbage dumps. And some family's livelihood depends on hawking disposable razors. But reducing garbage at the source will lessen the burden on incinerators, recycling programs and landfills, to say nothing of bring a little white-cloth gentility to the school lunchroom.

—Sharon Begley *with* Patricia King *in Chicago*

Let's take that story apart. It splits in four.

Part one is the *lead* or attention getter. It highlights the problem. It's meant to get the reader interested in garbage, which isn't all that easy:

Another day, another 3.5 pounds of garbage to generate. Sound like a challenge? It's a snap to fulfill your quota. Brush your teeth, rinse, toss the paper cup. Shave with a disposable razor. Comb your hair—oops, a couple of comb teeth snapped off; out it goes. For breakfast, a single-serving cereal box and a juice-in-a-box. There's no time to do dishes, so use a paper bowl and plastic spoon. Off to work, buying a cup of coffee and newspaper on the way. And on through the day . . .

Every American seems to be doing his part; we're producing twice the solid waste per person as the Europeans.

Part two tells us precisely what this article is about. It's the *thesis* or thrust statement, that sentence or paragraph or section crafted to tell the reader exactly what he is reading:

This dubious achievement, says Steve Romalewski of the New York Public Interest Research Group (NYPIRG), means that cutting down on trash is "a primary component in a safe and sensible solution to the garbage crisis." The less there is, the less that must be recycled, burned or buried. Known by the unglamorous name source reduction, its potential is huge.

Parts one and two—lead and thesis—unite to "Tell them what you're going to tell them."

Part three is the body of the article, the elaboration, the expansion, the *proof of thesis*. It's the logical development of the subject. In the *Newsweek* piece, proof of thesis comes during the progression of paragraphs that follows. Part Three equals "Tell them."

Part four is an ending, a finish, a windup. It may be conclusion, a final point, a quip or quote, a summary, a return to the beginning, but something to let the reader feel he's done:

None of the changes will be easy. Politicians like taxes even less than they do garbage dumps. And some family's livelihood depends on hawking disposable razors. But reducing garbage at the source will lessen the burden on incinerators, recycling programs and landfills, to say nothing of bringing a little white-cloth gentility to the school lunchroom.

Part four means "Tell them what you told them."

For complicated subjects, for readers who don't read carefully but need to be reached, the structure of Reinforcement offers coaxing and coaching. It is an important structure for you to be aware of. It is one you can use repeatedly.

Compartmentalization

This book is an example of compartmentalization. One subject has been divided, segmented, compartmentalized. Articles about multifaceted subjects can be constructed compartmentally. The handling of topic by the writer becomes simpler. The reading becomes easier, too.

If I were assigned by *National Geographic TRAVELER* to write an article about my place of residence, Bloomington, Indiana, I might plan my piece compartmentally: (1) university town, (2) commercial and industrial hub of south central Indiana, (3) liberal outpost in conservative region, (4) home for artists, (5) music center, (6) tourist attraction, (7) outdoor delights, (8) place for seniors to live, (9) madness for basketball. And so forth. To handle all these facets in a continuing flow of information would be difficult. Through division, each matter can be taken care of, given its proper position and length. Movement from section to section can be shown through subheads or asterisks or spaces.

Magazine editors increasingly use compartmentalization because they increasingly face complicated and many-splendored subjects. An article in the June 1989 issue of *Life*, for instance, covers a major exhibit, "Making Their Mark: Women Artists Move into the Mainstream, 1970-85," through individual biographical tidbits:

Faith Ringgold

"I'm writing little bitty short stories and putting them on quilts," says Ringgold, fifty-eight (here with granddaughter Faith), explaining her art. The tales she prints on fabric are about birth, marriage, death, a night on a rooftop, a reunion.

She began making her hangings in 1980. She had spent the 1960s painting landscapes and making murals and the 1970s working on soft sculptures. The shift to fabrics seemed natural. Ringgold's mother was a dress designer in Harlem, and the women were always telling stories.

But Ringgold grew frustrated when she couldn't get her work shown in New York. She packed thirty-six pieces in a trunk and went on the road to colleges around the U.S., hanging exhibits of her work, telling her stories. Twenty years ago this mother of two grown daughters also became involved in protesting museum discrimination against women artists. "If they don't see you in there, then you're not anywhere." New York's Guggenheim Museum now owns one of her quilts, which sell for $40,000.

Deborah Butterfield

"When I was starting out," says Butterfield, forty, "wildest expectation was that I might make enough money to buy art supplies." Twelve years after following her sculptor husband, John Buck, to Bozeman, Montana, her sculptures sell for as much as $100,000. At nine most weekday mornings, Butterfield leaves her sons, Wilder, four, and Hunter, two, with a baby-sitter and goes into her studio. She welds her life-size horses from pieces of autos, farm equipment and old metal buildings. Her first gallery show was in Chicago in 1976. Three years later at the Whitney she exhibited horses made of mud and sticks.

Butterfield has six real horses on the 150 acres she owns with her husband, and she rides often with friends who fly in an instructor to teach them and their mounts the complex maneuvers of dressage. "It's sort of good to make art in a place that's slightly boring," Butterfield says. "You spend more time in the studio." And she thinks that being a woman may have helped too: "I feel I've had more success than my husband because I'm a female."

Both the increasing complexity or scope of subjects and the television-influenced inclination of people to view scenes in short spurts of time have increased use of compartmentalization. Each in the above is a unit unto itself as well as an element of a larger informational organism.

Mother Jones (July/August 1989) tackles a controversial and confusing international situation in "Contradictions, A Decade in Documents." Here's how Peter Kornbluh's article begins:

Ever since the Sandinista Revolution toppled Nicaraguan dictator Anastasio Somoza ten years ago, U.S. relations with that tiny Central American country have dominated the ethical landscape of American foreign policy. From 1979, when the Carter administration began trying to stop the Sandinistas, through the recent vote in congress to sustain a standing contra army in Honduras with $57.5 million in "nonlethal" aid, U.S. officials have pursued a policy of unrelenting punishment.

The resulting war has brought death and destruction to the Nicaraguan people and lawlessness and scandal to the United States. What follows are excerpts of key policy statements and once-classified documents that chart this decade-long anti-Sandinista campaign:

Then he supplies, compartmentally (and chronologically, I might add), those documents and statements. For instances:

1979: The Sandinistas Triumph

. . . [W]e run the risk of having events overtake us if he [Somoza] does not leave soon. . . . The benefits we derive from orchestrating his departure will slip from our hands, and the survivability of any elements of the GN [National Guard] will be unlikely. Indeed, we will be placed in a very vulnerable

position if we are seen offering [a] safehaven to a Somoza fleeing from Nicaragua under military attack. We will be viewed as having saved his neck rather than as having negotiated his departure . . .
U.S. Ambassador Lawrence Pezzullo, in a July 13 secret cable to Washington.

1986: The Iran-Contra Scandal Breaks

Twelve million dollars will be used to purchase critically needed supplies for the Nicaraguan Democratic Resistance Forces. This material is essential to cover shortages in resistance inventories resulting from their current offensives and Sandinista counter-attacks and to "bridge" the period between now and when Congressionally-approved lethal assistance . . . can be delivered.
The paragraph in an April Oliver North memorandum on arms sales to Iran, which cited the diversion of profits. The discovery of this document precipitated the Iran-contra scandal.

1988: The War Winds Down

No amount of monetary reparation can truly compensate for the devastation wrought upon Nicaragua by the unlawful conduct of the United States. No such reparation can revive the human lives lost, or repair the physical and psychological injuries suffered by a population that has endured an unrelenting campaign of armed attacks and economic strangulation over seven years . . . Nicaragua has, nonetheless, quantified its losses as far as it is possible to do so.
From the Memorial on Compensation submitted by the Republic of Nicaragua to the World Court on March 29, asking for approximately twelve billion dollars in reparations from the United States.

You can divide by quotes, by days, by geography, by people, by differences of beliefs. And problems of structure can be solved. Don't compartmentalize just to compartmentalize. But if the subject benefits, think segments.

"In 1907, traffic jams neighed," we read in the September 1989 issue of *Chicago* magazine, "high-fidelity sound was a neighbor with a good singing voice, and Prohibition mobsters-to-be wore short pants and looked forward to kindergarten. Return with us now to those days gone by, as one-time Chicagoan Phillip Grant recalls the city between the Fire and the Great War, as seen through the eyes of a child." The year 1907 then becomes a chain of images and memories: Sunday dinners, The Nickel Show, his cousin Rosie, Big Jake's Saloon, and more. Compartments. Pieces. Fragments. Together they made a whole.

You can relish the results in one compartment, "Taffy Apples."

IT IS NOT EVERYONE WHO CAN BOAST THAT THE VERY FIRST pal of his life was legally hanged by the neck until dead. I can. In 1907, when I was four years old, my closest and only pal was Johnny Burke; and in 1924 he was arrested, charged with murder, and sentenced to be guest of honor at a Chicago "necktie party."

Poor Johnny. He deserved better. When we were four, he was the one who took me on an exploration of the rooftops of the one-story buildings at the end of our alley. As the leader, he was first to fall through the skylight of Morse's Ice Cream Parlor, almost landing in the hopper of the ice-crushing machine below.

As a devoted friend and loyal follower I, too, fell through the shattered skylight, caught just in time to prevent my blood from staining the crystalline beauty of Mr. Morse's ice. As survivors of a death-taunting experience, Johnny and I were rewarded with ice-cream sandwiches and then sent home.

When Johnny's hour arrived, and he was hanged by the good citizens of Cook County, Illinois, I was in New York. My first reaction on learning of his execution was that the judge who had sentenced my pal had not been supplied with all of the facts. Most likely Johnny's shyster had failed to mention Johnny's mother, Mrs. Burke, the most angelically popular person in our alley. A sober and thoroughly rested judge would have ruled that no son of Mrs. Burke, reincarnation of Mary, Mother of God, could have murdered another racketeer as charged. Her Johnny may have wiped out, rubbed out, bumped off, or croaked some other hoodlum; but never could Mrs. Burke's little boy have murdered.

Mrs. Burke was the neighborhood washerwoman, and on certain sunny days when her washtubs were scoured free of soap, she would select her smallest one and cook in it, over her backyard wood fire, perhaps a gallon of heavy red syrup. When the mix was so thick that it would not drip off her long wooden spoon, she would allow Johnny to affix an apple to a stick and dip it into the mixture. Then, satisfied she had done her best, Mrs. Burke would send Johnny out to scream the good news through our alley.

And how did the good news spread? Like wildfire. In no time at all, dozens of kids of all ages were screaming "Taffy apples!"as they ran. Into their houses they flew, staying only long enough to seize an apple. Then it was out again to search the alley for a piece of wood suited to skewering it.

Finding a stick of the right thickness was the great problem. Too thin a stick would snap under the apple's weight; one that was too thick would split the apple. More than once I had to degrade my reputation by borrowing a fork from my mother's kitchen and using it instead of an authentic alley-bred stick.

Still screaming "Taffy apples!" I would sprint to join the crowd that jostled about Mrs. Burke's washtub. Somehow or other, each of us managed eventually to elbow close enough to swobble his apple in syrup. The eating was anticlimactic. The truly exciting elements were the screaming, the promise of a free confection, and the hunt for a suitable stick.

Today, of course, Mrs. Burke's backyard shindig would be impossible. Modern parents don't allow their youngsters to wander freely through alleys. Secondly, a wooden stick found on an alley floor would certainly be regarded as too unsanitary to handle, let alone to plunge into apples and syrup that children will eat. Such unsanitary conditions cause typhoid, bubonic plague, schedebastication of the pancreatic juices, and of course cancer. Fortunately, in 1907, no one seemed to know much about germs.

The right structure will take you where you need to go. Someone likened the magazine article to a moving van, a conveyance with much room to hold things which nevertheless has to be packed just right. A conveyance with a place to go and a reason to get there.

Structuring means packing properly and heading the article in the right direction. So think structure before you write.

6

The Writing Begins

MONEY

Workers earn it,
Spendthrifts burn it,
Bankers lend it,
Women spend it,
Forgers fake it,
Taxes take it,
Dying leave it,
Heirs receive it,
Thrifty save it,
Misers crave it,
Robbers seize it,
Rich increase it,
Gamblers lose it . . .
I could use it.

—Richard Armour

Notice the nouns and verbs. They make the poet's point.

Notice the details. They command attention.

Seek the elusive detail and wrestle with language to find the right noun or verb to fit the message.

You'll discover once again, of course, that the writing—though made a bit easier by preparation—remains a blood, sweat, and tears activity.

Blood. Sportswriter Red Smith is credited with the comment: "Writing is easy. All you do is sit at the typewriter until drops of blood appear on your forehead."

Sweat. Philosopher Jean-Paul Sartre has written: ". . . apart from a few old men who dip their pens in Eau de Cologne and little dandies who write like butchers, all writers have to sweat. That's due to the nature of the Word. One speaks in one's own language; one writes in a foreign language."

Tears. Journalist/humorist/cynic H.L. Mencken addressed the agonies in writing, noting that such a person of creative imagination "pays a ghastly price for all his superiorities and immunities; nature takes revenge upon him for dreaming of improvements in the scheme of things. Sitting there in his lonely room, gnawing the handle of his pen, racked by his infernal quest, horribly bedeviled by incessant flashes of itching, toothache, eyestrain, and festering conscience — thus tortured, he makes atonement for his crime of having ideas. The normal man, the healthy and honest man, the good citizen and householder — this man, I daresay, knows nothing of all that travail. It is the particular penalty of those who pursue strange butterflies into dark forests, and go fishing in enchanted and forbidden streams."

A byline and a paycheck make one forget the trials until one faces the process again. Like using weights, the use of language never becomes easier. But as with weights, the user becomes better through usage. So the task becomes your opportunity.

THE TASK IS TO SHOW

The journalist wrote:

> We saw the sea sucked away by the heaving of the earth . . . a fearful black cloud forked with great tongues of fire lashed at the heavens and torrents of ash began to pour from the sky.
>
> Although it was daytime, we were enveloped by night — not a moonless night or one dimmed by cloud — but the darkness of a sealed room without light.

The journalist was Pliny the Younger. The event was the volcanic eruption that eradicated Pompeii in 79 A.D. Pliny wasn't satisfied telling us that the disaster was awful or terrible or unforgettable or awesome. He used nouns and verbs to show us what occurred.

Telling is easy, but it keeps the reader distant from the subject. Showing is hard, but it brings the reader close. Adjectives and adverbs carelessly used just tell. Nouns and verbs carefully used show. They intensify the material of the article because they immerse the reader.

A word like "unforgettable" means much more to the writer who experienced an event such as Pompeii or the eruption of Mount St. Helens. It contains no movement. The real information remains locked in the writer's mind. The reader cannot share in the experience. Pliny however, was too good an observer and writer. He wanted us to know what happened. We do. Nineteen centuries later we do because of a writer's use of nouns and verbs.

Even the best of us cannot fully re-create an event or a place or a person or an object on paper. Words are symbols, after all. But the right words satisfy a reader's desire to know, his or her need to understand. A powerful example comes from Jacob Timerman, the Argentinian journalist whose memoirs about prison and torture were published in the April 20, 1981 issue of *The New Yorker* (in translation from the Spanish by Tolby Talbot). In "No Name, No Number," he writes:

In the long months of confinement, I often thought about how to convey the pain that a tortured person undergoes. And always I concluded that it was impossible. It is pain without points of reference, without revelatory symbols or clues to serve as indicators. A man is shunted so quickly from one world to another that he's unable to tap a residue of energy that will permit him to confront this unbridled violence. That is the first phase of torture: to take a man by surprise, without allowing him any reflex defense, even psychological. A man's hands are shackled behind him, his eyes blindfolded. No one says a word. Blows are showered upon him. He's placed on the ground and someone counts to ten, but he's not killed. He is then led to what may be a canvas bed or a table, stripped, doused with water, and tied to the ends of the bed or table with his hands and legs outstretched. And the application of electric shocks begins. The amount of electricity transmitted by the electrodes — or whatever they're called — is regulated, so that it merely hurts, or burns, or destroys. It's impossible to shout — you howl. At the onset of that long human howl, someone with soft hands checks the state of your heart, someone sticks his hand into your mouth and pulls out your tongue in order to prevent you from choking. Someone places a piece of rubber in your mouth to prevent you from biting your tongue or destroying your lips. A brief pause. And then it starts all over again. With insults this time. A brief pause. And then questions. A brief pause. And then words of hope. A brief pause. And then insults.

What does a man feel? The only thing that comes to mind: They're ripping apart my flesh. They didn't rip apart my flesh. They didn't even leave marks. But I felt as if they were tearing my flesh. And what else? Nothing that I can think of . . . .

Words on paper do not match reality. But Timerman's nouns and verbs — simple, yet precisely chosen — bring us a little closer to an understanding.

The writer has chosen the helpful details, then expressed them in appropriate nouns and verbs. They are ham and eggs, details and the right words to express them. They are matter and manner. Read an award-winning article, and you'll find engaging detail engagingly expressed. Analyze any article you've enjoyed, and you'll find that combination in evidence.

You can be impressed, for instance, with a naval officer who serves as member of the White House ceremonial guard. You can point a camera at him and document his demeanor, his military snap, his wholesome good looks, the starch of his uniform, the ribbons. You can do that with words, too. The photo or the piece of video can go no further. With words you can, but you need more detail. Those ribbons? Four rows of them on so young a man, and it's peacetime. "How did you accumulate them?" you must ask. With a bit more prodding along the way, you find out that one is for serving at the White House, another for having worked on the President's inauguration. There are two flying crosses; one of these is for helicopter flights that rescued twenty-five people from a hotel fire in Puerto Rico. One ribbon came as a reward for volunteerism, more specifically, participating in a Navy program to teach primary school children about civics. Now you can write and surpass a photographer's work. The ribbons are a code. The writer through detail decodes them.

That's information gathering, of course, this hunt for detail. But it's a willingness to use such material, to be revealing. Sally Bedell Smith wrote in the March 8, 1984 edition of *The New York Times* of the dining room in the Dorset Hotel where each weekday morning, she discovered, dozens of television executives and entertainers gathered for breakfast. Among the dozens "who make the Dorset a habit," she wrote, are:

> Van Gordon Sauter, an executive vice president of the CBS Broadcast Group (at least two cans of Tab diet soda, sometimes rye toast), Frank Biondi, president of Home Box Office (scrambled eggs or cereal), and Herbert A. Granath, president of ABC Video Enterprises (whole wheat toast and coffee). Howard Cosell (corned-beef hash and a poached egg) is also a regular, and when they are in town, Cary Grant (scrambled eggs and juice) and Kirk Douglas (grapefruit and toast) stop by.

What captivates the reader falls within parentheses — not who ate there but what they ate. That special detail.

Writing With Nouns and Verbs

The unhappy story of Klaus and Sunny von Bulow was retold in a two-installment article for *Vanity Fair*. Consider these three paragraphs:

> Meanwhile, the subject, or object, of all this conflict, Sunny von Bulow, lies in the fifth year of her coma on the tenth floor of the Harkness Pavilion in the Columbia–Presbyterian Medical Center in New York City. She is not, as many believe, on a life-support system, nor is she the total vegetable she is often described as being. I was told that the yearly cost of maintaining her is considerably in excess of half a million dollars. Her $725-a-day room is guarded around the clock by a special security force, and private nurses and a maid look after her at all times. A maze of curtained screens further protects her from the remote possibility that an outsider should gain entry in her room. A current photograph of the comatose woman would be worth a fortune.
>
> Dr. Richard Stock, who has been her physician for twenty-nine years, as he was her mother's and grandmother's, visits her several times a week. She is fed through a tube in her nose. She receives physical therapy and dental care, and her hair is washed and set twice a week. Her own skin creams are used on her hands and face. She wears her own nightgowns and bed jackets and sleeps on Porthault sheets. Music plays in the room, and there are always highly scented flowers on her bedside table.

Ala and Alexander visit her regularly. Sometimes Ala brings her two-year-old daughter, also called Sunny, so that her mother can know she has a grandchild. They talk to her. They touch her. They tell her about things.

The detail brings the reader almost too close, but it produces a picture that clarifies elements of a confusing real-life drama. And with such detail, Dominick Dunne's reporting has made easier Dominick Dunne's writing. The story tells itself. The nouns and verbs become natural extensions of collected detail.

"Teenage Wasteland," in the July 14, 1987 issue of *The Village Voice*, uncovers the empty lives of young people in Bergenfield, New Jersey. Through detail:

Twenty minutes into this hang, the police cruise by. Bobby's mother is at work, so we go there. The small house is cluttered with the artifacts of lively teenagers living with a single parent who works. The rooms are normal teen messy — socks everywhere, piles of unfolded clothes, grooming artifacts, stuffed animals, and a collection of cassette tapes. Religious icons, awards, the kids' school photos, diplomas, and trophies are displayed. Wall-to-wall paste-ups from magazines of cute heavy metal haircut bands in an absent sister's room, skin-care cosmetics, Jean Naté powder and bath splash, economy-size cans of Aqua Net hairspray — Extra Hold, three sizes of styling brushes, costume jewelry, shoes, and makeup. The color TV is on with cartoons; Bobby's preteen brother watches with no sound. There's a boom box and blow dryer in every room. The guys climb up to the roof. Joan and Susie discuss layered haircuts. Nicky is teasing Doreen — "Here, Rover." She walks out in a huff but returns giggling and sits on his lap. I ask to use the bathroom.

When the now legendary E.B. White wrote the now legendary essay, "Here Is New York," he called on detail culled from observation and memory to help us as readers grasp his feeling about the city:

I am sitting at the moment in a stifling hotel room in ninety-degree heat, halfway down an air shaft, in midtown. No air moves in or out of the room, yet I am curiously affected by emanations from the immediate surroundings. I am twenty-two blocks from where Rudolph Valentino lay in state, eight blocks from where Nathan Hale was executed, five blocks from the publisher's office where Ernest Hemingway hit Max Eastman on the nose, four miles from where Walt Whitman sat sweating out editorials for the Brooklyn *Eagle*, thirty-four blocks from the street Willa Cather lived in when she came to New York to write books about Nebraska, one block from where Marceline used to clown on the boards of the Hippodrome, thirty-six blocks from the spot where the Historian Joe Gould kicked a radio to pieces in full view of the public, thirteen blocks from where Harry Thaw shot Stanford White, five blocks from where I used to usher at the Metropolitan Opera and only 112 blocks from the spot where Clarence Day the Elder was washed of his sins in the Church of the Epiphany (I could continue this list indefinitely); and for that matter I am probably occupying the very room that any number of exalted and somewise memorable characters sat in, some of them on hot, breathless afternoons, lonely and private and full of their own sense of emanations from without.

In the Details . . .

American Way published two excerpts from author Roald Dahl's *Going Solo*, the second volume of his autobiography. Covering the years 1938 to 1941, the book is filled with incidents made rich by detail. In the magazine excerpt published May 1, 1987, he recounts his voyage to Africa to work for Shell Petroleum. On board ship he meets representatives of "that peculiar Empire-building breed of Englishman who spends his whole life working in distant corners of British territory." One is "the elderly Miss Trefusis," who through Dahl's words becomes very nearly as three dimensional and different as she must have been in real life:

Miss Trefusis was all bones and grey skin, and when she walked her body was bent forward in a long curve like a boomerang. She told me she owned a small coffee farm in the highlands of Kenya and that she had known Baroness Blixen very well. I myself had read and loved both *Out of Africa* and *Seven Gothic Tales*, and I listened enthralled to everything Miss Trefusis told me about that fine writer who called herself Isak Dinesen.

"She was dotty, of course," Miss Trefusis said. "Like all of us who live out there, she went completely dotty in the end."

"*You* aren't dotty," I said.

"Oh yes, I am," she said firmly and very seriously. "Everyone on this ship is as dotty as a dumpling. *You* don't notice it because you're young. Young people are not watchful. They only look at themselves."

"I saw Major Griffiths and his wife running around the deck naked the other morning," I said.

"You call that dotty?" Miss Trefusis said with a snort. "That's *normal.*" . . .

She was eating an orange at the time and I noticed suddenly that she was not eating it in the normal way. In the first place she had speared it from the fruit bowl with her fork instead of taking it in her fingers. And now, with knife and fork, she was making a series of neat incisions in the skin all around the orange. Then, very delicately, using the points of her knife and fork, she peeled the skin away in eight separate pieces, leaving the bare fruit beautifully exposed. Still using knife and fork, she separated the juicy segments and began to eat them slowly, one by one, with her fork.

"Do you always eat an orange like that?" I said.

"Of course."

"May I ask why?"

"I never touch anything I eat with my fingers," she said.

"Good Lord, don't you really?"

"Never, I haven't since I was twenty-two."

"Is there a reason for that?" I asked her.

"Of course there's a reason. Fingers are filthy."

"But you wash your hands."

"I don't *sterilize* them," Miss Trefusis said. "Nor do you. They're full of bugs. Disgusting dirty things, fingers. Just think what you do with them!" . . .

"Toes are even worse," she said suddenly.

"I beg your pardon?"

"They're the worst of all," she said.

"What's wrong with toes?"

"They are the nastiest part of the human body!" she announced vehemently.

"Worse than fingers?"

"There's no comparison," she snapped. "Fingers are foul and filthy, but *toes*! *Toes* are reptilian and viperish! I don't wish to talk about them!"

I was getting a bit confused. "But one doesn't eat with one's toes," I said.

"I never said you did," Miss Trefusis snapped.

"Then what's so awful about them?" I persisted.

"Uck!" she said. "They are like little worms sticking out of your feet. I hate them, I hate them! I can't bear to look at them . . . ."

Much of Dahl's detail comes in the form of dialogue, but detail it is. Without it Miss Trefusis would have remained no more than a memory in Dahl's mind. Through detail he shared her.

In stressing detail, I want to caution you against overstressing. Don't overwhelm a reader with too much material. Move gingerly through the detail; remember that a person can take in only so much before mental overload sets in. Know which facts are helpful and which get in the way. You're not writing a textbook. You're writing an article. You want an arrangement of details, not a welter. The "yes" word is arrangement. The "no" on detail is collection of little value, dross. The "yes" is informational treasure, jewels.

That goes for quotes, too. Good quotes are a form of detail that enriches an article. Bad quotes deaden. "We're delighted the Martin Luther King Institute has enticed Sarah Goodale to become its historian. She brings a lifetime of experiences with her." That's a bad quote. "I marched with King in Washington. I marched with Tutu in South Africa. I broke the law in Birmingham. Police broke my arm in Decatur. I lived the history. Now I want to record it at the Institute." That's a good quote.

Using Quotes to Achieve Authenticity

A period quote, an eyewitness quote, a quote from someone eminent gives the reader a sense of closeness to the subject, a feel of being told something special. The recollections of S.H.M. Byers in *American History Illustrated* (April 1987) offer through his own words the sort of detail that stamps an article as authentic.

Sumter was fired upon. I was twenty-two. I longed for the excitement of battle, the adventure of war; and so I enlisted in a regiment that was to be wiped out of existence before the war was over.

More than a year passed after my enlistment. It was noon now, of the nineteenth of September, 1862. Possibly the fiercest battle of the Civil War was about to begin—a battle in which our small brigade of three half-regiments was to lose six hundred and eight killed and wounded. My own regiment had four hundred and eighty-two engaged, and two hundred and seventeen of them, with fifteen officers, were stretched out dead or wounded within an hour. It was appalling. That was war.

Know how much quoting to use. Don't permit the strong quotes to get lost in a sea of weak ones. Help the strong ones to stand out by being selective.

On the other hand, you may find—as you develop an article—that it is best handled in quotes. Some years ago James Stevenson wrote a profile for *The New Yorker* (February 18, 1980) on the esteemed art historian and critic Vincent Scully. He laid out the man's life almost totally in the words of Scully (his lectures, his writings, his conversation) and the words of colleagues. Stevenson took the reader through a lecture at Yale, for instance. We were told that dozens of slides are shown as Scully speaks rapidly "and—as always—without notes." During the final slides Scully said:

"Man-made conical hills, temples, an altar to Zeus. An environmental monument. Brutal and powerful forms. Typical cruel Greek images of victory. The dying and the dead. Absolute clarity and cruelty. All this is embodied in the Winged Victory of Samothrace. All that force. Command: victory over other men and the elements themselves; defeating nature. In the swells and in the wind, victorious above all."

Stevenson continued his article this way:

Applause fills the room. Most of the students disperse; several wait to speak to Scully. With one of them Scully gets into a discussion of Nietzsche and Dostoevski. "You ought to read 'Notes from the Underground,' " Scully says as they depart.

Scully in his office: "I had no talent for drawing as a kid—they had changed me from left-handed to right-handed, and it really screwed me up, made it all cerebral—but I was always interested, in a way, in architecture. From the earliest time, I remember walking around the neighborhood and looking at the other houses. I'd run with my dogs down Edgewood Avenue. It was all elm trees, like a cathedral, and I'd look at the houses, figuring out where all the rooms were. Most of the houses near us on Derby Avenue were two-family houses—two front doors, with one family downstairs and one upstairs. We lived upstairs. Then, suddenly, a six-family house was built next door to us. It threw everything out of scale. My parents were upset, and we might have moved, but they wanted to stay in St. Brendan's Parish. I think I felt our house was pinched, and when I looked at other houses I was trying to imagine a more generous kind of life."

Scully on Frank Lloyd Wright: "The American tradition of wood frame structure . . . played its part in the first great masterpiece among the Prairie
Houses. This was the Ward Willitts House, of 1902 [by Wright]. . . . Its
exterior is articulated by, and its windows set within, an expression of its
wooden skeleton, and it seems to recall in this way the Stick Style tradition
of Wright's childhood. At the same time . . . [it] seems to mirror Japanese
forms as well . . . . The windows themselves are set back in plane, so that
the walls tend to become merely space-defining screens and the roofs go
outward continuously: 'floating.' . . . [Wright] hailed '. . . the new reality that
is *space* instead of matter.' "

Scully in his office: "I was very spoiled as a child in the twenties. My parents
got me electric trains, and later they added houses you could light up, and I
remember at Christmas the trains running through the dining room. They
were small-gauge, though, and not Lionel. I remember that. My aunts lavished smashing presents on me. It all stopped overnight with the Depression.
I remember an aunt giving me a present, probably around 1931. All it was
was a pen-and-pencil set, and just like one she had given me before. I quietly
put it aside. I still feel guilty about that."

And so forth. The article is built on quotes. The right ones. The
good ones.

Life, in offering its readers "The View from Out There," uses pictures and the words of astronauts to give us an idea what space flight
is like. (Excerpted from the book, *The Home Planet*, edited by Kevin W.
Kelley, published by Addison-Wesley, 1988.)

When the engine shut down, I unbuckled myself from my seat and I was
floating. I knew we were in orbit. I looked out the window and couldn't
believe it. The Sun was streaming in, and you could look right down at the
Atlantic Ocean. I looked at [the guys] doing the countdown for the orbital-
maneuvering-system burn [to get into a higher orbit] and I thought, How in
the world can you do that? Look outside!
—*Joseph Allen, U.S.A., five days in 1982 and eight days in 1984. He is
president of a firm that is designing a new industrial facility for space.*

We orbit and float in our space gondola and watch the oceans and islands
and green hills of the continents pass by at five miles per second.
—*Joseph Allen*

We could not immediately detect that the Earth was shrinking as we sped
away from it. The sensation was like watching the hand on a clock move.
You know it is moving, but watching it you cannot see it move. Only after
looking elsewhere for a time, then returning to the minute hand, can one
realize it actually did move. The Earth was eventually so small I could blot
it out of the universe simply by holding up my thumb.
—*Buzz Aldrin, U.S.A., four days in 1966, eight days in 1969. He is a professor
of astronautics at the University of North Dakota.*

Around six p.m. we were flying north of the Mediterranean, almost right
above Marseilles. I know this region well, since I lived there more than
twenty years. At the same time I can see all of France, Corsica, Sardinia,
Italy, part of Spain, perceive the south of England, part of Germany, in fact,

a good part of the world; all the while distinguishing without difficulty the little details of the place where I was wandering on foot some weeks earlier. I smile then, realizing how laughable and relative the immensity of our planet is. Seconds later, we were flying above the U.S.S.R.!
–*Jean-Loup Chretien, France, eight days in 1982. He will be going on the Soviet-French mission this year.*

All quotation, an article built on the words of experts. Of such detail is the memorable article built.

Take this opening for "The Women of Palm Beach," another Dominick Dunne effort for *Vanity Fair*:

Palm Beach people talk about Palm Beach people constantly. It is a subject that never seems to exhaust itself, and any one of them, at any event where they are gathered, can give you an instant precis of any other one's life. "She's Mollie Netcher Bragno Bostwick Wilmot. She lives next to Rose Kennedy, and last year a tanker ran aground on her seawall and practically landed in her living room." . . . "The man in the receiving line, third from the end, is Paul Ilynsky. He's on the town council. His father was a Russian grand duke who married Audrey Emery, Paul's mother, and his second cousin was the last czar of Russia." . . . "The lady with the long blond hair who never misses a dance is Sue Whitmore, the Listerine heiress. She was practically born at the old Royal Poincianna Hotel. She single-handedly runs the International Red Cross Ball every year, which is the only one of the big charity parties the chic people go to." . . . "There, with the deep tan and the mustache, is Douglas Fairbanks Jr. I don't have to tell you who he is, except that his house, for some reason, is called the Vicarage." . . . "That elderly lady being helped across the dance floor by Charlie Van Rensselaer is Mary Sanford, Laddie Sanford's widow—you know, the polo player. They call her the Queen of Palm Beach. Don't say I called her elderly." . . . "The guy with the pale-pink lipstick and the plucked eyebrows and the big diamond ring in the color photograph in the window of Kohn's on Worth Avenue is Arndt Krupp, the German munitions heir. Last year he gave a big party for the Queen of Thailand, but nobody's seen him this year." . . . "She's Lilly McKim Pulitzer Rousseau. Everybody loves Lilly. She's Ogden Phipp's stepdaughter, and she used to be married to Peter Pulitzer, years before all that awful Roxanne business, and they were the most beautiful couple in Palm Beach.

And on it goes. Dunne plays out the monologue, giving us not only the personality of the speaker but the flavor of his society.

Sifting Through the Details

Detail, of course, makes articles longer. Detail takes up space. It will cause you to make critical decisions about what must go into an article and what can be left out. The poet John Ciardi once said, "Everything in a good piece of writing must be chosen into it." Indeed. If an editor has given me a limit of three thousand words for an article on Impressionism in the arts, I know immediately that not all aspects of the subject can be covered. Long tomes have been written even about selected aspects. I might handle the subject through one painting by Monet, the creative process in one poem by Rimbaud, and the initially confused relationship between music and audience in the performance of one work by Debussy. Concentration can clarify.

Breadth is important in an encylcopedia entry. Depth is important in an article. So choose wisely, carefully, selectively, sparingly. Select those elements that will help you achieve your purpose. It is far better to be thorough on two or three points than scattershot on a dozen. Make the most of space limitations. Don't shun detail.

When for my *Highlights for Children* series on composers I got around to George Frideric Handel (December 1982 issue), I decided that in eight hundred words I could do no more than concentrate on his *Messiah*. That would have to serve as a young reader's introduction to the Handel story, whether I really wanted it that way or not. I hoped that the focus, though limited, would give the reader some understanding of just who Handel was and what his work has meant to future generations. Reader reaction confirmed that my hope was realized.

Handel's Messiah

The weather was raw and stormy, making the water too rough for travel. George Frideric Handel, composer to the court of England, had to wait. He looked out over the gray Irish Sea and the sky that matched it. On the other side lay Dublin, where he was to give an important series of concerts.

It was November. November 1741. Not the best time of year to sail, he realized, but the months before had been frantically busy as he worked on two oratorios, one of which he now had with him.

The little port of Chester bored Handel. He missed the activity, the streets and beautiful gardens of London. He missed his friends and the good food, which he ate in amazingly large helpings. And the weather was bleak.

He decided not to waste time. Contacting the local church organist, he managed to find the best singers around. He gave them some of the choruses from the new work, which he called *Messiah*. He wanted to try out the music. So he rehearsed the little group, led by a printer with a solid bass voice. The rehearsal was a disaster. The poor fellow couldn't manage the music. Handel became furious. "You scoundrel," he shouted, "did you not tell me that you could sing on sight?"

The printer answered meekly, "Yes, sir, and so I can, but not at *first* sight."

After Handel's temper and the weather calmed, he sailed for Ireland. There he spent several weeks preparing the best musicians in Dublin, who were much better than those in Chester. The series of concerts began two days before Christmas.

With each concert the esteem in which the people of Dublin held Handel rose. But he was most eager to get to the final program. He had saved *Messiah* for last. It was special to him. His other oratorios were like operas, with stories and dramatic music, but not acted out. *Messiah* was different, not like an opera but like a musical church service.

Handel had asked a literary friend, Charles Jennens, to provide the words, called a libretto. And so Jennens did, out of Old and New Testament material. In fact, every word he set to paper came from the Bible. Carefully and skillfully he told of Jesus: what the Prophets said of His coming, what happened during His life on earth, and what we learned from His death and ascension.

Jennens gave Handel the finished libretto in July 1741. On August 22, after he had cleared up other work, Handel sat down at his desk to compose. On September 14 he was done. He had composed 265 pages, all within twenty-four days. He'd scratched out notes. He'd written notes on top of notes. He'd blotted and erased. And all that while he ate little and slept less, which was unlike him. Handel usually composed with ease and speed, but in *Messiah* he seemed inspired.

Now, here in Dublin, he was poised for the first performance. The theater was sold out and then some. The ladies were requested not to wear hoops in their skirts. The gentlemen were asked to leave their swords at home. That way more people could squeeze in. Handel was at the harpsichord, conducting the thirty other players and twenty singers. "Words are wanting to express the exquisite delight it afforded to the admiring crowded audience," reported a Dublin newspaper afterwards. The seven hundred people went away pleased but not aware, of course, that they had just witnessed history.

In Handel's time *Messiah* was played most often around Easter. But custom has changed. Now we hear it usually at Christmas.

George Frideric Handel, who lived from 1685 to 1759, wrote eighteen other oratorios. He also wrote more than forty operas. He wrote songs and concertos and cantatas and anthems and the famous *Water Music* and *Music for the Royal Fireworks*. But it is for *Messiah* that he is most remembered.

Handel continued through the years to make changes in his oratorio. So did others after he died, including Mozart, who changed the orchestration so much that it sounded like a different composition. Today we sometimes hear *Messiah* in the style Handel wrote it and sometimes with Mozart's changes. We almost always hear it with more musicians than Handel had in mind.

Rarely, however, do we hear it the way guests in Westminster Abbey did in 1784 when, one year early, the British marked the 100th anniversary of Handel's birth. That *Messiah* featured 253 players, 257 singers, plus soloists. King George III attended, and when he heard the "Hallelujah Chorus," he stood up. Because it is customary to stand when a king stands up, everyone else in the church stood, too. That started a tradition which continues today.

As if five hundred performers weren't enough! A hundred years later, both in England and the United States, sometimes several thousand singers would gather to perform the *Messiah*. The craze for bigness disappeared early in the twentieth century. Now we do have sing-alongs during which an entire audience performs, but otherwise performances are smaller-scaled. That's the way we've come to like it. That's the way Handel probably would like it. After all, he planned it that way.

7

Leads and Endings

You're the top!
You're the Colosseum.
You're the top!
You're the Louvre Museum.
You're a melody from a symphony by Strauss,
You're a Bendel bonnet,
A Shakespeare sonnet,
You're Mickey Mouse.
You're the Nile,
You're the Tow'r of Pisa,
You're the smile
On the Mona Lisa.
I'm a worthless check, a total wreck, a flop,
But if, Baby, I'm the bottom
You're the top!

— Cole Porter

Those lyrics begin "You're the Top," a classic of the American musical theatre. They'd make a good lead for an article on compliments or on wooing or on hyperbole or on writing song lyrics.

Songs, novels, stories, articles have beginnings. We call them "leads" in journalism. That's what beginnings are supposed to do: lead. They must lead a reader to what comes next. If a lead fails to do that, all that follows is of no account. A writer's project is dead, at least for those readers who've chosen not to continue.

But a lead has even more to do: It (1) attracts attention, (2) establishes the subject, (3) sets the tone, and (4) guides or bridges into the article.

WRITING LEADS WITH VERVE AND VALUE

Here from *Restaurant Hospitality* is a well-crafted article opening that would seem to serve a lead's four purposes:

> If cleanliness is indeed next to godliness, then the kitchen at Tony's belongs not in St. Louis but high atop Olympus, wherefrom its pleasures could be whisked to the table of Zeus. This is the sort of kitchen that gives Inspectors

of Health bad dreams about pink slips and unemployment lines, for if every kitchen were maintained so meticulously, we would have no need of them or their rules. The Health Code could go on the Honor System.

It's attention getting. It establishes the subject, sets the tone. And what follows, let me assure you, links comfortably.

Carter Wiseman fulfills all the needs for "The New Zoo," published in *New York* magazine (July 18, 1988):

Just weeks after he became New York City's commissioner of parks and recreation, in 1978, Gordon Davis took his three-year-old daughter to visit the Central Park Zoo. It was easy enough to do, since his office was in the Arsenal, at 64th Street and Fifth Avenue, and the zoo was his backyard. The little girl seemed oddly quiet as they walked around, and when the visit ended, she turned to her father and said, "Daddy, never bring me here again."

It was a blow to the new commissioner, who had always regarded the zoo as a "magical place" in the public imagination. But when Davis took a look beyond the cheerful image, the sight was not pretty at all. "I was embarrassed that my daughter could see better than I could," he says. The monkeys chattered and swung in cages that were squalid and dank, and the big cats paced with what seemed like a peculiarly urban expression of anger on their faces. There were gates and bars at every turn, and the plantings had grown ratty. Even the centerpiece of the place, the sea-lion pool, was an eyesore.

Be reminded of the lead that goes:

In the beginning God created the heaven and the earth. And the earth was without form, and void; and darkness was upon the face of the deep. And the Spirit of God moved upon the face of the water. And God said, Let there be light; and there was light.

That's a good lead. It gets right down to business. It intrigues. It mystifies. It surprises. It's pithy. It's potent.

What piques the reader, as the opening of *Genesis* does, is a good lead; what doesn't, isn't. The lead should entice, provoke the reader into action, that action being to continue reading the story. The approach must be honest, but aside from that, you have free reign — always keeping in mind however, what suits the subject and what seems appropriate for the audience.

Bill Hunter in his article on "Midnight Movie Madness" for *American Way* begins: "Listen, my children, and you shall hear of the midnight rites, appalled, revered." Why not a parody lead for a story about the silliness of movie cults?

Daniel Lehman wrote an article on adult homes for *The Village Voice:*

"All I wanted was a decent breakfast instead of that rot they had been serving us," Barbara Brubaker tells me. "But the administrator of that adult home looked at me and told me something I'll never forget. 'You know,' he told me, 'if you were in a concentration camp and complained like that you would be shot.' "

Why not a quote lead when the quote is strong?

The lead must grab attention, introduce the subject, set the tone, establish the pace, and prepare the reader for what will follow.

Blues singer Billie Holliday began her autobiography with these two sentences: "Mom and Pop were just a couple of kids when they got married. He was eighteen, she was sixteen, and I was three." That's a lead.

So is Roger Kahn's quite differently paced and toned beginning to "A Masque of Genius," an article for *Esquire* about violinist Jascha Heifetz:

> In the end we are finding out that Shaw was right. I am speaking of the playwright, and of a time, so current and so distant, when Jascha Heifetz traveled to London as a boy of nineteen, with curly hair, a serious mien and a fiddle.
>
> Shaw had been a music critic, a master of barbs, but hearing Heifetz overwhelmed his irascibility. Terribly moved, he went home to Ayot St. Lawrence and wrote an odd, touching, ominous letter:
>
> My dear Heifetz:
>
> Your recital has filled me and my wife with anxiety. If you provoke a jealous God by playing with such superhuman perfection, you will die young. I earnestly advise you to play something badly every night before going to bed, instead of saying your prayers. No mortal should presume to play so faultlessly.
>
> G. Bernard Shaw
>
> Heifetz presumed and today, robust in his seventies, he continues to play with a touch that would draw tears from an audience of stone.

Subject determines lead. The lead should develop out of your growing command of the subject matter. And whether the lead should shock or tell a story or describe or tie what follows to history or explain how to do something, whether it is understated or hyperbolic, whether it is extended or brief, whether it is first person or third, whether it is simply constructed or complex, whether it is cool or warm, cold or hot, whether it is gutter talk or grandiloquent, whether it is question or exclamation, all depends on the subject matter and what you consider appropriate for it. Not only should the information lead to further information, but it should set a climate at the same time.

A mark of the professional is the taste he or she shows in constructing the lead, the ability to balance between going far enough to gain reader interest and not going so far, as to distort the story or its purpose.

There's no one way to begin a story. Take the staff writers of

Newsweek and *Time*, responding in words to the October 30, 1989 San Francisco earthquake. Both sets of writers and editors turned to the reaction of observers. But there the similarity ends. *Newsweek* began:

"God just clapped his hands," Annette Henry said. "The ground was like a wave under a surfboard, and the cars on the highway were jumping up and down like in a Disney movie." Henry, who watched the horrifying carnage on the Nimitz Freeway from her Oakland home, had it exactly right. From the first rumbling spasm of the San Andreas Fault to its nationally televised eruption all across the Bay Area, the Quake of 1989 was an event that seemed part Biblical, part Hollywood—and all California.

When the dust and smoke finally cleared, at least fifty-five Bay Area residents had lost their lives and property damage was in the billions. "Every time we have an earthquake in California, we giggle, we're cool, we're blasé," said Ellen Newcomb of Santa Cruz. "This time was different. I was just hanging on, thinking it's not so funny anymore. We're in store for The Big One."

Time opened its coverage this way:

Even for those born long after San Francisco's great 1906 earthquake and fire, it had become a habit to recall the warm, breezy conditions during that cataclysm. Looking out a window from her home in suburban Sunnyvale, Neta Lott remarked to her husband Byron that the Indian-summer evening of October 17 seemed like "darned good earthquake weather." Moments later, the shaking and rolling began. Byron, an electrical engineer, fell to the floor. Neta tried to get up but remained pinned to her chair until she rolled onto the floor. "I sat under the desk and thought I would be buried," she recalled. "I thought, 'This is it. I'm going to die.'"

To the north in Oakland, auto mechanic Richard Reynolds glanced at the traffic on the double-decker I-880 freeway across the street and urged a friend not to drive to night school until after the rush hour. Minutes later, Reynolds felt "a ripple." Then a neighbor screamed a warning. He ran out of his shop to find "the whole goddamn ground lifting up." He grabbed a telephone pole as the sidewalk buckled beneath his feet, and looked up at a horrifying sight. A mile-long section of the freeway's upper deck began to heave, then collapsed onto the lower roadway, flattening cars as if they were beer cans. "It just slid. It didn't fall. It just slid," said Reynolds.

Newsweek writers used a single eyewitness to set the scene, then turned to the totality of disaster. The *Time* staffers expanded on people's experiences using them to unfold the tragedy. It's important to create a lead that works for the story; the lead should work for you, too. You know full well how hard you have to work for a lead, so, in turn, make the lead work for you. Writers of good leads play with information. The word "play," as used here, is not meant to suggest frivolity. It does not mean to toy with the reader. But you must learn to make the most of some facet of your subject: to build on a set of facts or combination of concepts, or simply the sounds of words.

Richard Teresi made a lead work for him in a piece for *Omni*: "Since Erasistratus starved a sparrow to 'note the decrease in weight,' billions of animals have been starved, suffocated, shocked, shot boiled, baked, frozen, thawed, refrozen, force-fed, crucified, crashed, crushed, asphyxiated, irradiated, poisoned, and laser-beamed – all in the name of science." He then attached a thesis: "Notwithstanding the countless medical breakthroughs from animal experimentation, animals are far from the ideal research tool."

Reader reaction is assured. Agreement or disagreement. Wow or silly. Wishy-washiness from a reader is unlikely. And that, undoubtedly, is what Teresi wanted. That list of verbs forces itself into a reader's head, and perhaps heart as well.

Make the lead work for you.

And make it as long as it needs to be. That's the answer to the usual question about leads: "How long should they be?" A lead should be as long as it takes to get the story underway, but not a word longer.

"I love Fred Astaire," wrote Adolph Green in *American Film*. No more needed. Or:

"Hi, Honey, how tall are you?"

"Five, two."

"Good. Tomorrow you're an ape."

So wrote William Murray in an article for *Playboy* about movie extras.

Yet look at this lead-thesis combination by Martha Brannigan from *The Wall Street Journal* (August 23, 1989), one of its front page feature articles:

When Joseph Maccaquano rushed his twenty-one-month-old son, Joseph, to a Secaucus, N.J., hospital in March, he never dreamed he would have to fight to get his only child back.

But after physicians had tended to a broken leg, a state social worker arrived to tell Mr. Maccaquano and his wife, Kathryn, that their little boy might not be allowed to go home.

The social worker told Mr. Maccaquano he was suspected of abusing the child. He said, "The injury couldn't have happened the way I said," recalls Mr. Maccaquano, a warehouse worker who says the child apparently fell in the kitchen just a few feet from him.

Two private physicians – a pediatrician and an orthopedic surgeon – swore in affidavits filed in Superior Court in Jersey City that they saw no evidence of abuse and that the family seemed to be a loving one. But a third physician – a state employee – was suspicious. He said the boy's injury was a spiral fracture, a type caused by twisting and thus often associated with abuse.

Fitness Tests

After two weeks in the hospital, the child was allowed to go home, but only after Mr. Maccaquano agreed to move out of his house temporarily, and only after he and his wife had agreed to undergo psychological testing intended to establish their fitness as parents.

Mr. Maccaquano, a thirty-three-year-old former high-school football coach, lost eighteen pounds during the period and had trouble sleeping. He took a leave of absence from his job because of anxiety over the ordeal. "They make you feel like you did something wrong, even though I know I didn't," he says. Mrs. Maccaquano, a legal secretary who sought help from her boss, attorney Richard Seltzer, believes the boy might have been taken away if the couple hadn't aggressively fought the agency.

For three months after Mr. Maccaquano moved back home, a social worker from the New Jersey Division of Youth and Family Services made unannounced visits. Then, last month, the agency closed the case. In a letter to the court, it said the child "appears well cared for and happy with his parents, and there have been no further reported incidents of physical abuse." The agency won't comment, and it isn't clear whether it reached an opinion about the boy's injury.

An Anonymous Call
It is clear, however, that the child-protection system throughout the country has come to wield tremendous power over families. All it takes to launch an investigation in most states is an anonymous phone call. Teachers, physicians and other child-care professionals are required by law in every state to report suspected abuse. And evidence that wouldn't hold up in a criminal court can, in family court, cost parents custody of a child.

The final paragraph is the article's thesis. The rest of the copy is the lead. Long? Not really. The writer has taken the necessary space, but no more. I've read articles in which leads continued across hundreds of words, even more. Of course, you should always strive to make leads concise. Don't waste words (or ideas). But give a lead the room it needs for you to accomplish those necessary services.

Those of us who write for magazines or for newspapers on which editors savor good writing can learn from fiction. *The High King* won for its author, Lloyd Alexander, the coveted Newbery Award for excellence in children's literature. Consider the mood, the action, the character, and the reader attraction Alexander establishes with his opening paragraphs:

Under a chill, gray sky, two riders jogged across the turf. Taran, the taller horseman, set his face against the wind and leaned forward in the saddle, his eyes on the distant hills. At his belt hung a sword, and from his shoulder a silver-bound battle horn. His companion Gurgi, shaggier than the pony he rode, pulled his weathered cloak around him, rubbed his frost-nipped ears, and began groaning so wretchedly that Taran at last reined up the stallion.

"No, no!" Gurgi cried. "Faithful Gurgi will keep on! He follows kindly master, oh yes, as he has always done. Never mind his shakings and achings! Never mind the droopings of his poor tender head!"

Taran smiled, seeing that Gurgi, despite his bold words, was eyeing a sheltering grove of ash trees. "There is time to spare," he answered. "I long to be home, but not at the cost of that poor tender head of yours. We camp here and go no farther until morning."

They tethered their mounts and built a small fire in a ring of stones. Gurgi curled up and was snoring almost before he had finished swallowing his food. Though as weary as his companion, Taran set about mending the harness leathers. Suddenly he stopped and jumped to his feet. Overhead, a winged shape plunged swiftly toward him.

Our task in a magazine article is to create with facts the mood, the compression of details, the establishment of scene or character that Alexander does through his imagination.

John Leonard in one of his "Private Lives" columns for *The New York Times* (some of which were published in a book by the same name) set mood, action, character, and did so attractively:

We were standing at a party. Every fall I do a lot of standing around at parties, having forgotten over the summer how much I don't care for standing around at parties with my teeth hanging out. Every fall I imagine once again that something wonderful will happen at a party. This is like imagining that the telephone book will prove to be a wonderful novel. Parties and telephone books have their reasons, but wonder lurks elsewhere, sitting down, in small groups, without any shoes on. Still, in the fall, I will go to a party so long as it isn't on a boat. In my experience, parties on boats are bad news because when I want to go home I am in the middle of the Hudson River with a rock band and an assistant professor of mortuary science.

This particular party, last Thursday, on the day when New Yorkers made the first of the three votes that will be necessary to achieve a new Mayor, contained many of my friends, all of whom had voted. Of my friends' politics, what is there to say? We have lost many, many elections. We all grew up together, losing those elections, reading the same newspapers, magazines and books. We tend, as if history were a kind of pollen, to sneeze the same sneeze.

Alexander and Leonard managed to capture the essence of their subject. A reader becomes immersed, gaining immediately not only information but an atmosphere. Two travel writers did that, Stephanie Brush for *Northwest* (January 1987) and Donald Dewey for *TWA Ambassador* (July 1987). China, according to Ms. Brush, "began with a gnat."

I was standing on the deck of the *Pearl*, straining to see something—a jetty, a headland, a floating bit of straw—that belonged to the coastline. But the fog had hung over us all morning, and the silence, like the weather, was eerie, dense, and absolute. Out there (close enough to touch?) was the coast of Manchuria. The captain blew a long blast on the foghorn every few minutes, and then all you could hear was the hum of the giant engines and the slap of the sea.

Then, out of nowhere, a wet and dizzy gnat landed on my arm and I started to shake; I knew the Chinese mainland had to be nearby.

We are into it. We are arriving with her. The author has used the element of surprise, moving from the seemingly insignificant to what will become the important impact of a great nation. Not only has the fog been lifted, but life—in very small form—has welcomed us to the world of China.

In the following excerpt, Donald Dewey intorduces us to Rome:

> Few cities have less of the eternal about them than Rome. From its ancient stones to its medieval churches, from the Palazzo Farnese of the Renaissance to the Porta Pia of nineteenth-century statehood, from the monarchist narcissisms of the Wedding Cake to the facist fantasies of EUR, the Italian capital evokes temporality on the grandest of scales, displaying the relentless development of its history by reducing entire epochs to streets and piazzas that are best appreciated by being trod upon. The sobriquet of Eternal City has never reflected some special social or philosophical dynamic, but only sectarian propaganda, and is closer in origin to the "city of champions" distinguished after every Super Bowl and World Series than to judgments of Paris as the City of Light or of Amsterdam as the City of Canals. The history of Rome—pagan and Christian, imperial and republican, aggressive and besieged—is first of all a history of mortality.
>
> A constant of mortality, of course, is death, and Rome is filled with the dead, the dying, the doomed, the slaughtered, the murderous, the fatal, and the lethal. Everyone remembers the questions as "Quo vadis Domine?" (Where are you going, Lord?) but how many remember the answer as "Eo Roman interum crucifigi (I go to Rome to be crucified again)"?

Notice how the writers set pace, moving the reader into each article at an appropriate clip. Think how swiftly or deliberately you want to propel or ease the reader into your article.

Types of Leads

All kinds of leads are available for you to choose from, as you'll see from the following list. Use a lead that serves your purpose and that of the article—you may want to experiment with several different ways of handling the same information before settling on one, but remember those four purposes of a lead. You can choose from:

- News peg
- Description
- Establishing a mood
- Anecdote
- Personal involvement
- Summary
- Context
- Philosophic
- Definition

- Multi-example
- Opinion
- Startling or surprise statement
- Question
- Quote
- Gimmick
- Mystery/kicker
- Make-believe

News Peg. Events of the moment can prompt a story, either directly or indirectly. The editors of *The Progressive* (January 1990) take a reality of international affairs and shape a commentary. They open:

> Body counts are back. U.S. advisers carry weapons in a foreign war zone. U.S. embassy officials provide media briefings. The foreign government says it has dealt a decisive blow to the rebels, even as they mount offensive after offensive.
>
> Sound familiar? It's Vietnam revisited. But this is not *China Beach*. It's El Salvador.

Description. Sometimes an article calls for mood or scene setting or a getting-to-know-you start. That's when descriptive material may function as a starter. Consider the scenic atmosphere established in this descriptive lead by John Eastman in his article "The Ghost Forest," published in *Natural History* (January 1986):

> Up hill and down, extending miles across northern Michigan, the pine stumps endure. They squat in hard-core silence, cracked and ravaged by age, insect, lichen, and fire, eroding like upthrusts of an old geology in a modern sea of bracken fern and aspen. They are time warps in the landscape, relics of the golden age of timber, amputees of an America I never knew. Today they form a ghost forest of sullen carcasses littering the slopes and plains that bridge the inland seas.

Or consider the following getting-to-know-you lead from "Alligators Are Back, Breeding Like Crazy and Making a Big Splash," by Donald Dale Jackson, published in the *Smithsonian* (January 1987):

> The problem starts up front, with the face—the cavernous, leering mouth filled with spiky teeth; the cold, predatorial eyes; the knobby reptilian skin. There's no sense mincing words: we're talking ugly here, nightmare dwellers, creatures from the black lagoon. Show me an alligator and I'll show you somebody truckin' hard the other way.

Establishing a Mood. Such a lead is descriptive in nature, but it may also contain elements of narration, exposition, and even argumentation. Sallie Tisdale, in a memoir for *Harper's*, "Bound Upon a Wheel of Fire" (January 1, 1990) turns to mood and then explains why:

Every winter night of my childhood, my father built a fire. Every element of the evening's fire was treated with care—with the caress of the careful man. The wood, the wood box, the grate, the coal-black poker and shovel: He touched these more often than he touched me. I would hold back, watching, and when the fire was lit plant myself before it and fall into a gentle dream. No idea was too strange or remote before the fire, no fantasy of shadow and light too bizarre.

But for all the long hours I spent before his fires, for all the honey-colored vapors that rose like smoke from that hearth, these aren't the fires of memory. They aren't my father's fires. When I remember fire, I remember houses burning, scorched and flooded with flame, and mills burning towers of fire leaping through the night to the lumber nearby like so much kindling, and cars burning, stinking and black and waiting to blow. I loved those fires with a hot horror, always daring myself to step closer, feel their heat, touch.

My father is a fireman. My submission to fire is lamentably obvious. But there is more than love here, more than jealousy—more than Electra's unwilling need. It is a fundamental lure, a seduction of my roots and not my limbs. I am propelled toward fire, and the dual draw of fascination and fear, the urge to walk into and at the same time conquer fire, is like the twin poles of the hermaphrodite. I wanted to be a fireman before, and after, I wanted to be anything else.

Anecdote. A common solution to the lead problem is the anecdote, the concentrated narrative or fragment of action that typifies the problem or situation to be covered in the article. Anecdotal beginnings tend to be more active than others. Since we are attracted to action 'round and about us, an active lead is likely to lure. Perhaps the method has become overused, but writers recognize what succeeds, and so do editors. What's more, many articles legitimately call for an anecdotal opening.

A good example of this technique is provided by Nancy Schommer in "The Embryo Connection" in *Hog Farm Management*, (August 1982):

> Like an expectant father, Dave Stewart paced back and forth as the doctor wheeled the first patient into the operating room. Bright lights overhead glistened on her smooth-shaven skin. On her back she lay, head hanging upside down, a gas mask cupped over her nose. Her foil-wrapped feet dangled awkwardly, unladylike, about the table.
>
> One of Stewart's best sows. Eleven performance-tested generations behind her. His finest genetic material, except for one tragic flaw: pseudo-rabies. But, like the twenty-one positive sows waiting their surgical turn, she might be carrying a future generation of PrV-negative pigs. *Might be.* What if she hadn't conceived, Stewart wondered. And what about the others? It was too late to worry now. The surgical team stood ready in the rented ISU laboratory; a chartered plane waited outside; and Stewart had already plunked down $11,000. The embryo connection was underway.

Reg Potterton turned to narrative in *Playboy*'s "Land of the Risen

Sun," a travel-sociology/world affairs piece about a Japan tied to yesterday's customs, today's economic competition, and tomorrow's technology, a serious land of serious people seemingly comic at times to outsiders, people at once worldly and parochial. Here is his lead section for the 1971 piece:

The message was slipped under the door of each guest's room early in the morning. It read: "Welcome congenial guest and honored Japan visitant! Announcing process emergency proper fire drilling the clock eleven." That was the English version. Most guests threw it away or kept it as one of the more intriguing examples of Japanese translation. At precisely 11:00 that morning, an anxious voice was heard over the guest-room speakers: "Emergency! Emergency! Fire in the main elevator shaft! Fire in seventh and eighth floors! Emergency! Firemen taking good care these fires. Evacuation commencing. Listen for further speaking."

Many guests commenced their own evacuation when they heard this. Most milled nervously in the corridors, some in pajamas with shaving soap on their faces, others still chewing breakfast or carrying luggage. Bright green and purple smoke billowed outside the windows, maids ran around giggling in hard hats and victims wrapped in bandages were lifted onto stretchers and removed to ambulances lined up in the hotel entrance way. When one of them careened into the street at top speed and ran into an approaching fire engine, the two "victims" got out and went sprinting back to the hotel to have their dressings checked.

"Very authentic fire drill," beamed the hotel manager to an American guest. "Very thorough to prepare for possible emergency." The guest asked about the collision between the fire engine and the ambulance. "Yes, yes," was the happy response. "Authentic mistake. Sometimes people slightly killed in fire drills, but never any guests. Ha-ha! Very authentic, thank you." And he excused himself to join some hard-hatted, smiling hotel executives who were posing for a group photograph.

Many guests, once they learned the alarm was in fact only a drill, started to return to their rooms. Those on the seventh and eighth floors were informed politely that they were temporarily dead and unidentified, but to the chagrin of the organizers, the occidentals in this group became truculent and refused to play. The Japanese guests went along with the game and took pictures of one another in front of the fire engine, while a couple of Europeans and Americans muttered threats about checking out. Their rooms were full of brightly colored fumes from the smoke bombs detonated outside their windows.

"Further speaking," said the voice on the room speakers. "All guests and participants greatly thanked for their cooperation." A middle-aged English guest stamped into one of the elevators to go back to his breakfast. "Mad buggers," he growled at the smiling operator. "Ruined my bloody boiled eggs."

Many travelers who have been to Japan would argue that this anecdote is hardly typical of everyday life there, but then, few people would agree on what is typical about Japan. What is certain is that to the visiting foreigner, Japan is culture shock on a massive scale.

Potterton used an extended anecdote to get matters underway and also to represent his view of a strange land. It its detailed telling, that point of view becomes shared. The author works away at our impressions. He has a message to communicate. For that to happen, the author decided the fire drill fits better than viewing Tokyo from the air as one arrives by 747 or the description of rugged countrysides around Hokkaido. His lead attracts attention, establishes the subject, sets the tone, and guides into the story. He is taking us along on the tour, one that he, not someone from Thomas Cook or American Express, has mapped out for us.

The anecdote may be expansive, inclusive, detailed as is Potterton's. It may, on the other hand, be merely suggested:

> When Alicia de Larrocha was two and one-half, they took her favorite toy away, and she banged her head on the floor in a tantrum until she got it back.
>
> The toy was the family grand piano.

Writer Louise Sweeney has given the reader a quick push into an article about the renowned Spanish pianist for *The Christian Science Monitor* (December 8, 1978).

Personal Involvement. If you're part of the story, an opening action can become intensely personal. William Broyles, Jr., managed that in "Pushing the Mid-life Envelope," his *Esquire* verbalization of a search, at age forty-two, for the ultimate adventure and self-discovery:

> I am hanging, exhausted, by my fingertips from a rock ledge twenty-three thousand feet above sea level. My right foot searches for a dimple in the rock to push from, fails, then my left foot does the same. Finally, my toe catches on a tiny protrusion. I take eight desperate breaths, then push. My left hand goes up to another rock, finds a hold. I breathe eight more times, trying to muster some last shred of strength, and pull.
>
> Somewhere above me is the summit of Aconcagua, the tallest mountain in the Western Hemisphere. Storm clouds are gathering. It is past 5:00 in the afternoon, and soon the temperature will fall to twenty below zero. I have climbed four thousand feet through a forty-five-degree pitch of loose boulders. For three days I have been unable to eat. I am dehydrated. My breathing comes in irregular gasps. My brain, starved for oxygen, has all but ceased to function. I have become senile, an old man. In the snow on the summit is the body of an Argentine who froze to death after reaching the top a few days before. Five other climbers have died on the mountain in the past month.
>
> This is what mountaineers call a "nontrivial situation." I have, however, never climbed a mountain in my life, and until a few weeks earlier I owned barely a Swiss army knife. I am also intensely afraid of heights, and break out in a sweat when I stand near a high window. I cannot look down on a ski lift. I have nightmares about falling.

What am I doing here?

Gary Haynes' outdoor adventure, "Where Elephants Die" for *Natural History*, (June 1987), was of another sort, a different danger. He faced it in Zimbabwe's Hwange National Park where he'd gone to study elephants. He, like Broyles, must have wondered at a critical moment why he was there:

> An emaciated elephant is lying in the shade of a thicket of small trees. My game scout, Morven Mdondo, says quietly, "I don't think this one is dead," but I step right up to it with my instant camera in hand and take its photograph. A very fresh dead one, I think. The camera clicks and whirs and spits out the developing print, and the elephant opens its eye, staring at me in alarm. It rises abruptly, and Morven and I take off running, the elephant racing behind us through the trees. I wonder breathlessly whether it will kill me or Morven first. My hat flies off. The elephant crashes right through a tree behind me. I hold on to the camera.
>
> Morven veers off toward the open grass to our left. He cocks his automatic rifle but stumbles and falls. The elephant runs after me. I leap over the fresh carcass of a small elephant calf and look back to see the elephant drop to its front "knees" at full speed and repeatedly plunge its tusks into the calf's body.
>
> When it has flattened the carcass, it slowly rises and walks over to stand in the shade of some trees about twenty yards away. There it remains, as if dazed, for the rest of the afternoon.

The personal involvement, however, can be more reflective. C.L. Rawlins wrote in "Lines on the Land" for *Sierra* (October 1989):

> When I was too young to say "public domain," let alone know what it might be, I still knew three sorts of places. The first was *where we live*. The second was *where they live*. The third was *out there*. *Where we live* had the right smells and the right food—I knew it the way a badger knows its burrow. *Where they live* was strange—in the houses of friends, different smells, different ways. Artichokes. Egg salad. A different word for toilet. The frontiers of *where they live* were dangerous places. An old woman like the witch in night stories might burst screeching from a door. A black man in a T-shirt might catch a chicken and—*ka-chunk*—chop off its head with a hatchet, the body flailing and spouting as the head lay still on the block, one eye going blink-blink-blink. Strange kids might get a notion to put dirt in your hair. *Out there* was the desert, where nobody lived. There were stickery bushes that didn't grow where we live, and lizards tracking the sand. You could pee anytime, anyplace. There were things you did only once, like stand on an anthill to watch the ants or pick the bloom from a prickly pear, but nobody told you not to do them. You suffered and learned. *Out there* you could sneak to the ditch and take off your clothes and lie in the mud because the mud was cool. Back *where we live* you would be cussed out and hosed down, though there was never any doubt that the pleasure was worth the risk. You could dig holes in the sand and roof them with plywood signs or the hoods of cars. You could have wars with kids from the houses on the other side of

the strip of desert; you could throw clods and rocks, punching and kicking and spitting and running away, for the rush of real fear. *Out there* was the bush, the rock, the bull, the beast, the ghost. *Out there* was the golden sand, the patch of cottonwood shade where no one could say "Go home." You could wear your own skin, look and listen and hide, watch cars shimmer by on August asphalt through a thorny screen of mesquite, and see, above the road, a blue line of peaks, the solid, cool promise at the edge of the world.

In the Anglo-imperialist notion of the frontier, *out there* coincided with the *where we live* of Lakota, Cheyenne, Shoshone, Crow, Blackfoot, Paiute, Apache, Hopi, and Comanche. The logic of manifest destiny was brutally simple: If there are no streets or deeds or lawyers, then rightfully speaking no one lives there. We drew the lines, hard and fast.

The public domain is what was left of *out there* by the turn of the century, land that none of the miners, ranchers, farmers, bankers, speculators, or congressmen wanted urgently enough to file papers or pay taxes.

Rawlins's involvement is in the mind, in past experience and present contemplation.

Summary. If you prefer to tell the reader immediately and precisely what your article is about, then summarize. That's like putting your thesis first. Meg Gaige did that in "The Deadliest Profession" (*Farm Journal*).

As sure as weeds grow in corn, farmers will die at work this year. More than fifteen hundred will die horrible deaths — crushed by tractors, suffocated in grain bins and silos, battered by bulls, electrocuted. They'll bleed to death, their limbs torn from their trunks by PTOs and augers. And their children will die — hundreds of them — riding tractor fenders, helping out, trying to master tasks too sophisticated for their years.

Why don't we care until mutilation and death scar our own family, or our neighbor's? Why do we believe it will never happen to us?

Wham!

Context. The reader may, in your view, need background to understand the significant or the new in your subject. Manuela Hoelterhoff celebrated in words the centenary of the Eiffel Tower for *Travel & Leisure*, (April 1989). She began:

The writer Guy de Maupassant called it a "disgraceful skeleton" and liked to say that he regularly lunched there because it was the only place in Paris where he didn't have to look at it. The irremediable ugliness of the Eiffel Tower was probably one of the few things French tastemakers agreed upon in the late 1880s.

As it rose one thousand feet above the green Champ de Mars across the Seine from the Trocadero, a petition demanding the removal of this blight grew to three hundred names, among them those of the poet Paul Verlaine and the composer Charles Gounod. They asked, "Is the city of Paris going to continue her association with the wild ideas, the mercenary aspirations of a machine maker, only to be shamefully disfigured and dishonored?" Idle words in the wind. From the day Gustave Eiffel first climbed to the top of his creation (one hundred years ago this month) the iron tower has been a hit—and not only with the Parisians. It is the city's most widely recognized landmark and, along with the Tri-color, an emblem of France.

When David Whitman of *U.S. News & World Report* reported on "America's Hidden Poor" for the January 11, 1988 issue, the story's opening served to remind the reader of a problem that changes little despite political manifestos and governmental programs:

Tom Fletcher didn't realize Lyndon Johnson was going to inaugurate the War on Poverty from his front porch. But one sunny April morning some twenty years ago, two Secret Service agents walked into Fletcher's back yard in Inez, Kentucky, and told him the President was planning to drop by the three-room tar-paper shack that housed Fletcher, his wife and their eight children. Sure enough, several hours later, there was ol' LBJ in his navy suit, pumping Fletcher's hand up and down while Lady Bird in her white sunbonnet chatted with the neighbors and news photographers clicked their cameras out on the dusty highway. Fletcher told LBJ how he had managed to make only $400 the previous year working odd jobs at a sawmill and "scratching" in the mountainside for coal. A few minutes later, the President bade Fletcher farewell, Lady Bird called out, " 'Bye, chillun," and Johnson's motorcade vanished into the Appalachian hills.

Tom Fletcher never forgot that day, but much of America—including LBJ's Democratic and Republican successors—has forgotten the Tom Fletchers of the world. For a short time, Fletcher and his family were celebrities. The three weekly newsmagazines all featured photos of Johnson on Fletcher's porch, and the unemployed coal miner with a third-grade education and lots of mouths to feed soon became a national symbol of the need for a War on Poverty. Yet two decades later, Fletcher's life is much the same. The checks and donations he received after LBJ's visit have long since ceased. He has found work only sporadically in the intervening years. And he still resides in the same house with the same crude front porch.

Now, it seems to me, we're ready to move into the world of the nation's hidden poor. We are prepared to comprehend.

Philosophic. Some subjects tempt writers to tempt readers to think. Lincoln Barnett, writing about Earth's origin for the December 8, 1952 edition of *Life*, turned contemplative. He used poetry to trigger a train of thought:

Earth! Thou mother of numberless
children, the nurses and the mother.
  Sister thou of the stars, and beloved by
the Sun, the rejoicer!
  Guardian and friend of the moon, O
Earth, whom the comets forget not.

Yes, in the measureless distance
wheel round and again they behold thee!

— Samuel Taylor Coleridge,
"Hymn to the Earth"

Poisoned in his paved cities, blindfolded by his impulses and necessities, man tends to disregard the system of nature in which he stands. It is only at infrequent moments when he finds himself beneath the stars, at sea perhaps, or in a moonlit meadow or on a foreign shore, that he contemplates the natural world — and he wonders.

One must be careful of philosophic leads. They must suit the subject, the objective of the article, the kind of reader likely to read the article, and even the author. Consider whether the reader is likely to accept such thoughts from you. Have you the appropriate aura of authority to be so weighty with the reader?

Definition. If you want the reader to know what a subject means to you, then explain by defining it, marking the boundaries you've set for it. In *Channels of Communication* we find out:

The talk show is not, contrary to the belief of many Americans under thirty, a natural form of human communication that evolved along with the capacity for speech — though it does seem likely to last till the crack of doom. This infinitely mutable and varied form was born with television, and represents, for better and for worse, its most distinctive contribution to human discourse. The talk show, like television itself, is a commercial transaction — bringing a celebrity with something to sell into contact with would-be consumers — delivered in the form of entertainment. But it is also a national stream of consciousness, in which all the rumors, obsessions, heartaches, verbal ties and, yes, ideas at large in the culture go floating by.

That's not only informative but a strong clue as to how the writer will approach the subject in what follows. It sets the tone and direction.

Multi-Example. To immediately prove the extent of "Middle-Class Squeeze," the staff of *U.S. News & World Report* (August 18, 1986) fashioned this lead:

"I have three college degrees, and I make less than a public-school teacher," says Kimberly Quintero, editor of a 6,600-circulation weekly newspaper in Gilbert, Arizona. She would rather be a stay-at-home mother, but she and her husband Joseph, a customer-service representative for Premier Industrial Corporation, need their joint income of about $35,000 to support their four children.

"My $225 car payment is more than my parents' mortgage payment," laments Barbara Stevens, thirty, who earns $30,000 as a media buyer at a Los Angeles advertising agency. She owns a 1985 Volkswagen Jetta; her parents own a four-bedroom house with swimming pool in San Marino, an affluent Los Angeles suburb.

Desmond Moody, twenty-four, was graduated from the University of Massachusetts with an economics degree two years ago. He'd like to work in banking or finance but can't break in. As an assistant manager in a Cambridge, Massachusetts, photocopying store, he earns $260 a week. "College just wasn't the big ticket my parents and I expected it to be," he sighs. Most humiliating to him, he has had to move back home with his parents.

America's middle class is in a fix. After decades of rising living standards, many in the middle now find they're clambering up a descending economic escalator. They are having a harder time than ever buying houses and cars. Despite the Reagan income-tax cuts, total taxes are taking a bigger chunk of family incomes than they once did. When all the bills are tallied and inflation is accounted for, a typical middle-class family actually has *less* money to spend these days than it did more than a decade ago. Says social critic Alvin Toffler, author of *Future Shock*: "It has become clear that it's not all onward and upward."

Three human examples followed by a thesis. We're prepared for what's ahead.

Opinion. If point of view is what you're pushing, get right into it. Digby Diehl ponders turning forty in "Looking at 40" for *Esquire* (March 1981):

Some guys give up their dental practice and go to Tahiti. Some have a torrid affair with a pizza waitress in a sleazy hotel. Others return to graduate school and find solace in the groves of academe. A few discover drugs and make fools of themselves freaking out. A friend of mine had a complete mental breakdown, a trip to the funny farm, and a revitalized reentry into respectable upper-middle-class life, and his corporation never even got wind of it. One way or another, we must all face a middle-age rite of passage just as surely as a bar mitzvah, a train ride to college, or a first glass of beer.

The terror of turning forty is not that you are midway through life; it is that suddenly, irrevocably, you are half-dead.

Or as Cynthia Parsons put it in *The Christian Science Monitor* (March 30, 1981):

They are in serious trouble, the public schools in major U.S. cities. As one schoolman remarked, only half in jest: "If you think you see some light at the end of the tunnel, obviously you're going in the wrong direction."

Startling or Surprise Statement. Catch the reader off guard for effect, as did Richard Stengel, in "Here Today, Here Tomorrow" for *Spy* (December 1989). *Spy* is a publication dedicated to amusing or outraging its audience, usually through low voltage shock.

Funerals are for the living. An implicit nod passes among the guests: *We're still here.* Few rituals affirm the social order like a funeral. In the hierarchy of grief, mourners jostle one another for the best pews, eulogists duel one another with sharpened superlatives, pallbearers bask in shouldering their heavy burden.

A point is made pointedly, potently in *Farm Journal*:

If farmers had to listen to this story instead of read it, over half would have a hard time hearing the words. Loud noises associated with farming have made farmers some of the most hearing-impaired workers in the U.S.

The article was titled "Farming in Silence." We swiftly get the idea.

Question. Every article could begin with a question. Too many do. That's why you should be careful. Use the question only if you firmly believe it the best introduction to what follows. Does the question pose a fetching mystery? Does the question lead directly to a vital answer? Does the question turn playful?

Who would have guessed that beneath the bone-hard shell of the American lobster beats the heart of a gentle and seemingly flirtatious romantic? Or that the creature has a mating routine as clever and coy as any encounter between people?

If such assertions seem difficult to swallow, it may be because of our own narrow view of lobster.

Daniel Haney posed the question in "Getting to the Heart of a Lobster Love" (*National Wildlife*, April/May 1987). And David Jeffery, investigating the restoration efforts in the Vatican's Sistine Chapel "A Renaissance for Michelangelo" (*National Geographic*, December 1989), asks:

Who would dare change the arms of God on the first day of Creation? Michelangelo. First he scribed outlines for God's arms into wet plaster with quick strokes of a sharp tool. Then he abandoned those outlines in a flash of brushstrokes. He painted God's left arm so it swept directly overhead, made that arm plunge a divine hand into the turbulent light and wrench it from the darkness.

Haney asks a surprising question and immediately answers.

In *World Monitor*, Earl Foell asks:

Is your local president, prime minister, or dictator up to dealing with the greenhouse effect? Or the superconductivity race, "star wars," biotechnology competition, chemical weapons, or a joint Mars expedition? Or even retooling of factories with computers and robots?

Can he or she persuade some 160 other members of the heads-of-state club to join in making sensible decisions on such issues for the benefit of this and future generations?

On present evidence the answer to all these questions is a blunt "no."

Foell uses questions to summarize a host of problems, tying them to rational leadership, or a lack thereof. He then propels himself and the reader into a discussion of what leadership requirements are in a modern world. Questions get him going.

Quote. As with the question lead, so the quote: don't overuse it. Make sure you have a strong quote, one that powers the informational engine.

From Thomas Sancton, reporting "The Fight to Save the Planet," for *Time* (December 18, 1989):

> "When a man knows he is to be hanged in a fortnight," Samuel Johnson once wrote, "it concentrates his mind wonderfully." The threat of impending ecological doom seems to be having the same effect on public opinion. If historians remember 1989 as the year the Iron Curtain collapsed, it has also been the year that concern for the environment reached a new peak.

In *Fortune* (May 11, 1987), Myron Magnet introduces us to "America's Underclass: What To Do?"

> Listen: "He made me scared, so I pulled the trigger. So feel sorry? I doubt it. I didn't want to see him go down like that, but better him than me."
>
> "I'm gonna work forty hours a week and bring home maybe $100, $150, when I can work fifteen minutes and come back with $1,000 tax-free?"
>
> "I ain't working for no minimum wage."
>
> "Man, you go two, three years not working, and hanging around and smoking reefer or drinking, and then you get a job—you can't handle it. You say, 'I don't want to get up in the morning, get pushed and shoved. I'm gonna get on welfare.' "
>
> "Everybody else I knew was having babies, so I just went along."
>
> "It just seems that everybody here is down on their luck."
>
> The voices, reported in the press, are the voices of the underclass, and their message is that the troubles of this group at the very bottom of the American social ladder need fixing fast.

One quote or even a batch may not suffice. Try dialogue. Peter Buckley entered the lives of "Theater's Seasoned Duo" (*American Way*, April 1983):

> "I suppose that the first thing you want to know is how the hell we've managed to make it through forty years together," says Hume Cronyn even before the question is asked.
>
> "Oh, my God," says Jessica Tandy in mock horror. "Not *that* one again."
>
> "Well, Jess, everybody wants to know *that* one," continues Cronyn, "but to tell you the truth, we just don't seem to have an answer."
>
> "Oh, it's no big secret," says Tandy, smiling. "All I have to do is just keep on forgiving him."
>
> Outside it's a gray Manhattan morning, but inside it's as bright as a summer's afternoon as the first couple of the American theater pad around the comfortable hotel suite that has served as their home ever since they sold their big lakefront house in Pound Ridge, New York, two years ago.

The words of the two actors help to set scene, tone, direction.

Gimmick. Don't be different just to be different, but if the trick profits the topic, go for it, as Lisa Grunwald did in her *Esquire* (April 1989) piece, "The Passive-Aggressive Male":

These are some of the things that a passive-aggressive man says:
- "Nothing, I'm just thinking."
- "No, why do you ask?"
- "Angry?"
- "I don't hate it."
- "I won't stop you."
- "What's the problem?"

These are some of the things that a passive-aggressive man does:
- Has a new lock put on the front door and forgets to give his wife the key.
- Calls an early staff meeting and shows up forty minutes late.
- Talks on the phone for an hour when he knows that his girlfriend is trying to call.
- Hears about passive-aggression and decides that it doesn't apply to him.

These are some of the things that a passive-aggressive man can find tough:
- Meeting deadlines.
- Firing people.
- Getting angry.
- Saying no.

This is what a passive-aggressive man fears:
- Himself.

So let's talk about my friend Moe.

The staccato prose through a rush of opinions serves to "educate" the reader swiftly into the author's realm of thought. The pace is lively. A more measured pace might have wearied the reader, bogged him down in a welter of ideas.

Mystery/Kicker. Malcolm Browne offers an example of a buildup toward the unexpected in "The Ultimate Video Game: Mock War" for readers of *Discover*, (August 1983):

The Soviet forces had invaded Iran swiftly, but now they were confronted by a range of mountains and foothills pierced only by a few narrow valleys. In one of these, an American brigade commander waited, readying his force of a few thousand troops to meet the onslaught. At his disposal were a score of tanks, several batteries of artillery, various anti-tank weapons, and half a dozen ground-attack aircraft armed with cannon, missiles, and bombs.

Quickly checking terrain elevations and measuring fields of fire, the U.S. commander ordered a series of maneuvers that would give his troops the best possible views of the enemy while exposing them to the least amount of fire. The focus of the fight, he had decided, would be an obstacle of mine field, tank traps, and barbed wire thrown across the narrowest part of the valley. Here the Soviet tanks would have to slow down, and here he would concentrate his fire.

As the American commander made last-minute preparations and issued orders for sorties by his helicopters and planes, his Soviet counterpart also deployed his forces and refined his plans, trying to guess his adversary's intentions.

Then, with both sides braced for combat, the Soviets attacked. The first wave of their big T-64 tanks swept out of a forest toward the field of obstacles and within minutes had reached the American outposts. Shells and missiles began to fly, and explosions signaled the destruction of gun positions and strong points on both sides. As the battle raged, the Soviet advance halted, but now the American commander recognized that enemy reinforcements, although still unseen, were on the way. To head them off, he ordered his long-range guns and tactical missiles to begin hammering areas in the enemy rear through which the reinforcements were probably moving.

Now another possibility began to worry the U.S. commander: A region of fairly low ground southeast of the main action might be vulnerable to the Soviet force. There was just a chance the enemy would try to advance through it, attacking the American defenders from the flank. It was essential that the U.S. commander know what was happening on the low ground, so he hastily ordered his helicopters and planes up for a look.

They soon confirmed the commander's suspicions. The Russians were, indeed, on the move for a flank attack. The warning came in time, but at a high price: Soviet anti-aircraft missile crews opened fire on the Cobra helicopters and A-10 ground-attack planes, bringing down one after another. Only two of the six aircraft survived.

"Damn, I blew it," the American commander said. "I've thrown away my air support." With that he pushed away the hand controller he had been using to direct the battle on the video screen, lighted a cigarette, and strolled over to compare notes with his "Soviet" opponent, who was seated at another computer terminal a few yards away. The two men had been waging war inside the building that houses the new JANUS war-gaming system at Lawrence Livermore Laboratory in Livermore, California.

Nonfiction turns out to be fiction used on behalf of nonfiction. A surprise element that works.

Make-Believe. In his June 1989 *Smithsonian* article, entitled "In 1789, a Farmer Went to New York to Become President," Michael Kernan places the reader into early American history—a feat of make-believe within a real event:

> Put yourself under George Washington's wig for a minute. It is April 16 exactly two hundred years ago and you have recently been elected the first President of the brand-new United States, and you are riding in your carriage from Mount Vernon to New York City for your Inauguration.

The crowds are unbelievable. All along the way people stand by the road to cheer. Horsemen ride alongside in a continuous guard of honor, raising a storm of dust. At every town, dignitaries are drawn up expecting you to get out and shake their hand. People make speeches, each more grandiloquent than the last. Cannon go off and at night fireworks blossom in the sky. You pass beneath triumphal arches piled with flowers, cross rivers on decorated barges, find yourself caught up in parades. And dinner parties. And even, at one particularly fulsome celebration, "a numerous train of white-robed ladies."

Variety is at your beck and call when you create your lead. Select the approach that fits information and focus. If a bit of game-playing might help, play the game. If you feel more comfortable playing it straight, then play straight. Engage the reader. Make a lead work for you.

And make the ending work, too.

FINISH STRONG

If you've managed to cajole your reader to the end of that article, its finish — if well crafted — may be what he or she remembers most. It is, after all, what's read last.

You may not put as much effort into a finish as into a start, but give it time and consideration. Articles *do* need endings. Endings should be carefully led to. They should leave the reader satisfied, giving a sense of completion, of fulfillment.

A number of techniques you use to open stories can be used to close them: mood-setting description, narrative, a summarizing point, a final point, a twist, a quote. Do you want to leave a sense of conclusion? Do you want to suggest continuation? Do you want the reader concerned or elated, educated or inspired? These are important decisions. To help you see how various endings work, share some examples with me.

For instance, Thomas De Carlo summarized for readers of *Esquire* ("The Unracked Back," December 1981):

The back is a magnificent piece of craftsmanship. With a little maintenance, a little work, it can be as wonderful to live with as it is to behold.

He offers a reminder to take care of your back. Period. End.

T. Kent Jones, writing in the January, 1990 issue of *M* about Leonard Goldenson, "The Father of ABC," selected quotes to wrap up:

And television still excites him all the time. "The pressure is always there to do something better and to outwit the competition. That's the greatest thing in the world," he says. "When you come in every day and see the ratings for your shows compared to CBS, NBC and Fox you say to yourself, 'Well, we could have done that better,' or, 'They fumbled,' or whatnot. For instance on the earthquake in San Francisco, I watched that right through the night. I looked to see what CBS and NBC were doing and there's no question about it, we took 'em" he says, adrenalin pumping, proud of his people. He flashes a big, toothy, Monday-Night-Football-just-torpedoed-your-new-sitcom smile. "I hate to be second."

And that, after fifty years in show business, earning millions of dollars and the respect of an industry, is what it boils down to. As for the rest, talks should be concise and meetings shouldn't go on too long. "You know," he says, "You can only eat three meals a day, you can only sleep in one bed at night. Everything else is extra."

The quote is oft-used, perhaps too oft-used. But if someone has given you an effective and conclusive one, how can you not use it?

Art expert Robert Hughes ended his report on the high-stakes art market in *Time* with some informed opinion, a nugget one might expect from him, even subconsciously demand:

For Chicago's James Wood the damage comes down to a confusion between aesthetic and material value. "When a work of art passes through our doors, it should leave the world of economics," says Wood. "Walking through a great museum is not going to give you a profile that reflects the auction market. You have to educate people to grasp that the money paid for a work of art is utterly secondary to its lasting value, its ability to make them respond to it."

The problem is that although art has always been a commodity, it loses its inherent value when it is treated only as such. To lock it into a market circus is to lock people out of contemplating it. This inexorable process tends to collapse the nuances of meaning and visual experience under the brute weight of price. It is not a compliment to the work. If there were only one copy of each book in the world, fought over by multimillionaires and investment trusts, what would happen to one's sense of literature—the tissue of its meaning that sustains a common discourse? What strip mining is to nature, the art market has become to culture.

Mood suffuses the end of Gretel Ehrlich's essay "Spring" for *Antaeus* (which was reprinted in the book, *Best American Essays of 1987*, edited by Gay Talese). But out of mood come a writer's thoughts, even a touch of philosophy:

Spring teaches me what space and time teach me: that I am a random multiple; that the many fit together like waves; that my swell is a collision of particles. Spring is a kind of music, a seething minor, a twelve-tone scale. Even the odd harmonies amassed only lift up to dissolve.

Spring passes harder and harder and is feral. The first thunder cracks the sky into a larger domain. Sap rises in obdurateness. For the first time in seven months, rain slants down in a slow pavane—sharp but soft—like desire, like the laying on of hands. I drive the highway that crosses the wild-horse range. Near Emblem I watch a black studhorse trot across the range all alone. He travels north, then turns in my direction as if trotting to me. Now, when I dream of Joel, he is riding that horse and he knows he is dead. One night he rides to my house, all smiles and shyness. I let him in.

The observational anecdote winds up Christopher Hope's *New Republic* reaction to a startling political event, the fall of the Iron Curtain ("Seeing is Believing," December 18, 1989):

> At the entrance to a large department store I watched a family of East Berliners, freshly arrived, wide-eyed and eerily silent. Father, mother, and a boy of about six were passing the chocolate counter. Suddenly the little boy stopped dead. He had seen the chocolates, homemade and gleaming darkly under the lights, perfection behind the glass, a costly pyramid, profligate, tempting, untouchable. His adoration passed like an electric current into his mother and father and rooted them to the spot. No one spoke. After a while, like sleepers awakening, they shook themselves and went on their way. Seeing is believing. It's not the same as having, but it will do, for a while at least.

Scene and action seem not to end in "Beyond the Mountains," Mark Danner's final paragraph for his lengthy study of Haiti for *The New Yorker*. Were we to go there now, only small details would be different, he's telling us; the fundamentals, the verities would be unchanged:

> Suddenly, through the rain lashing the jeep's windows, I became aware of dark shapes outside, moving silently along the road. Looking more closely, I realized that I was sitting in the midst of a village; on either side of the road, scores of mud huts extended back into the trees. Now the rain had come, and—as would happen many times every year, hundreds of times in every lifetime—the villager's homes had instantly been flooded, and the entire village had been forced from sleep out into the rain. With each flash of lightning, I could see them all, hundreds of them, standing mutely on either side of the road, thigh-deep in water. On the radio, Bazin's low voice droned on, smoothly, gracefully, forming its perfect sentences, continuing a brilliant analysis of Haiti's political crisis. When it rains in Haiti, the country's one highway is immediately impassable. When it rains in Haiti, the people have no shelter.

Death is conclusion, at least for experience on one plane, our plane. And so two writers treated death in their stories about that most grievous loss: the death of one's mother. Nancy Burson, an artist, made "Unmasking Death" (*New Age Journal*, June 1986) a sensual process and event:

> There was no last gasp that I had been prepared for. There were no lines in her face, something I never understood about the way my mother aged. But she looked much thinner. That last day she had aged twenty-five years—but at the end those ravages seemed filled in by repose.
> She wasn't the horrid color I had imagined. She was gray. Gray is an important color in my artwork. It is neutral, dispassionate. The gray seemed

to emphasize the indifference with which the world would go on without her. It felt strange that I was what was left of her and that her life now seemed to be about my survival, my existence.

At the same time that I felt my mother's spirit lifting, I felt my own body become heavier and heavier. By the time the doctor came in to pronounce her officially dead, I ached all over. Part of this, I knew, was stress, but I also couldn't help feeling that she had left me something, some part of her spiritual self or perhaps new life. And that additional weight, I knew, was anchoring me more firmly to the earth.

Writer Helen Epstein, recounting "A Death in the Family" for *New York* (November 27, 1989), seemed to keep herself, and us as readers, at a distance. All the facts have been conveyed. The emotions, however, remain private. They're inferred, not shared. Epstein ended her story this way:

> David presents the safe-deposit-box key casually, as though this visit with his siblings is routine, and the three of us sit down in an empty room with the long, thin metal box. Its contents, like those of my mother's apartment, have been meticulously kept. At the very bottom, under my mother and father's old Czechoslovak passports, lies a small white piece of parchment: a living will.
>
> If the situation should arise in which there is no reasonable expectation of my recovery from physical or mental disability, I request that I be allowed to die and not be kept alive by artificial means or "heroic measures." I do not fear death itself as much as the indignities of deterioration, dependence, and hopeless pain. . . .
> This request is made after careful consideration. I hope that you who care for me will feel morally bound to follow its mandate. I recognize that this appears to place a heavy responsibility upon you, but it is with the intention of relieving you of such responsibility that this statement is made.
>
> My mother had signed it in 1974. My brothers and I read it over in silence. We breathe deeply. We reread. Then we return to my mother's apartment.
> We are sitting around her dining table, sorting through papers, when the doorbell rings. Dawn is out of breath and sobbing. We all rise; there is no need for her to deliver the message in words. While we were in the bank, one of the neurologists was trying to reach us: My mother is dead.

No more needs to be said. No more should be said. End of a life. End of an article.

As with leads, so with endings: you must consider the graphic detail or the telling moment or the edged quote or the moral with which to shake or change the reader and wish him adieu.

8

Narration and Description – Humanization and Visualization

It was as if God had taken a pen of fire
  Into his flaming blue hand
And scrawled a chapter of horrors
  Across the city at night,
Burning the world in a day-and-a-half . . .

It was as if, after 98 days of drought,
  The furious oranges and reds
Of the Last Judgment erupted
  In a barn on DeKoven Street:
God had burnished the Gem on the prairie.

Fire seethed through the shams and shingles,
  Through the parched bodies
Of cottages and sheds, of cow-stables,
  Corn-cribs, and pigsties,
All the tinder-dry precincts of Garden City.

The raised sidewalks were piles of kindling
  Sticks under pine and hemlock
Fences, the shanties were logs
  Lit by kerosene. The barns
Were giant ovens exploding in a lumbermill.

—Edward Hirsch

Those four stanzas are but the beginning of Mr. Hirsch's mental image of Chicago, 1871. He's read, thought about, watched fires, and now written. He's painted a picture in words. Like a painter, he has permitted himself embellishments, poetic license in this case. But a reader can envision a plausibility, possibility, even probability of the scene.

When we write about a more distant past—an historic piece, for instance, about the signing of the Declaration of Independence or the assissination of Abraham Lincoln—we, like Edward Hirsch in "American Apocalypse," depend on records, and then fill in the blanks with mental pictures, hoping as we do that what we present does not distort history. But we cannot know. We weren't there. Our readers cannot know. They weren't there. What we hope is that our words feel right to readers and that they'll believe, or at least go along.

Most of what we write as magazine journalists involves more current history, something of the recent past or something happening as we work. Here the dreaming must stop. What we put on paper must represent as closely as possible what happened to whom and where. The participants are around, quite likely, to let us know where we've gone wrong. Or eyewitnesses will. So, while we're free to use any reasonable words at our command and to employ rhetorical and informational devices we believe will help the reader understand what we're trying to picture, we're commanded by duty and tradition to be accurate. That requires us to be carefully observant.

In no kinds of writing is it more important for us to be judiciously and scrupulously watchful than in narration and description. And since all too many of us aren't natural or effective observers, we find the writing of narrative and descriptive material difficult, sometimes harrowing.

Years ago, the scientist Thomas Huxley wrote, in an essay "On Science and Art in Relation to Education," that if he were to reconstruct the elementary educational system in England, he would require all children to be taught to draw as early as possible. The program, he explained, would not produce masterpieces of art or more future masters. But, as he put it: "I do not think its value can be exaggerated because it gives you the means of training the young in attention and accuracy, in which all mankind are more deficient than in any other mental quality whatever."

Accurate perception, he argued, was the first step to education, and a prerequisite for a career in science. It also is an essential for the writer: that ability to see the world clearly. The proper words must then still be sought, but without that clear vision, meaningful and readable narration and description become impossible.

Like a visual artist, as a writer you must train yourself to see and experience meticulously, to take note (mentally or on paper) of detail, then hunt for the verbal symbols and write.

NARRATION AS HUMANIZATION

Through storytelling we first learn. Through mimicry we first enunciate words. What we first experience, we cling to. Most of us maintain an affection for stories, fictional and nonfictional. We like to hear them. We like to read them. They bind the generations. As individuals, we find they bind our yesterdays and today together. Through stories we learn and remember and gain a sense of continuity. They're important. We who write, we who write articles, shouldn't forget the persuasiveness of the story.

A story humanizes information. It has the power to transport a reader into a realm inhabited by another human being, be it a foreign potentate or a homeless beggar. The reader comes to participate in someone else's experiences. That results in enhanced empathy and understanding. Not only does that happen in stories about individuals, but of events and developments and processes. The right narrative material clarifies personality of situation. It brings the reader closer.

Today's magazine and newspaper feature writers strive to bring the reader close. They work for the "show" versus "tell" effect.

When *Time* developed a cover story on the plight of the homeless ("Slow Descent into Hell," February 2, 1987), the senior writer of the project chose these words to introduce the article:

> In winter it becomes harder not to see them, tougher to avert our gaze as we pass them by. The brutal storms of January tear through the cloak of statistics, and once again an abstract problem — discussed in terms of percentage increases and changing demographics — becomes a shivering man or woman struggling for survival, a pair of eyes that painfully remind us of our human bond. In cities across the nation shelters overflow, leaving the spillage to cope on steam grates or in subway tunnels or wherever else warmth can be found.

The article held evidence of considerable research and reporting: statistics and demographics, the words of politicians and civic leaders, sociologists, urbanologists, psychologists, church people, health experts, housing officials. But, to explore their plight, the editors explained, "*Time* correspondent Jon D. Hull took up residence on the streets of Philadelphia. Some of the people he met, like a former construction worker named George, are still struggling to find a way up. Others, like a former machinist named Gary, seem hopelessly caught in the undertow. Many once led normal lives, with jobs and families and homes."

The article becomes people-centered. Hull and colleagues knew that the real story could not be found in statistics or among "experts." The true authorities were the homeless. Reporting focused on the homeless, and so did the writing. Here is Hull's first paragraph:

> A smooth bar of soap, wrapped neatly in a white handkerchief and tucked safely in the breast pocket of a faded leather jacket, is all that keeps George from losing himself to the streets. When he wakes each morning from his makeshift bed of newspapers in the subway tunnels of Philadelphia, he heads for the rest room of a nearby bus station or McDonald's and begins an elaborate ritual of washing off the dirt and smells of homelessness: first the hands and forearms, then the face and neck and finally the fingernails and teeth. Twice a week he takes off his worn Converse high tops and socks and washes his feet in the sink, ignoring the cold stares of well-dressed commuters.

As you develop your articles, you must remember audiences, as

I've stressed. For some kinds of readers humanized material is more important than for others. But who's to say that a factual excursion into truck maintenance cannot or should not have those elements of action and description and personality that make consumer-oriented articles so pleasurable to read? We're talking about degrees, perhaps, and nuances, but not exclusions versus inclusions. Editors of general consumer, specialty consumer, professional and trade publications should consider narrative material, as long as it captures the informational slant and purpose of the publications. It's a matter of sifting facts through personality, the personality of people involved in the topic you're covering and your own personality as a writer.

The human dimension has become increasingly important in journalistic writing, particularly magazine and newspaper feature writing. Can you wonder why? With society in all its bigness and oppressiveness washing away so much of the personal and individual, a reader wants to be reminded that it's people—the artist, the scientist, the teacher, the member of the city council, the athlete, the chef, the city planner, the fireman, the social worker, the parent, the child, the builder, the priest, the volunteer, the engineer, the lab technician—who create change and progress. It is they who solve problems and answer questions.

Their thoughts and actions interest readers. What they ponder and do, if it is to be communicated, suggests, sometimes demands, the narrative approach from the writer.

In "Scanners," for *Helix* (Spring 1988), the University of Virginia Medical Center quarterly, Jeffery Lindholm wrote:

> They told him the only other way to know was to cut him open. He stares dubiously up at the gleaming machine towering before him. The cool, efficient technician hands him a glass of milky liquid. "Please drink this contrast fluid, sir. It's designed to coat your intestinal tract so that we can more easily see other tissues." He hesitates, then gulps it down, noting that it tastes like a chalky milkshake.
>
> The technician lifts him effortlessly onto the padded silver platform. He lies back and gazes up at the huge, round apparatus, a smooth steel doughnut of a machine into which the platform glides easily. It reminds him of the rings of Saturn.
>
> He stares toward the far wall, covered in glass, through which he can see dim outlines of technicians huddled around banks of computers. An electronic voice breaks the silence, and he realizes it's one of the people in the other room, speaking over an intercom.
>
> "Don't worry," the voice says. "This won't hurt a bit. When I tell you to stop breathing, please stop. If you breathe, you may blur the film." He nods at the man, who waves back through the glass.
>
> Then they begin. "Stop breathing," says the wall. He holds his breath and the machine hums. In less than two seconds, the X-ray unit housed in the doughnut whirls around. "You may breathe now." Then the platform slides

ahead a centimeter and the process is repeated. "They were right," he thinks absently. "It doesn't hurt."

Inside the control room, the computers reconstruct the X-ray images into clear, high-contrast, cross-sectional views of the man's internal organs. The technicians push buttons, quietly and efficiently altering the images to look at different organs.

A scientific subject for serious readers. Information humanized. A narrative.

You can use narrative in a short burst, in an anecdotal, incidental manner; within an extended essay or investigative piece or issue discussion you can insert helpfully reflective bits of narration. Or the narrative might be full length; then your entire article becomes a story.

Narrative Purpose

Whether short burst or full length, narrative can serve one or more of four purposes:

1. Narration as narration — you have a good story to tell, so you tell it.
2. Narration as exposition — the well-selected narrative can turn into excellent explanation.
3. Narration as argument — you can make a point or state a position, indirectly and yet forcefully, through story.
4. Narration as symbol — the human example you offer can serve as exemplar of a situation or problem.

Narrative, if properly chosen and written, does not waste space. It potentially compresses information, giving the reader more than one lesson at a given moment. That's a plus for most editors (and for readers, too).

We know narratives make good beginnings. They immerse the reader in the subject matter. Erik Larson writes in *Smithsonian* (June 1987):

> That mango is loaded and Jesus Ramirez knows it.
>
> Ramirez stands at one end of a table that could do double-duty for the local coroner. About the size of a pool table, it is stainless steel with sides that slope to an open drain. Travelers never see this room at the American Airlines terminal at John F. Kennedy International Airport. After a visit here, no supermarket produce section can look quite the same again.
>
> The mango, confiscated from a woman from the Dominican Republic, is plump, satisfying in heft and just now turning a forsythia shade of yellow: it is one fine-looking piece of fruit. But Ramirez points his knife at two punctures, each invisible unless you know what to look for. "These are exit holes," he says.
>
> He shaves around the holes, exposing a bruise that has spread through

the mango's orange flesh like a plume of brown ink in water. He cuts deeper. The bruise darkens. "Look," he says.

Suddenly this mango does not seem so delicious. Something white wriggles up and breaches the pulp. A worm. Ramirez clears away some juice. This worm is not alone. "They're big suckers. Caribbean fruit fly larvae. Full-grown and ready to drop."

That opening for "A Close Watch on U.S. Borders to Keep the World's Bugs Out" is a multi-purposed lead. It's narrative for narrative's sake — a good story. It's narrative as exposition — we gain an introduction to how inspection works. It's narrative as argument — the importance of the process is indicated.

Story, explanation, and symbol are prominent in Thomas Friedman's "Surviving Beirut" for *Wilson Quarterly* (Summer 1989):

I watched a man being kidnapped in Beirut. It took only a few seconds.

I was on my way to Beirut International Airport when my taxi became stalled in traffic. Suddenly I saw off to my right four men with pistols tucked into their belts who were dragging another man out his front door. A woman, probably his wife, was standing just inside the shadow of the door, clutching her bathrobe and weeping. The man was struggling and kicking with all his might, a look of sheer terror in his eyes. Somehow the scene reminded me of a group of football players carrying their coach off the field after a victory, but this was no celebration. Just for a second my eyes met those of the hapless victim, right before he was bundled into a waiting car. His eyes did not say "Help me"; all they spoke was fear. He knew I couldn't help him. This was Beirut.

Moments later the traffic jam broke and my taxi moved on to the airport. The Lebanese driver, who had kept his eyes frozen straight ahead the whole time, never said a word about the horror which had just unfolded. He talked instead about his family, politics, about anything but what had happened alongside us. While he spoke, my mind remained locked on the kidnap victim. Who was he? What had he done? Maybe he was a bad guy and the others good, or was it the other way around?

The narrative lead is common. You must make sure you don't abuse the technique. Consider: Is it your best approach? Will it comfortably lead the reader to what comes next? Are you serving the message of your article?

Narratives make good middles. Peter Goldman and Tony Fuller, writing about the execution in Texas of killer J.D. Autry, brought the readers of the March 26, 1984 issue of *Newsweek* close through this scene after several paragraphs of background:

Autry did not die alone. He had struck up a pen-pal liaison with Shirley Tadlock, a pretty Dallas woman of thirty-one who had been moved by his case. She had wept with him in the death house in Huntsville that afternoon — "Shirley, I want to live," he told her through the mask of his bravado — and when he lay buckled to the gurney, his searching eyes found her among the nearly two dozen witnesses. The warden asked if he had any last words. "No," Autry answered, and a massive overdose of sodium thiopental — the first of three lethal chemicals — began to flow into his veins. It was 12:26 a.m.

"I love you," Mrs. Tadlock said. She was kneading a square of pink tissue. Autry stared at her.

"I love you so much," she said. "I love you a lot, pretty brown eyes."

Autry smiled, his lower lip quivering. "I love you, J.D.," she said again. "Give it up. Give it up."

The minutes dragged. Autry's brow furrowed. His breathing rasped loud in the stillness.

"I love you, baby," Mrs. Tadlock said. "I'm here. I care."

"I love you, too," Autry said. His face contorted. His head rolled back. His eyes closed, then opened and found Mrs. Tadlock again.

"You feel pain?" she asked. His eyes were closing her out. She blew him a kiss, then another. The eyes flared open. "Love you," she said, but he seemed not to hear. "My arm's hurting!" he cried. His left palm opened wide, as if to ask what was taking so long.

"Pretty brown eyes," Mrs. Tadlock said.

"I love you," Autry answered. It was 12:36. His body shook, then stiffened, and he was gone.

Dramatic story, of course. Exposition, too: death by chemistry. And argument: behind the writers' words lies the question, "Autry spent ten conscious minutes dying; is this the best method?"

Sally Quinn used narration to end her portrait of dancer Rudolf Nureyev for the Style section of the Washington *Post* ("Not Only Is He Beautiful But He Can Dance, Too" June 1, 1974). The dialogue and action tell us much, as well as little, about the ballet legend:

He turns to the waiter and asks for a cup of tea.

"I think I am getting drunk. I want to be able to think straight. This interview is so acid it's good we didn't have vinegar with the salad." He laughs.

"I want to be sober when you drop the bomb question, when you do a Hiroshima on me," he giggles again.

Well, then, Mr. Nureyev, how's your sex life?

"I knew it, you see, there it is," and he clasps his hands and throws his head back and laughs with Slavic glee.

"Sporadic," he announces.

Well, tell us more. The ladies will be disappointed with that little morsel and nothing else.

"The ladies will just have to remain tense," he says sadistically.

He leans back smugly, ponders his own words, then leans forward and asks with real earnestness: "This is a city of politicians. How am I doing in this interview? Am I as good as the politicians?"

When told he has revealed absolutely nothing of himself, that he is still a complete mystery, that he is impenetrable as an interviewee, he beams like a Boy Scout receiving a medal.

"Now we must go," he says, his success complete. "We will pay the bill, then you will feel guilty and your conscience will make you write nice things."

And he gets up from the table and stalks triumphantly out of the restaurant, as though he is taking bows for a magnificent performance.

Your choice, on the other hand, may be to cover your entire subject via narrative. Frazier Hunt offered the readers of *Redbook* a brief one with sermonette attached:

One July afternoon at our ranch in the Canadian Rockies I rode toward Helen Keller's cabin. Along the wagon trail that ran through a lovely wood we had stretched a wire, to guide Helen when she walked there alone, and as I turned down the trail I saw her coming.

I sat motionless while this woman who was doomed to live forever in a black and silent prison made her way briskly down the path, her face radiant. She stepped out of the woods into a sunlit open space directly in front of me and stopped by a clump of wolf willows. Gathering a handful, she breathed their stange fragrance: her sightless eyes looked up squarely into the sun, and her lips, so magically trained, pronounced the single word "Beautiful!" Then, still smiling, she walked past me.

I brushed the tears from my own inadequate eyes. For to me none of this exquisite highland had seemed beautiful: I had felt only bitter discouragement over the rejection of a piece of writing. I had eyes to see all the wonders of woods, sky and mountains, ears to hear the rushing stream and the song of the wind in the treetops. It took the sightless eyes and sealed ears of this extraordinary woman to show me beauty, and bravery.

Serenity and dignity emerge. Not so in "The Late Show," Dan Santow's story for *Chicago* (September 1989) of a doorman's shift at a Chicago nightspot:

License to Grill

YES, NO. NO, YES. ALL NIGHT LONG.

"Sorry, babe, I can't let you in without an I.D.," says Dave, Esoteria's doorman. "No one gets in without an I.D."

"Like, I've been twenty-one since May 23, 1989. Spare me! Here's my VISA, my Saks card, Nieman-Marcus, the East Bank Club," a woman cries, spreading open her Louis Vuitton purse to show Dave its contents, as if it contained the meaning of her life. "Whaddya want, a letter from my mother?"

"Sorry, can't let you in."

"You have to!"

Streaming past Dave, who checks I.D.'s, and Bart, who collects the four-dollar cover, they come, the women with their frosted lipstick, gladiator sandals, and off-the-shoulder tops like Madonna wore three years ago; the guys in their polo shirts, collars turned up against the still of the night.

"He's got it," half the women say as they point over their shoulders to their boyfriends and blithely walk in, leaving the guys to pay the cover.

Yes, no. No, yes. On and on it goes until 3:00 a.m. or so, when things slow down a bit. Here, as at other clubs around, the door scene is often the best scene—the comings, the goings, the little dramas. "But we just found the greatest parking space," another woman whines as she feverishly fumbles in her purse for her license. "My friends Joanie and Cindy just went in. You have to let me in!"

"Four-dollar cover tonight; this gentleman will take your cash," says Dave, pointing to Bart. "Four-dollar cover tonight; this gentleman will take your cash," he repeats over and over again.

"Yeah, I'm Mark, Mark from Lettuce [Entertain You Enterprises], you know, in accounting," says one guy, trying to avoid paying the cover. "You remember, we met two weeks ago?" Dave doesn't remember. "Who'd lie about being an accountant, though?" Dave says to no one in particular. Mark's in—comp.

"Hey, you should mark those steps," another guy says, stumbling into the club. "Some of us are wasted."

The line ebbs, the line flows, but the line always exists. There are few moments of rest, no moments of quiet.

"Hey, hey, hey, my wife just had a baby tonight," a man says, flapping his arms like a chicken.

"A baby? What are you doing out, then? asks Dave.

"I'm out celebrating, man. What? I'm supposed to stay in because she's laid up in the hospital?"

Yes, no. No, yes. They drop their Binaca and tampons as they reach into their pockets and purses, fishing for dollars, tripping on their heels, protesting ("But they let me into Clubland without an I.D.!"), looking for Joey, or Annette, or Kenny, and asking about other places ("Which direction I must take to other club?" asks a man with a French accent and a leather passport pouch around his waist). "Oo, tonight's crazy, tonight's going like this," says Dave, snapping his fingers twice. "Before you know it, we'll all be home in bed." Amen.

That short article says volumes within the words and behind the words. Narrative.

Beyond Storytelling

Otto Friedrich kept a diary of a memorable personal experience. Narration was the only workable method to give the reader an understanding of what Friedrich experienced while "Gone Blind." Here, from *Harper's* (March 1989) are entries from the diary:

May 28, 1988, Saturday, 10:00 a.m. Now I am blind. I have put on the two black eye patches, and I am supposed to sit motionless (or as nearly motionless as possible) for the next four days and four nights. In theory, that will make all the blood from the hemorrhage inside my right eye settle on the bottom, where it won't interfere with my vision. But if the theory doesn't work . . . Well, the doctor says I'll just have to see if the blind eye can heal itself. Otherwise, surgery . . .

The immediate question is, What in God's name does one do with oneself while sitting upright in an easy chair for four days and four nights? Most of the things I normally do can't be done. Can't read, can't write, can't play the piano, can't work in the garden, can't even watch TV. It's a rather frightening prospect. Pascal's warning: "Tout le malheur des hommes vient d'une seule chose, qui est de ne savoir pas demeuer au repos dans une chambre." That's me, the unhappy man who does not know how to remain at rest in a room. . . .

Saturday, noon. How little I know about exactly where things are in the house that I have lived in for twenty-five years. And how easy it is to get lost. And when I'm lost—maybe only a few feet from where I think I ought to be—how hard it is to recognize anything. What is this sharp corner in this wall? Which door is this?

I very soon learn that just about every mistake leads to some kind of punishment, to barked shins or a lampshade hitting you in the face. So you slow down, just creeping along in what you used to think were familiar surroundings. And so you get scared, not really scared but anxious, wary. . . .

Monday, 6:00 p.m. People keep calling, and so I have to keep telling the story of my blindness over and over again, even making the same wisecracks. What a bore I've become!

Tuesday, 6:00 a.m. Another awful night, again very little sleep. I cannot stop thinking about blindness, particularly at night, in the darkness.

Harrowing material. Certainly it goes way beyond just storytelling.

Some years ago, one of my students, Andrew Wolfson, developed an article on medical interns. He worked almost entirely through the narrative structure, departing from it only when he needed to insert expository statements. Throughout the article he stressed the point that interning is too tough and maybe not the best way for the hospital system to be served. He lets the happenings during an intern's rounds teach the lesson for him. The *Chicago Tribune Magazine* ran the article, "Ordeal by Intern." Here is how it gets underway:

It's 8:00 a.m. on a cold morning in Chicago, and Pam Fennewald, M.D., has just reported to work. Before she can return home, the sun will set and rise and set again.

Fennewald is an intern at Chicago's Cook County Hospital. She and her fellow interns on County's "Green Service" will work straight through today, tonight, and tomorrow—thirty-three hours in all, with only a chance for a few brief catnaps during the night. This is all part of the system, basically unquestioned for more than a century, in which interns work eighty, ninety, and even up to 120 hours a week as medical shock troops in the nation's teaching hospitals.

Fennewald toils eighty to ninety-four hours a week, serving on the hospital's thirty-three-hour marathon shift one night in four. She works seven days a week and has not had a day off in more than a month.

Forget about the popular image of the eternally chipper, high-spirited young doctor; the intern is unremittingly fatigued. The treadmill of internship—the long hours, the endless responsibility—wears down nearly everyone who must walk it. That much is clear. But what effect does the intern's staggering work week have on the care he gives to patients? That's a question only recently asked.

Nearly every intern remembers having fallen asleep on the job—at least once. But even those who manage to keep awake know that the sleepless inevitably become the reckless. "The intern is like a drunken driver," says a County staffer. "You think you're being efficient and you're doing all right, but the next day you realize you didn't do it right at all. When you're tired, your efficiency goes straight downhill."

It's morning here now, though, time for the changing of the guard on Ward Sixty-five. Doctors, nurses, and orderlies scatter in a dozen directions, the lucky ones on their way home. Fennewald got off work from the hospital yesterday at 5:00 p.m. She starts her work today in the Doctor's Conference Room, an office no larger than a walk-in closet, poring over her patients' charts. In the background you can hear the pitiful moaning and groaning of a patient, sounds of pain so persistent they almost sound canned.

"Oh, that's the Yelling Lady," Fennewald says. "She's not one of my patients. She gets so loud we have to stick her in the lab at night."

Fennewald begins her rounds. She has only four patients now, but that count could more than double during the shift, and it is not uncommon for interns at County to share responsibility at night for thirty or forty patients with just one other doctor.

Mr. Belding, Fennewald's first patient this morning, has stabilized during the night. But that's hardly cause for optimism. He is fifty-eight years old and looks like ninety. "You'd need a scorecard to keep Mr. Belding's problems straight," Fennewald says. "He's got a whopping pneumonia and a bad liver. But mostly we're worried about his brain. We're wondering if he's still got one. He came in here three weeks ago. Couldn't talk, couldn't give us a history. His daughter told us he'd been drinking a half gallon of whisky a day ever since she was born. And she's eighteen."

At County Hospital, the monolithic doctor to this city's poor, patients like Mr. Belding are common. Interns bear the double burden of their own fatigue and the oppression of their patients. Doctors say that two, three, up to four of every ten patients who come to County come with problems at least indirectly tied to living in Chicago's sprawling South and West Side ghettos. Gunshot and knife wounds, tuberculosis and hypertension, drug addiction and lead poisoning—these are the cases that County interns specialize in and interns at most other hospitals rarely, if ever, see.

Why would any rational medical school graduate come to County to intern? One reason is purely selfish. Just as the auto mechanic thrives on blown gaskets, thrown rods, and burned-out clutches, the intern flourishes on human sickness—and by one grisly standard, the sicker the patient, the better.

Interns don't like people to get sick. But the wider the variety of illnesses they can treat during their year of internship, the better clinical skills they will develop, the better doctors they will become. "You'll see more diseases here in a month," says Fennewald, "than you'll see at most other hospitals in a year."

We then follow Pam Fennewald, M.D., through her crushingly long shift. Patients are treated and dismissed. One dies. When we've finished reading, we've seen what Wolfson saw, and have a better notion what interns endure because one intern has endured before our reading eyes.

Wolfson's story fulfills all four potential purposes of the narrative. It is narrative for narrative's sake—a good, gripping tale. It is narrative for exposition's sake—the intern's duties under pressure are explained. It is narrative for argument's sake—the writer suggests that the system is flawed. It is narrative as symbol—Pam Fennewald becomes the exemplar of interns.

There's energy, there's potency in the narrative—if you use it properly.

DESCRIPTION AS VISUALIZATION

Back on October 11, 1963, foreign correspondent George Weller cabled his paper, the Chicago *Daily News*, reporting the aftermath of a disaster. The story opens with a classic descriptive section:

> Longarone, Italy—Longarone does not exist.
>
> Longarone is beyond medicine, blankets, food or sympathy.
>
> What was Longarone is a hillside of battered boulders, white as bones.
>
> Longarone is Hiroshima without houses, Pompeii without streets. Burn the telegrams. Throw away the incoming letters. Longarone was alive and now it is nothing.
>
> When the 784-foot-high Vaiont Dam spilled over after a landslide at 10:35 Wednesday night, Longarone's twelve hundred sleeping people, a third of those lost in the whole disaster, were given a Biblical death. They were not merely drowned by the waters and suffocated by the mud, they were pounded to death by stones like criminals in the Bible.
>
> Nobody is left to tell the world what it must be like to be pinned under the beams of a house, to be ground to death in a cement mixer.
>
> The eerie thing about death by stoning is that it leaves less than cremation. There are not even bones. Longarone has boulders the size of footballs, of barrels, of water tanks, of cottages—but nothing human, not a wall, timber nor a roof tile. When water brings mud something survives but when water brings stones it doesn't leave even corpses.

There's nothing overdone in Weller's description. It is gripping in its simplicity. It is true also to his style of writing. And that's important for you to remember about description: it works best if you retain the style of writing that is naturally yours and not infect the passage with strains of expression that aren't. Avoid the phony. The phony will embarrass you, distress the reader, and demean the subject.

Sharpen those observational powers, too. And think of yourself as a painter in words. The problems are similar. You must make decisions about inclusions and exclusions, angles, color and light, sharpness or lack thereof, and distance. You can use impressionistic techniques or expressionistic, the real, the super-real, the surreal.

But . . .

A Bosch or Breugel painting of superabundant detail, translated into words, won't work. Too fussy. Too complicated.

A Picasso or Braque abstract, translated into words, won't work. Too vague. Too puzzling.

An Edward Hopper or Grant Wood, translated into words, works fine. Just enough detail. Concrete.

Writers face descriptive dilemmas constantly. How to describe a tickle, a scratch, or an itch, the perception of a rose upon the nostrils or the touch of a raindrop on the skin, a kiss, the caress of tongue by meat and soup, heaven's blue, the feathery softness of a bed, the steel of steel, the sting of a gnat, the sensation of a cough or a sneeze, sand sifting through fingers, the many sounds of music, a howling child, a fire, a hand parting hair, a dog lapping milk, a cat's purr, leaves carried by wind, walking barefoot through mud, a waterfall, snow, the face of a child, the crack of a ball against a bat, red, the snap of a stick, the moon, the whirr of a machine, salt and pepper, an eggshell smashing against the side of a dish, a skin's wrinkle, a wave upon the sea, a field of wheat, the pungency of hay and alfalfa, the eyes of a woman or man, a word on paper, a painting and the feel of brush strokes on canvas, smoke and ashes, glass, the power of air in the lungs, the smoothness of silk, the sparkle of an emerald, the dizzy contentment of wine, flowers, velvet, a heartbeat.

A heartbeat describes itself, I guess. So does a sneeze. But often we must go beyond the already stated to picture things and images, people and places. Observation, accuracy, imagination, and honest language must come together.

As when Robert Hughes described Edgar Degas and his work in "Seeing Degas as Never Before" (*Time*, October 17,1988):

> Nothing escaped Degas's prehensile eye for the texture of life and the myriad gestures that reveal class and work. He made art from things that no painter had fully used before: the way a discarded dress, still warm from the now naked body, keeps some of the shape of its owner, the unconcern of a dancer scratching her back between practice sessions in *The Dance Class*, 1873-76, the tension in a relationship between a man and a woman (*Sulking*, 1869-71) or the undercurrent of violence in an affair (*Interior*, sometimes known as *The Rape*, 1868-69): a laundress's yawn; the stoned heaviness of an absinthe drinker's posture before the dull green phosphorescence of her glass . . . .

As Hughes did for Degas in *Time*, Edward Rothstein did for

Herbert von Karajan in *The New Republic* (November 7, 1988):

> It was eerie, for example, to see Karajan conduct. Karajan is a small man. His back was stiff, his legs were immobile (he has long had health problems that would have crippled other conductors); his body irrelevant, it would seem, to his project. Moreover, Karajan leads with his eyes closed: the score is always committed to memory. Conducting without eye contact means controlling the space rather than thinking of the players, knowing how with hands alone to articulate a particular phrase, signaling with minimal movement. Bernstein is the ecstatic wild dancer. Karajan's ecstasy seems entirely contained in the shapes created by his hands. It was as if the hands created a physical model, a tactile translation of the composition. The result was a sort of musical musculature as clear and precise as the shape of the conductor's gestures.

In each case, the writer has verbalized technique. Through their description, we come closer to an understanding of what a great painter and a renowned conductor accomplished. In neither case is the language difficult, far-fetched, overdone. You'll notice the attention given to nouns and verbs, proving that nothing describes better than a noun and the verb which gives action to that noun. They are your most effective verbal tools. Adjectives and adverbs can help, but their best work is done in support of nouns and verbs rather than standing virtually alone, attached to a form of "to be." "I think the painting is glorious," means almost nothing. "As a swimmer, the woman is incredibly fast," says not much more. Figures of speech can help you describe. So can comparisons that are accurate, readily clear, and common to the experience of your readers. Metaphors are the implied comparisons between two objects or ideas that differ—heart of stone, ships that plow the sea. Similes actually compare two unlike things or actions. Some New York fourth graders completed the sentence, "Let's be as quiet as . . ." with phrases such as "a leaf turning colors," "a feather falling from a bird," "an uninhabited creek," "time passing," "a plant growing," "an old hat sitting up in the attic," "the first star coming out," "children sleeping," "an ant while it is walking," "a butterfly flying," "a pumpkin lit up." Analogies can help you. So can the use of multi-dimensional sense appeal. Don't employ sight alone if and when other senses are available and useful. Hearing, smell, touch, taste can be important to you.

Writing Sensuously

Alan Gross took "A Trip to the Barber" (*Chicago*, May 1986), using the senses simply:

> Oh, the perfume of eau de Pinaud, Jeris, and talc. Lucky Tiger. The feel of fresh Butchwax, the sting of witch hazel.
> A row of colored bottles under fluorescent mirror lights, bright as gemstones—green, and violet, and amber.

The sound of the razor strop. The chirping beaks of a jungle of scissors. The voices of men in private moments – moments of hair being clipped from nostrils and ears – moments not even wives can share.

You can hardly feel the lather go on the back of your ears and neck. It is warm and close, and the straight razor tingles all the way down to the small of your back.

The magazines remind you that you are in a man's world. *Men* and *Men at War*, saving U.S. Navy nurses from bands of endomorphic Nazi thugs. Oh, how those blouses tore.

In summer my dad took me to Danny's on Devon Avenue. We'd pick up my grandfather, and three generations of Grosses would breakfast at the Californian, then spend the morning at the tonsorial parlor.

The description then moves into narration of "a time-honored ritual of manhood," according to Gross.

If scene requires poetic mood, then supply it. Barry Lopez in "Arctic Dreams" (*American Way*, April 15, 1988) depicts icebergs as phantom presences:

The first icebergs we had seen, just north of the Strait of Belle Isle, listing and guttured by the ocean, seemed immensely sad, exhausted by some unknown calamity. We sailed past them. Farther north they began to seem like stragglers fallen behind an army, drifting, self-absorbed, in the water, bleak and immense. It was as if they had been borne down from a world of myth, some Gotterdammerung of noise and catastrophe. Fallen pieces of the moon.

Farther to the north they stood on their journeys with greater strength. They were monolithic: their walls, towering and abrupt, suggested Polala Palace at Lhasa in Tibet, a mountainous architecture of ascetic contemplation. We would pass between them, separated from them by no more than half a mile. I would walk from one side of the ship to the other, wondering how something so imposing in its suggestion of life could be approached so closely, and yet still seem so remote. It was like standing in a dirigible off Annapurna and Everest in the Himalayas.

Good description is difficult to achieve. But what an extraordinary opportunity it offers the writer to astound or elate or frighten or delight the reader. Jonathan Raban is a British writer who traveled the Mississippi like Huck Finn. To him, the river seemed

. . . as big and depthless as the sky itself. You can see the curve of the earth on its surface as it stretches away for miles to the far shore. Sunset has turned the water to the color of unripe peaches. There's no wind. Sand bars and wooded islands stand on their exact reflections. The only signs of movement on the water are the lightly scratched lines which run in parallels across it like the scores of a diamond on a windowpane. In the middle distance, the river smokes with toppling pillars of mist which soften the light so that one can almost reach out and take in handfuls of that thickened air.

Raban's Mississippi (as described in "A Modern Huck" for *The New York Times Magazine*, August 16, 1981) differs from Richard

West's Nile ("Its Ancient History," *Travel & Leisure*, September 1989).
To West, the Nile is a synonym for unchanging history:

> Ancient Egyptians rejoiced in the thought that their country was without
> history. Their view of the world was static: the best life was one in which
> everything remained the same. The Nile rose, flooded and receded; the sun
> crossed the sky; the pharaoh, whoever he was, was always considered the
> son of the sun-god.
>
> Floating down the Nile in benign hypnosis, I felt this sense of continuity
> strongly. Hour after hour I watched ancient sites and huddled settlements
> that hadn't changed since God was a boy. Figures of women in raven-black
> cloth carrying water jars; pajamaed children scattering chickens in puffs of
> dust down bald lanes; men waist-deep in the river washing oxen; minarets
> and palm groves and soil so fertile you could plant a shaft and harvest an
> oxcart. All of it, even the faces—the narrow foreheads, the black-almond
> eyes, the sunbaked pointed skulls—closely resembled pharaonic frescoes I
> had seen a few days earlier in the Egyptian Museum in Cairo.

The events of history, if to be remembered, must turn into images
as well as actions. It is the moment, the place, the situation that description preserves. Ernie Pyle, the revered World War II correspondent, used
the senses mentally and emotionally in this dispatch from the Tunisian
front. The dispatch was eventually reprinted in the book, *Ernie's War*
(Random House: 1986):

> War has its own peculiar sounds. They are not really very much different
> from sounds in the world of peace. But they clothe themselves in an unforget-
> table fierceness, just because born in danger and death.
>
> The clank of a starting tank, the scream of a shell through the air, the
> ever-rising whine of fiendishness as a bomber dives—these sounds have their
> counterparts in normal life, and you would be hard put to distinguish them
> in a blindfold test. But, once heard in war, they remain with you forever.
>
> Their nervous memories come back to you in a thousand ways—in the
> grind of a truck starting in low gear, in high wind around the eaves, in some-
> body merely whistling a tune. Even the sound of a shoe, dropped to the floor
> in a hotel room above you, becomes indistinguishable from the faint boom
> of a big gun far away. A mere rustling curtain can paralyze a man with
> memories.

The imprint of war is clarified. The horrors of war are clarified in
Newsweek's July 29, 1985 cover story on the atomic age at forty. At
one point we read:

> It wasn't her neighborhood alone that had been hit; all Hiroshima lay before
> her, a lake of fire and coal-black smoke. Long lines of people were trudging
> up the winding hillside roads, a spectral procession out of the holocaust
> below. They were women and children, mostly; the men had gone to war.
> They walked like somnambulists, arms thrust forward to keep their burns
> from brushing against their sides. Sheets of skin trailed from their fingertips.
> Their hair stood in spikes, held up by an impasto of sweat, dust and dried

blood. Features had been burned away; eyes had melted in their sockets, and noses and mouths had been reduced to open holes. Women's backs were marked with intricate patterns; the flash had tattooed the designs from their kimonos onto their flesh. There was no sound except the shuffle of feet and, here and there, a stifled moan.

A more recent struggle is memorialized through scenic depictions by Adam Hochschild for *Mother Jones* (September 1986) in "Green Is Detained. Yellow Is Missing. Red Is Confirmed Dead. An Eyewitness Report from South Africa."

From the distance, Johannesburg's Alexandra Township looks as if wisps of fog had collected above it, islands of mist in a sun-scorched day. Coming closer, you see that it is not fog but dust, for the streets here, unlike those in the white suburbs that surround Alexandra, are almost all unpaved. And this morning tens of thousands of pairs of feet are kicking the dust aloft as they walk over the hills in long streams that converge on one spot like a pilgrimage. Seventeen Alexandra youths, from age twelve up, are to be buried today. They are among some two dozen victims of a recent battle with police here, the latest skirmish in South Africa's civil war.

The writer moved into action, but first his scene had to be set. That, too, was the aim of Nicholas Von Hoffman, in one of his reports for the Chicago *Daily News* during the 1964 summer struggle for civil rights in this country. His articles were collected into *Mississippi Notebook*, a book-length lesson on how narration and description can be used for explanatory and opinion purposes. Description:

Devil's dust, the little wind-stirred geysers of dry earth that blow up between the rows of cotton plants, puff here and there across the fields.

Two Negro women walk by the side of the highway. Their parasols protect them from the sun, which even now in the early morning has laid down its heat over the Mississippi Delta.

The blues and reds of the women's cotton dresses are vivid. The orange umbrella atop the tractor moving down the rows of cotton plants is unfaded in the sun's summer light.

This Mississippi sun does not bleach. It brings out color and magnifies detail so that no man can mistake another.

The lean men of Mississippi are unmistakable. They pause at the gasoline pumps in front of roadside general stores, their lifeless eyes full of suspicion, forcing your own to glance downward as you get out of your car.

In this summer the stranger is the enemy, and the men of Mississippi wait and watch for him.

Momentous and monumental topics. But description also works for the material of everyday. Daniel Jack Chasan proved that once again in this paragraph from *Smithsonian:*

In the beginning, there's the crunch. Always. Bite into a red apple or a green one, a red one streaked with yellow, a yellow one with a rosy blush, round or oblong, baseball-size or softball-size, and before the flavor, before even the tang of acidity, there's the crunch. At least, there'd better be. If you bite into a peach or a plum or any other fruit and it crunches, you figure it's either dead green or frozen solid. If you bite into an apple, you expect it to crunch. A soft apple is . . . disgusting. You put it aside. Or you choke it down. Or you feed it to a grateful horse.

Thus, the apple gets its due. In thoughtful and yet simplest of terms, the author has summarized the special nature of the apple.

Winifred Gallagher attempted to give words to a feeling that's everyday but always special:

> The heart races, blood pressure soars, the breath comes in gasps. The skin flushes, and tissues swell with blood, changing the size, shape, color, and position of organs. As the nervous system is electrified, the face contorts, muscles tense and convulse. Sensations of vibration and pulsation, expansion and contraction, heat and cold, herald a loss of contact with the environment, a hallucinatory immersion in the moment, often accompanied by fragments of speech, sighs, groans. This "brief clouding of consciousness," as one sex researcher describes it, makes time seem to stand still, exalts emotions, alters perceptions. Yet after it's over, few can describe it accurately or even truly remember it.

In "The Etiology of Orgasm" readers of *Discover* (February 1986) discover that "the more scientists learn about the nature of sexual climax, the more they're convinced it takes place mainly in the depths of the brain." Gallagher gains reader empathy through use of description.

Painting an Accurate Picture

Tom Wolfe likes to set scene. This exponent of the "New Journalism" has a style of his own, flamboyant, dripping with detail. He makes description show and teach a lesson, as in this excerpt from his June 8, 1970 *New York* article, "Radical Chic: That Party at Lenny's." The Lenny is Leonard Bernstein. The occasion is his forty-eighth birthday.

> Mmmmmmmmmmmmmmmmmm. These are nice. Little Roquefort cheese morsels rolled in crushed nuts. Very tasty. Very subtle. It's the way the dry sackiness of the nuts tiptoes up against the dour savor of the cheese that is so nice, so subtle. Wonder what the Black Panthers eat here on the hors d'oevre trail? Do the Panthers like little Roquefort cheese morsels wrapped in crushed nuts this way, and asparagus tips in mayonnaise dabs, and *meatballs petites au Coq hardi*, all of which are at this very moment being offered to them on gadrooned silver platters by maids in black uniforms with hand-ironed white aprons . . . The butler will bring them their drinks . . . Deny it if you wish to, but such are the *pensees metaphysiques* that rush through one's head on these Radical Chic evenings just now in New York. For example, does that huge Black Panther there in the hallway, the one shaking hands with Felicia Bernstein herself, the one with the black leather coat and the dark glasses and the absolutely unbelievable Afro, Fuzzy Wuzzy-scale in

fact—is he, a Black Panther, going on to pick up a Roquefort cheese morsel rolled in crushed nuts from off the tray, from a maid in uniform, and just pop it down the gullet without so much as missing a beat of Felicia's perfect Mary Astor voice . . . .

People need to be described. It's how personality comes to paper and then transfers to a reader's consciousness. Stephen Schiff's subject in "Gore's Wars" for *Vanity Fair* (June 1987) was an author/celebrity figure:

> The bulk of Gore Vidal crumples into a couch in his suite at the Beverly Hills Hotel, and if the couch looks tattered, so does its occupant. At sixty-one, he finally resembles the grand old senator he's always wanted to be: his hair is profuse and gray and curlicued in the Everett Dirksen manner, his face still regally beautiful, and his avoirdupois marches steadily toward the dimensions of his idol, the late Huey Long. But Vidal is tired, as friends say he so often is these days. His face, which is the color of January tomatoes, sags; and the familiar verbal torrents have slowed to a dribble. Raking his hair with his fingers, he turns to Howard Austen, his companion of thirty-seven years. "I'd like a little bit of whiskey and a lot of soda water," he groans in that George Sanders accent of his. "I'm full of gamma globulin at the moment."
>
> Vidal, it seems, has contracted Epstein-Barr, Hollywood's most fashionable and mysterious disease, which counts among its putative victims every third screenwriter, movie director, and studio executive in Los Angeles; its most common symptom is fatigue unto death. "It's something about the T cells—God knows what *they* are," Vidal intones. "And it's like jet lag. You're in perfectly good health and you just cannot move. Just total inertia." Despite the droop in his voice, he seems rather pleased about the whole thing. "It's very hard, because I have never actually been ill before—although I am a hypochondriac."

Bulk crumples . . . A face the color of January tomatoes . . . He rakes his hair . . . The voice droops . . . Schiff has selected words carefully. He's attended to his nouns and verbs.

Joe Flaherty took on the fighter Jake La Motta in "Sympathy for the Devil," a profile for *Inside Sports* (January 31,1981):

> The La Motta you meet today hardly qualifies for a portrait in ferocity. If it weren't for his classically failed souffle of a face and the thickness of his articulate speech, you wouldn't suspect he had made his living at demolition. His weight is back to the 160-pound middleweight limit, and his manner is deferential. His hands belie their destructive force in that they are small, slim, and tapered.
>
> "I should have been an artist, or a fag," he jokes. But the jibe has insight. They look like the hands of someone who would beat helplessly on the chest of a bully.
>
> Only the eyes give a clue to his former life. They are so sad and placid, they almost look burned out. Twin novas which didn't survive the Big Bang, memos to some terrible past.

Note that final sentence. It lifts commonplace description to a level of significance. Such description makes readers think. A lesser writer would have stopped writing after the words "look burned out." The added sentence completes the thought.

A writer *shows* through narration and description, through an infusion of personality, through pepperings of feelings and atmosphere. Showing is more telling than telling. Through narration and description we show.

In 1962 a Northwestern sophomore, Robert Cochran, fulfilled a descriptive writing assignment for me with an observational essay I've cherished. The piece was never published, as best I know. It should have been. Now it has.

Green and white Seven-Up signs proclaim to the bored neighborhood the existence of Walker's Grocery and Short Lunch. Traffic passing by on Greenleaf Street gives little notice to the dilapidated frame building.

Children from the nearby school come to Walker's to buy candy, gum, and groceries for their parents. As they grow older, they come to steal from Mrs. Walker, realizing sooner or later that she knows. As they grow still older they no longer come to the store very often, and when they do, they exhibit a new deference toward the huge, Buddha-like black woman with the yellowed smile who stands forever behind the pitted wooden counter.

Finally, when they themselves have children they will remember fondly the hot summer days of their childhood when Mrs. Walker passed out ice cubes among them, and they will be ashamed when they recall having stolen from her.

Walker's was a place of education apart from the academic formality of the school down the street. Vast knowledge of the world outside the confines of the neighborhood could easily be gleaned from the conversation of the lonely men who sat endlessly on the cement front steps in the summertime.

Many first cigarettes came from the little glass case behind the old blue Pepsi machine, and innumerable love accusations had been chalked into the hardwood floor, only to be obliterated each day by passing feet like a blackboard being erased in warm, 3:30 afternoons in preparation for wisdom to come.

Yet something is missing, gone. The entire store stands wreathed in museum-like antiquity, holding mysterious secrets somehow precious to unknown participants. An eeriness, strangely akin to an empty schoolroom during the summer vacation, prevails. Things organic and alive—like the children who will come next fall to the musty, glow-lit, schoolroom—have visited this little store and passed on, leaving only pathetic initials on counter tops as testaments of a one-time presence. Mrs. Walker herself is somehow inanimate and unreal, a caretaker of memories, mortician of dead dreams.

Perhaps this missing element went up the street, to the new Kroger shopping center. Then again, perhaps it just floated up to the ceiling, lodged in the grimy cracks, and stayed there wondering why it had to go.

Everywhere in the mummified silence lurks an air of expectancy. One day something will happen, the laughter will come out of the walls, the tears will well up out of the floors, the wrinkles will vanish from the faces of the men, and they will no longer be lonely.

Walker's is waiting, like a decaying railroad terminal, for airplanes to be disinvented. Walker's is waiting—waiting to die. It will die. It is not immortal or everlasting because it lived, and things that live, must die. Like an old, old man, the store has become senile. It gently rocks away the years, reminiscing and nodding quietly while the dust gathers. The Pepsi machine will soon break, and the glass door to the refrigerator cabinet already has. After several such breakdowns, Walker's will die. Demolition crews will attend to the burial, and perhaps a shiny new parking lot will serve as a tombstone.

People will continue to shop at the Kroger shopping center, a place too antiseptic for the storage of dreams or memories. But in compensation for this shortcoming, Top Value stamps are doled out to customers.

The children will never see Mr. Kroger, or be ashamed that they had stolen from him. Mr. Kroger will not help them with their school work or give them ice cubes in the summer. They cannot inscribe initials or witty adolescent obscenities in the Formica counters, and any old men foolish or lonely enough to sit on Kroger's electric doorstep would be arrested for loitering.

Surely it will be different. Something alive and meaningful is missing. It must be different.

9

Exposition, the Meat of Most Articles — Making It Tasty and Digestible

A HOLE IS TO DIG
The ground is to make a garden
Grass is to cut
Grass is to have on the ground with dirt under it and clover in it
Maybe you could hide things in a hole
A party is to say how-do-you-do and shake hands
A party is to make little children happy
Arms are to hug with
Toes are to wiggle
Ears are to wiggle
Mud is to jump in and slide in and yell doodleedoodledoo
Ahh-h-h-h! Doodleedoodleedoo-oo!

— Ruth Krauss

TO MAKE A PRAIRIE
To make a prairie it takes a clover and one bee, —
One clover, and a bee,
And revery.
The revery alone will do
If bees are few.

— Emily Dickinson

THE PANTHER
The panther is like a leopard,
Except it hasn't been peppered.
Should you behold a panther crouch,
Prepare to say Ouch.
Better yet, if called by a panther,
Don't anther.

— Ogden Nash

And "Mashed potatoes are to give to everybody enough," according to Ruth Krauss in *A Hole Is to Dig, A First Book of First Definitions*. Definitions explain.

The Dickinson recipe for prairie making is idiosyncratic, but who would argue with her analysis? Analysis explains.

Ogden Nash instructs by analogy and direction. Analogy explains.

As human beings, we probably do more explaining when we communicate with others than argue or describe or storytell. As writers, we most surely do more explaining than anything else in the course of our work.

Since we do more of it, we should be good at it, better at it than all too many of us are. We tend to get bogged down. Our writing tends to turn leaden. Result: reader boredom.

That shouldn't be.

Exposition should be palatable, and can even be exciting—that is, if we as writers turn to a subject with exuberant spirit. We must first be interested in the subject and its material if the reader ultimately is to be won.

Ask yourself: "Do I love facts?"

Connie Fletcher obviously does. "Cops know things you and I don't," she noted in "What Cops Know" for *Chicago* magazine (May 1987). Like what? Well, that when a motorist is pulled over for speeding, "that motorist will always look at the speedometer, even though the car is now at a complete stop." And that "in families of drug dealers, it's common to hide drugs in a baby's diaper—with the baby in it." And that "the most time cops have to execute search warrants on dope houses— before dope can be flushed, thrown out the window, or dissolved in a pan of water—is thirty seconds." And that "more women kill themselves on Mother's Day than any other day in the year."

Fletcher heard those facts. She was captivated by them. She passed them along to her reader. Hers is exposition, and not at all boring.

Roger Angell loves facts:

Here we are, and here it all is for us: already too much to remember. Here's a meerschaum pipe presented to Cy Young by his Red Sox teammates after his perfect game in 1904. Here are Shoeless Joe Jackson's shoes. Here's a life-size statue of Ted Williams, beautifully done in basswood; Ted is just finishing his swing, and his eyes are following the flight of the ball, into the right-field stands again. Here is John McGraw's little black mitt, from the days when he played third base for the old Orioles: a blob of licorice, by the looks of it, or perhaps a small flattened animal, dead on the highway. Here's a ball signed by seventeen-year-old Willie McCovey and his teammates on the 1955 Class D Sandersville (Georgia) club—Stretch's first address in organized ball—and over *here* is a ball from a June 14, 1870, game between Cincinnati and the Brooklyn Atlantics; Brooklyn won, snapping the Red Stockings' astounding winning streak of two full years. Babe Ruth, in a floor-to-ceiling photomural, sits behind the wheel of an open touring car, with his manager, little Miller Huggins, almost hidden beside him. The Babe is wearing driving gauntlets, a cap, a fur-collared coat, and a sullen assured look: Out of the way, world!

Angell is telling us about Cooperstown, what we can see—if we're observant—while visiting the National Baseball Hall of Fame and Museum. His list of facts goes on as he takes readers of *The New Yorker* (August 31, 1987) on a tour of a place which also is a state of mind. "Up at the Hill" is exposition and not at all boring.

Cullen Murphy loves facts. His information-packed article, "Kids Today," for *The Wilson Quarterly* (Autumn 1982) begins, continues, and ends with facts. But look at how he uses them in his opening:

Why is there air? "To make basketballs," answered comedian Bill Cosby. Why are there children?

One reason, of course, is that children provide jobs. Jobs for more than 1.3 million elementary school teachers, for thirteen million stay-at-home mothers, for the makers of 1.3 million infant and toddler car seats sold in the United States in 1980; jobs, too, for many of the 2,768 psychologists who received their Ph.D.s that same year. The very existence of children, moreover, implies that the economy is in for a long run.

Children keep democracy fit. Without kids there would be no PTA. Local town meetings would be reduced to acrimonious disputes over solid waste disposal. Congress would be little concerned about family subsidies, and utterly unconcerned about abortion, day care, and prayer in the schools. Children help to lure adults into political activity.

Children also challenge their parents to think about the future, and hence about values and standards. Children represent what society is going to become. While moral relativism makes for lively reading in the pages of *Us* or *Esquire*, the notions of right and wrong acquire a certain importance when adults contemplate their own offspring.

Thus, unintentionally perhaps, children do America a lot of good. Against all of this, however, is the fact that children are an immense burden on everyone, arriving in this world at odd hours, consuming precious resources. To their parents, they are a relentless inconvenience and a perpetual source of worry. They cause taxes to rise to pay for schools and welfare. They force many mothers into the work force just to help the family make ends meet and at the same time place obstacles in the path of mothers who wish to work, or must. They complicate divorce and they complicate remarriage. Even in the best of circumstances, they get sick, irritate friends, repeat their parents' errors, flunk school tests. They force adults, both as individuals and as members of a community, to make painful choices concerning time and money.

Because children mean so much to society, for better or worse, their elders long ago set up a kind of Distant Early Warning system—a DEW line monitoring the approach of serious trouble.

Murphy enlightens. He clarifies. It's exposition, and not at all boring.

Good exposition takes work, as does any and all good writing. But we tend, more than when we fashion narration or description, to just let the facts fend for themselves. Our task is to make the expositional article understandable, readable, and even pleasurable. Yes, we must know how to handle the complex, to reduce complications of a subject without diminishing them, to simplify information without oversimplifying it. We must also find a way to make the material interesting, and we do that by finding the right facts in the right combinations and then reflecting our enthusiasm and vision through appropriate language. We need not always turn stylistic cartwheels to gain reader attention. We must, however, know our reader's personality, the level of comprehension, and the extent of built-in inquisitiveness and fervor.

An editor of *RN*, Paul Cerrato, seems to have understood his professional reader in a series of columns labeled "Nutritionist on Call," which won honors for him from the American Business Press. "Why Johnny Can't Sit Still" (December 1987) is a no-frills, straightforward, well-ordered piece that explains hyperactivity, its possible causes and effects. The writing is clean. The information has been carefully chosen and organized. Either nurse or lay person can learn from Cerrato's account. One suspects that the author labored over the article so that to a reader it seems unlabored, an efficient and easy flow of information.

"Problem child." That's how his teachers, and even his parents, used to label Johnny Evans. In school, he disrupted classes and provoked fights in the playground. At home, he cried and kicked and screamed whenever he didn't get his way.

Johnny eventually calmed down when, after being diagnosed as hyperactive, he was put on methylphenidate (Ritalin). But now, two years later, his parents are worried about the long-term effects of drug therapy.

Isn't there another way, they wonder, to control Johnny's hyperactive behavior? Just recently they read a magazine article claiming that food additives and sugar exacerbate behavioral problems. Now they're asking you if they should put Johnny on a diet that limits these substances.

What can you tell them? A good starting point when working with Johnny's parents, and others like them, is to explain what the research shows.

The Effects of Additives
In the 1970's, some researchers thought that food additives influenced the behavior of large numbers of hyperactive children. One study, for example, suggested that a diet free of artificial colors, artificial flavors, and salicylates — a natural substance found in aspirin and some fruits and vegetables — could improve the behavior of up to 50 percent of such children.

However, follow-up studies in the 1980s cast doubts on the effectiveness of additive-free diets. One study of twenty-two children with behavioral problems, for example, found only two of them to be sensitive to artificial colors and flavors.

In another study, two groups of hyperactive children were put on an additive-free diet. Subsequently, one of the groups was fed cookies containing artificial colors. After four weeks or so, the behavior of the cookie-eaters was only somewhat worse than the behavior of those in the control group. In fact, medication was found to be far more effective than an additive-free diet in controlling behavior.

Not surprisingly, a panel of experts convened by the National Institutes of Health concluded that there's not enough evidence to justify putting *all* children diagnosed as hyperactive on additive-free diets. The panel went on to say, though, that such diets are certainly worth trying and should be continued if benefits have been noted.

You can obtain a list of commercial products — including pediatric medications and vitamin preparations — that contain no artificial colors or flavors from the Feingold Association, for a charge. You can contact the Association, an organization that promotes an additive-free diet, by writing to: P.O. Box 6550, Alexandria, VA 22306. Or phone (703) 768-3287.

The Role of Sugar

Although sugar has long been reputed to make hyperactive children more restless, moody, and irritable, the research does not totally support this contention.

In one study, for example, a psychiatrist gave sweetened lemonade to a group of fifty hyperactive children. Only one became more easily frustrated and difficult to control. In another study, sucrose actually *reduced* behavioral symptoms. A possible explanation: Like many other carbohydrates, sucrose increases the brain concentration of serotonin, which has a calming effect on the nervous system.

Though these two studies would appear to get sugar off the hook, yet another study produced quite different results: One-half of 265 hyperactive children developed hypoglycemia after they drank a concentrated sugar solution. Hypoglycemia can cause nervousness and irritability.

Where does such contradictory evidence leave parents? For one thing, they'd be wise to observe the effects of sugar-laden snacks on their child's behavior.

If they suspect he may be hypoglycemic, they can ask the doctor to perform a five-hour glucose tolerance test.

If the results are positive, they should be sure that, in addition to three meals a day, their child eats mid-morning, mid-afternoon, and late-evening snacks that are high in protein — cheese or nuts, for example — to keep his blood sugar level up. He should also steer clear of candy, cookies, cake, ice cream, and soda — even sugar-free soda if it contains caffeine, a substance that can bring on the symptoms of hypoglycemia.

One More Possibility to Check Out

Parents might also want to find out whether their child is allergic to certain foods.

A well-documented study of the role that food allergies play in behavioral problems discovered that, among other foods, milk, wheat, citrus fruit, eggs, beef, chicken, carrots, corn, and potatoes can all trigger difficulties. The best way to determine if a child has a food allergy is to put him on a diet that excludes most of these common allergens. If his behavior improves after two to three weeks, then suspected allergens should be added to his diet, one at a time. If problem behavior begins after introduction of one of the foods, it should be eliminated from his diet permanently.

While the research suggests that only a minority of children with behavioral problems have food allergies or will respond to an additive or sugar-free diet, that's no reason to discourage parents from experimenting with reasonable dietary changes. For some children—and perhaps Johnny is one of them—nutritional therapy can spell the difference between a well-adjusted childhood and many years of mental anguish.

EXPOSITORY TECHNIQUES

Various techniques are available to help the writer add spark to expository pieces. Narration and description can make exposition livelier, as we discussed in Chapter Nine.

So can the following expositional methods:

- Examples
- Identification
- Definition
- Classification
- Comparison and contrast
- Analysis
- Analogy
- Statistics

These can be used singly or in combinations, depending on your needs. Let's examine each individually.

Examples

The most frequently used approach is through example or illustration. It's the "for instance" way of explaining. Robert Deal asked the reader, "Are you a napper?" He then asserted, "If so, you have some prestigious company." Such a statement needs support or proof which Deal went on to provide in "The Benefits of Napping" for *USAIR* (August 1986):

—Thomas Edison napped to supplement his four-hour nighttime sleeping. Recalled one of his associates: "His genius for sleep equaled his genius for invention. He could go to sleep anywhere, anytime, on anything."

—First Lady Eleanor Roosevelt napped to collect her thoughts before delivering a speech. She would sleep at the speakers' table up to the moment of being introduced.

—John F. Kennedy and his family would nap religiously in their White House living quarters from 1:00 to 3:00 p.m. Presidents Grant, Truman, and Ford were also White House nappers.

—Artist Salvador Dali devised a unique method of timing his naps by sleeping in a chair with his right arm dangling over the side. In his right hand he would hold a metal spoon, then nap until he dropped the spoon, striking a metal plate below his arm.

—Winston Churchill found the nap to be a useful ally in World War Two. In *The Gathering Storm*, he wrote: "I always went to bed at least for one hour in the afternoon and exploited to the full my happy gift. By this means I was able to press a day and a half's work into one. Nature had not intended mankind to work from eight in the morning until midnight without the refreshed oblivion, which, even if it lasts only twenty minutes, is sufficient to renew all vital forces."

Now we know we're in prestigious company if we give in to our inclination to sleep. And we'll know that Lloyd's of London will "insure anything—well, almost anything" after we read Trevor Holloway's examples in *Sky* (March 1989), part of his celebration of the world-famous insurer, "Lloyd's at 300":

... A few of the more unusual risks they have accepted:

- Cutty Sark Whisky offered a prize (worth about $1.8 million) to anyone who could capture the Loch Ness monster alive, wisely guarding against their loss by taking out a Lloyd's policy.
- A grain of rice with a portrait of the Queen and the Duke of Edinburgh engraved on it was insured for approximately $36,000.
- The world's largest existing gold nugget, Golden Beauty, weighing 145 ounces, was covered for more than $144,000 while in transit from Perth, Western Australia, to Los Angeles.
- At the other end of the scale, forty members of the "Whiskers Club" in Derbyshire insured their beards for about thirty-six dollars against fire and theft.
- The National Federation of Building Trade Employers offered the prize of a house to anybody who correctly guessed the combination of a Chubb safe in which the deeds of the house were locked. They took the precaution of insuring at Lloyd's in case of a successful attempt.

A host of film, stage, and sports stars have insured themselves at Lloyd's, including Gene Kelly, Elizabeth Taylor, Frank Sinatra, Bob Hope, Bing Crosby, Richard Burton, and Lord Laurence Olivier. Christopher Reeve was covered for about thirty-six million dollars during the filming of *Superman*, Betty Grable, whose "million-dollar legs" sold millions of theater tickets, was another one of Lloyd's insured stars.

People whose livelihood depends on one of their senses often insure at Lloyd's. Composer Richard Stockler insured his ears; a whiskey distiller, his nose. One of the most bizarre objects Lloyd's agreed to insure was the world's largest cigar, exhibited to launch a new brand. It was over twelve feet in length and was covered for approximately $32,477, representing its retail value.

Example explains through specificity. It proves an assertion. It completes a point. It clarifies.

Identification

To identify is to place someone or something in a context, thereby to make the subject more meaningful to a reader. Simple identification would remind you that Ralph Lauren is a successful fashion designer and trend setter. For its May 1989 issue, *Life* visited Lauren. Staffers decided he was worthy of more expansive identification, of a sort that explains what the man really is all about:

> Welcome to Ralph Lauren country, where everyone has the classic dog, the classic tan, the classic house and, of course, the classic look. Lauren can't sell you the tan or the dog, but he can set you up with everything else, from hats to a place to hang them. He markets American archetypes — Wild West Cowboy, Down-Home Folks, East Coast WASP — so well that architecture critic Paul Goldberger of *The New York Times* called Lauren's neotraditionalism the leitmotiv of the 1980s, while *The New Republic* declared that Polo-driven snobbism elected a Yalie to the White House.
>
> Not everyone can dream what the rest of America dreams — and sell it. A good eye, top quality and unerring timing have made Lauren the nation's most successful designer, with sales each year of some thirty-five million items worth two billion dollars. "I have visions, and I go at it," says Lauren. "Everything I've done, I've done because I loved it and saw a need."
>
> He is a man for whom the word *lifestyle* could have been invented. He has a thirteen thousand-acre ranch in Colorado, a Long Island beach cottage, two hundred acres in Bedford, New York, a villa in Jamaica and a Fifth Avenue duplex. He has a Gulfstream II jet, but he has a rusted-out turquoise Willys jeep too. Unlike Donald Trump and his ilk, Lauren spends his nouveaux riches with old-money restraint. He's a chief executive who didn't start out in a log cabin but may wind up in one.
>
> This year the self-made man turns fifty. He has a personal net worth of almost a half billion dollars. He has 125 stores, including a sumptuously restored nineteenth-century mansion on Madison Avenue that is his flagship. He has two thousand employees — an empire. But time is passing. What's left to conquer?

In "*Life* Visits Ralph Lauren," the designer has been so identified that he can be mistaken for no other, and no other can be mistaken for him. Through identification he has been explained.

Boring? Never. Good exposition engages the reader, keeps him or her going.

Definition

Definition, literally, is the meaning of words found in the dictionary and of proper nouns more likely to be found in the encyclopedia.

The journalist, however, may find dictionary-styled definitions unsatisfactory, lacking oomph, minus the twist of surprise or newness, without personality or wisdom or grace.

I once asked Bob Williams, editor of the *Pennsylvania Farmer*,

"What's a cow?" I wanted to hear from a man steeped in agriculture, knowing he wouldn't be satisfied repeating the dictionary's "mature female of cattle or of any animal the male of which is called a bull" or "a domestic bovine animal regardless of sex or age." He jotted down:

> If God created one creature to save the starving masses of the world, surely it was the dairy cow. Old Bossy can convert grass and pea vines and discarded ice cream cones—even nitrogen fertilizers—into nature's most complete, most life sustaining food.
>
> And she does it with abundance, producing ten to twenty times her body weight in milk each ten-month lactation.
>
> This docile creature harvests her own food, replenishes the soil with her waste, and furnishes her own replacement. When she eventually wears out after four or six years in the milk string, she's converted into McDonald's hamburgers, Florsheim shoes, and steamed bone meal for your dog food and garden.
>
> On the millions of square miles not suited for corn and soybeans and wheat, she can live in animal splendor.
>
> Given the chance, this grand old dairy cow would easily nourish the world's poor and underfed.

That definition speaks to the importance of the subject. It makes me, as a reader, think anew about the animal my first-born son used to call moo-maker. We're not just talking cow here. Or bovine. To Williams the cow, or more specifically, the dairy cow, is a lifesaver. We keep returning to the matter of approach. This definition of the cow is an approach that makes the subject special and tends to alter a reader's view.

The Aztecs had no dictionaries. But they defined. As transcribed by Fra Bernardino Sahagún, they defined creatively, fervently, frankly:

> The traitor is a gossip. [He is] excrement, dung. He sows discord among people. He excites revolt, he causes turmoil. He makes one swallow falsehoods. He spits in one's mouth. Hot-tempered he arouses passions, causes riots, stirs rebellion. (From Charles E. Dibble & Arthur J.O. Anderson, *Florentine Codex General History of the Things of New Space by Fray Bernadino de Sahagún, Book II.)*

Definitions can heighten a reader's sensitivity.

Compilers of the dictionary, not attempting sensitivity, say our Constitution is the document that "sets forth the basic principles and laws of our nation, determining the powers and duties of the government and guaranteeing certain rights to the people." So, who doesn't know that? But *Time* devoted its July 6, 1987 issue to the Constitution when we marked its 200th anniversary.

It told readers what the Constitution really is:

> The Constitution has the aura of the sacred about it. It occupies a shrine up in the higher stretches of American reverence. A citizen imagines sun-shot

clouds, the founders hovering in the air like saints in religious art. But the constitution has its other, mundane life. Down at sea level, where people struggle along in law courts and jailhouses and abortion clinics, where lives and ideas crash into each other, the Constitution has a more interesting and turbulent existence. There the Constitution is not a civic icon but a messy series of collisions that knock together the arrangements of the nation's life. Those arrangements become America's history—what its people do, what they are, what they mean. Walt Whitman wrote, "I contain multitudes." That is what the Constitution does—an astonishing feat considering the variety of multitudes that have landed on American shores, and continue to land.

May a man be detained in jail before being tried? Is prayer to be permitted in the public schools? Or a Christmas creche in the town square? What of the Reagan Administration's arranging military help for the Nicaraguan *contras* when Congress has forbidden it? If a man murders someone, may the state kill the killer in retribution? May government employees be forced to have their urine tested to search for the trace of drugs? May American Nazis march in an Illinois suburb that is home to Jewish survivors of the Holocaust? May a man be arrested for performing a homosexual act in his own home? Is it right to promote a woman ahead of an equally qualified man in order to redress past inequities toward women?

Issues passionate and human and difficult surge up against the Constitution. Every day it attends to the pleas of lust, rage, unborn life, the killer's remorse, the President's prerogatives, the First Amendment rights of a Ku Klux Klansman. The Constitution even makes a ritual appearance in the American television cop shows: there comes a moment of denouement when the detective, triumphant but sardonically obedient to the *Miranda* decision, snaps the cuffs on a suspect and growls, "You have the right to remain silent. You have the right to . . ."

The Constitution forces Americans to think about uncongenial matters, to think about tolerating everything they may hate. It is the American superego. It holds Americans to a high standard, even though it has sometimes countenanced filthy deeds—most notoriously, the owning of slaves.

There is power in such a definition, a power to explain and persuade at the same time, if that is your desire.

In another heartrending example, Nobel Peace Prize winner Elie Wiesel, a survivor of Auschwitz, defined that infamous spot for *The New York Times* (June 11, 1989):

Let us repeat it once again: Auschwitz is something else, always something else. It is a universe outside the universe, a creation that exists parallel to creation. Auschwitz lies on the other side of life and on the other side of death. There, one lives differently, one walks differently, one dreams differently. Auschwitz represents the negation and failure of human progress; it negates the human design and casts doubts on its validity. Then, it defeated culture; later, it defeated art, because just as no one could imagine Auschwitz before Auschwitz, no one can now retell Auschwitz after Auschwitz. The truth of Auschwitz remains hidden in its ashes. Only those who lived it in their flesh and in their minds can possibly transform their experience into knowledge. Others, despite their best intentions, can never do so.

"In Praise of Rolltop Desks" author Mark Orwoll wrote:

The tiny compartments and pigeonholes of a rolltop desk hold magic. They also hold rubber bands, unpaid bills, shopping lists, snapshots that haven't been put into the family album yet, reminder notes from three years ago, paper clips, and the good pair of scissors that have been missing for a month.
The cavernous lower drawers of a rolltop contain mystery. They also contain an unfinished novel, old love letters, an autographed baseball, personalized stationery with an out-of-date address, a yearly diary whose entries stop abruptly in mid-February, and a football pennant for a team that long ago moved to a distant city.
The rolltop desk is arguably the most wonderful piece of furniture ever made. It is a desk that does not command you to work; rather it urges you to create. Its hidden corners and dusky cubbyholes contain more than the mere trappings of home or business accounting; they contain the very *life* of a home or business. For more than a century America has carried on a love affair with the rolltop desk. Rolltops are not furniture. They are a way of being.

Devotion is lavished on that subject (the article ran in *USAIR*), and again, as readers, we come to understand what a rolltop really is. *Reader's Digest* excerpted "A Skier's Dictionary" from Henry Beard's and Roy McKie's book *Skiing*. From them you learn:

Alp: One of a number of ski mountains in Europe. Also a shouted request for assistance made by a European skier on a U.S. mountain. An appropriate reply: "What's Zermatter?"
Avalanche: One of the few actual perils skiers face that needlessly frighten timid individuals away from the sport. See also, *Blizzard, Fracture, Frostbite, Hypothermia, Lift Collapse*.
Bones: There are 206 in the human body. No need for dismay, however; two bones of the middle ear have never been broken in a skiing accident.
Skier: One who pays an arm and a leg for the opportunity to break them.
Skis: A pair of long, thin, flexible runners that permit a skier to slide across the snow and into debt.

Classification

You may be able to shed light on a subject by putting the objects or the people or institutions or events under discussion into classes, not the way a scientist might, simply with precision, but the way a writer can, through color. Peter Richmond classified in "The Sultan of Spike" (*Rolling Stone*, June 1987) when he claimed:

There are three kinds of volleyball: picnic volleyball, beach volleyball and real volleyball.
Picnic volleyball is played by parents, kids and dogs, which makes for

short rallies. The boundaries are marked by half-empty cans of domestic beer. A picnic-volleyball match ends when you run out of sunlight, suds or both.

Beach-volleyball is played by men, women and human beach flotsam looking to kill time for the rest of their lives. A beach-volleyball match lasts until the coals are ready or someone lights another joint or both.

Real volleyball is a ballet of feathery finesse and bludgeoning power performed by exceptional athletes who leap to heights of eleven feet and throw themselves around the court like madmen. Real volleyball whispers and slams. It flies on tangents. It is dead serious. It brooks no end-zone foppery, no slam-dunking self-celebrations. It is played in stadiums in Brazil before fifty thousand people, in S.R.O. arenas in Japan, in packed houses all over Europe.

Richmond then began to drive home his point that volleyball deserves more clout in the United States and that Karch Kiraly, the sultan, is the man to do it.

Classification systematizes. Science writer Isaac Asimov used the technique in "The Green Enemy" for *American Way* (October 1987):

Humanity has three classes of living nonhuman enemies.

First, there are the great predators: lions, bears, sharks, and so on. We treasure stories of Samson rending a lion and we shudder over the movie *Jaws*. Actually, however, those poor animals have been outclassed for thousands of years and could be driven to extinction with very little trouble if humanity really puts its mind to it.

Second, there are the invisible parasites: the viruses, bacteria, protozoa, worms, and so on, that, in one way or another, live at our expense and interfere with our health. These are far more dangerous than the large predators; we need only compare the Black Death (bubonic plague) of the Fourteenth Century with anything man-eating tigers could do. In the last 125 years, however, we have learned ways of dealing with the disease producers, and the danger has vastly diminished.

That leaves the third group: unwanted plants, or weeds. With very few exceptions these are not apparently dangerous in themselves and are certainly not dramatic, for they do nothing but grow. And yet in some ways they are the most insidious and dangerous of all.

That classification out of the way, Asimov was ready to explore the uselessness of weeds. So are we.

Comparison and Contrast

I touched on this technique, as well as classification, in the chapter on structuring. Comparison, I said, shows how two or more items are alike; contrast shows how they differ. Comparison emphasizes similarities between or among subjects, people, things. Contrast highlights dissimilarity.

Tim Page, writing about composer Philip Glass in the June 1988 issue of *Opera News*, described his music and then turned to comparison:

> His mature music is based on the extended repetition of brief, elegant melodic fragments that weave in and out of an aural tapestry. Listening to these works has been compared to watching a challenging modern painting that initially appears static but seems to metamorphose slowly as one concentrates.

In the October 1988 edition of the same magazine, Jonathan Keates discussed the music of Handel and the composer's use of castrati ("Handel in His Element"):

> Among several sections of the audience there was an enthusiasm for the castratos that parallels the acclaim given in our own day to Michael Jackson, Bruce Springsteen or Madonna. Women in particular found a distinct allure in the manufactured sexual ambiguity of these creatures, and the fair spectator who accompanied her applause with the cry "One God, one Farinelli!" was typical rather than exceptional. Even more temperate aficionados responded warmly to the eunuch's singular versatility. Several years after the original *Giulio Cesare*'s return to Italy, a jaundiced listener to a performance of Handel's *Alexander's Feast* scribbled in the margin of his wordbook, "Oh for Senesino!"

Contrast comes from Hollie West in her Washington *Post* (February 9, 1975) article about an Oklahoma town that had a yesterday but has very little of a today, "Once a Town of Hope, Now a Fading Dream:"

> Say, have you heard the story,
>   Of a little colored town.
> Way over in the Nation
> On such lovely sloping ground?
>   With as pretty little houses
>   As you ever chanced to meet,
> With not a thing but colored folks
>   A standing in the streets?
>   Oh, tis a pretty country
> And the Negroes own it, too.
> With not a single white man here
> To tell us what to do — In Boley.

Boley, Okla. — That's how E.J. (Uncle Jesse) Pinkett sang the praises of Boley as its town poet more than sixty years ago. Today, a traveler speeding east along U.S. Highway 62 through rolling slopes of Oklahoma sandstone and shale could whisk by here without ever knowing this "little colored town" still stands.

Only McCormick's gasoline station, cafe and motel face the highway. The community, a mile square, sits on a hill screened by briar bushes and catalpa trees. The first, and only, advance notice of the town is a simple road marker, "Boley — 5."

Boley is a dream that faded. Its thriving farming base withered, the town today is made up largely of the middle-aged and elderly. Pecan Street, known by most as Main Street and built wide, once bustled with mule-drawn wagons laden with bales of cotton. Today it moves at a drowsy pace except on Saturday nights when the few remaining bars and cafes throb with jukebox soul music, the click of pool cues hitting balls, the thump of dominoes on a wood table, and the dancing feet of the town's dwindling youth. But on a Monday noon, chickens walk leisurely across Main Street, stopping traffic.

In "Fast and Smart," *Time* (March 28, 1989) covered experiments that "illustrate the paradox at the heart of today's computer science," arguing that "The most powerful computing machines — giant number crunchers possessed of speed and storage capacities beyond human comprehension — are essentially dumb brutes with no more intellectual depth than a light bulb." Note the contrast:

> *The computer at the University of Illinois is simulating something that no one saw: the evolution of the universe in the aftermath of the Big Bang. Re-creating conditions that may have prevailed billions of years ago, the computer reveals on a remote screen how massive clouds of subatomic particles, tugged by their own gravity, might have coalesced into filaments and flattened disks. The vivid reds, greens and blues of the shapes are not merely decorative but represent the various densities of the first large structures as they emerged from primordial chaos in the near vacuum of space.*
>
> *At the Massachusetts Institute of Technology, another computer is struggling to learn what any three-year-old child already knows: the difference between a cup and a saucer. What the youngster sees at a glance, the computer must be taught, painstakingly, one step at a time. First it must comprehend the concept of an object, a physical thing distinguished from the space around it by edges and surfaces. Then it must grasp the essential attributes of cupness: the handle, the leakproof central cavity, the stable base. Finally, it must deal with the exceptions, like the foam-plastic cup whose heat-insulating properties are so good that it does not need a handle.*

What follows is thesis, that "giant number crunchers" are "dumb brutes" but at "the other extreme are computers that have begun to exhibit the first glimmers of human-like reasoning."

Analysis

A "how-to" article is analysis. Taking apart a whole to see how it works or what's inside is analysis. Examining the structure of process of something is analysis. "Taming the Wily Rhinovirus" begins with analysis:

> A cold virus enters your body through the twin portals of the nose. Swept along by hairlike cilia in the nasal passage, it's borne on a carpet of mucus to the back of the throat, a journey that takes at most ten or twelve minutes. Almost always it's the end of the line. The virus either flows into the adenoids, the throat's garbage-disposal unit, or is washed down the esophagus to the gut, where it's obliterated by digestive acids.
>
> But once in a while the virus remains, lodging against the lining of your

nasal passage and, through a precise docking mechanism, binding tightly to a cell's receptors. Almost immediately an astonishing violation takes place. The virus enters the cell, disassembles, and unleashes its genes, taking over the cell's reproductive machinery. The cell stops making new copies of itself and starts making new viruses instead. At this point you're still unaware of the invasion. But in a few days it'll be all too clear. Sore throat, a stuffed and runny nose, headache, perhaps a touch of fever—you've got a cold again.

Peter Radetsky lets me know, as a reader of *Discover* (April 1989), how I get to feel so bad. Dreary? Not at all, because good exposition enlivens a subject.

Ryszard Kapuscinski, taking readers of *Granta* (Winter 1986) on "A Tour of Angola," said: "You have to learn how to live with the checkpoints and to respect their customs, if you want to travel without hindrance and reach your destination alive." The author continued:

Every encounter with a checkpoint consists of:
  (a) the explanatory section
  (b) bargaining
  (c) friendly conversation.

You have to drive up to the checkpoint slowly and stop at a decent remove. Any violent braking or squealing of tyres constitutes a bad opening; the sentries don't appreciate such stunts. Next we get out of the car and approach the barriers, gasoline drums, heaps of stones, tree trunks or wardrobe. If this is a zone near the front, our legs buckle with fear and our hearts are in our mouths because we can't tell whose checkpoint it is—the MPLA's, FNLA's or UNITA's. The sun is shining and it's hot. Air heated to whiteness vibrates above the road, as if a snowdrift were billowing across the pavement. But it's quiet, and an unmoving world, holding its breath, surrounds us. We too, involuntarily, hold our breath.

We stop and wait. There is no one in sight.

But the sentries are there. Concealed in the bushes or in a roadside hut, they are watching us intently. We're exposed to their gaze and, God forbid, to their fire. At such a moment you can't show either nervousness or haste, because both will cause things to end badly. So we act normal, correct, relaxed: we just wait. Nor will it help to go to the other extreme and mask fear with an artificial casualness, or joke around, show off or display an exaggerated self-confidence. The sentries might infer that we are treating them lightly and the results could be catastrophic. Nor do they like it when travellers put their hands in their pockets, look around, lie down in the shade of the nearby trees or—this is generally considered a crime—themselves set about removing the obstacles from the road.

At the conclusion of the observation period, the people from the checkpoint leave their hiding places and walk in our direction in a slow, lazy step, but alert and with their weapons at the ready. They stop at a safe distance.

The strangers stay where they are.

Remember that the sun is shining and it's hot.

Now begins the most dramatic moment of the encounter: mutual examination. To understand this scene, we must bear in mind that the armies fighting each other are dressed (or undressed) alike, and that large regions of the country are noman's land into which first one side and then the other penetrates and sets up checkpoints. That is why, at first, we don't know who these people are or what they will do with us.

Now we have to summon up all our courage to say one word, which will determine our life or death: '*Camarada!*'

If the sentries are from Agostinho Neto's MPLA, who salute each other with the *camarada*, we will live. But if they turn out to be Holden Roberto's FNLA or Jonas Savimbi's UNITA, who call each other *irmao* (brother), we have reached the limit of our earthly existence. In no time they will put us to work—digging our own graves. In front of the old, established checkpoints there are little cemeteries of those who had the misfortune to greet the sentries with the wrong word . . . .

And so on. How to travel. How to stay alive. How to understand the realities of a geopolitical situation. Narration and description are blended in, but the writer used analysis as the article's foundation.

John Lamm's subject is an automobile. His treatment is analytical, his market is *Road & Track* (June 1987):

It's this easy: Find a lonely stretch of straight road, preferably a drag strip. Make certain the engine of the Buick Grand National GNX is up to temperature. Hold your left foot lightly on the brake while your right foot presses down gently on the accelerator. Engine revs will climb as you take up the slack in the torque converter. The car will try to move forward. You might have to press a bit harder on the brake to keep the GN stationary, but be subtle, almost gentle.

Then slam the gas pedal down as you lift off the brake. The back of the Buick will slew a bit as the fat tires scratch for traction, but keep your foot down because the Goodyears will quickly grab and send you rushing down the road. Less than 6.0 seconds after you mashed the throttle, you will be going 60 mph. If you're on a drag strip and keep your foot down, come 14.0 sec you'll have covered the quarter mile and be traveling around 105 mph. If you still haven't had enough, keep your right foot working, and when you feel the engine rev limiter cut in, you'll be doing 124 mph. And that was a gentle run.

Earthquakes need explaining, too. All that stuff about faults and pressures. *Life* published "How Earthquakes Happen: The Inside Story" in 1989. Written by the editors, it provides a good and compact example of analysis, a method so useful to a science writer:

The globe is encased by a shell of rock, divided like a jigsaw puzzle into more than a dozen interlocking pieces. These plates, about seventy miles thick, float on the earth's semimolten mantle, the layer that surrounds the core. Propelled by forces in the earth's interior, the plates shift as much as four inches a year, gradually increasing plate-to-plate pressure. When the stress exceeds the strength of the rock to contain it, the edges of the plates break and snap into a new position. This is the initial upheaval of an earthquake.

The realease of energy results in seismic waves that radiate far from the earthquake's epicenter. Tremors from the 1964 Alaska quake, for instance, swayed buildings in Seattle and lifted the ground four inches as far south as Houston, Texas. Quakes can also generate huge ocean waves called tsunamis. More than seven hours after the first shock shattered Anchorage, tsunamis, moving down the Pacific coast at speeds of more than four hundred miles per hour, demolished 150 stores and drowned ten people in Crescent City, California. Still later they battered the shores of Japan — four thousand miles from downtown Anchorage.

A seismograph translates tremors into spiky lines on paper. Seismograms help scientists calculate an earthquake's power, duration and location, as well as the depth of the earthquake's origin. The U.S. Geological Survey's National Earthquake Information Service in Golden, Colorado, collects information from three thousand seismological stations in about 125 countries.

Although our understanding of the way earthquakes work is increasingly sophisticated, seismologists admit that predicting the timing of an earthquake is impossible. It is believed, simply, that the longer a vulnerable area goes without a major earthquake, the more chance there is that one will occur. By closely monitoring seismic gaps, areas along a fault that have been unusually quiet for some time, scientists hope that they can measure foreshocks and learn to make accurate predictions. "The weather forecasters have an easier task," says USGS seismologist Allan Lindh. "They can fly around in airplanes and study hurricanes and tornadoes. We have an intrinsically harder problem — our subject matter is buried ten kilometers down with a big piece of real estate in the way."

Analogy

The dictionary says it's "a resemblance in some particulars between things otherwise unlike." Analogy focuses on a similarity that helps explain what otherwise might be difficult for the reader to comprehend, or might simply not have occurred to him.

"I like to sail alone," E.B. White wrote in one of his essays. "The sea was the same as a girl to me — I did not want anyone else along."

"A home is like a reservoir," he wrote in another, a reservoir "equipped with a check valve: the valve permits influx but prevents outflow. Acquisition goes on day and night — smoothly, subtly, imperceptibly. I have no sharp taste for acquiring things, but it is not necessary to desire things in order to acquire them. Goods and chattels seek a man out; they find him even though his guard is up."

Karen Elliott House, writing about problems of world leadership as part of a series for *The Wall Street Journal*, prophesied in the February 21, 1989 issue:

There is every reason to believe that the world of the 1990s will be less predictable and in many ways more unstable than the world of the last several decades. The need, then, is all the greater for a global leader to protect peace and promote prosperity.

She then turned to analogy:

It is rather basic. So long as there were only two great powers, like two big battleships clumsily but cautiously circling each other, confrontations—or accidents—were easier to avoid. Now, with the global lake more crowded with ships of varying size, fueled by different ambitions and piloted with differing degrees of navigational skill, the odds of collisions become far greater.

Among the ships certain to be careening about in this global lake over the next generation are a jerry-built European Common Market craft answering to no single captain or command; a Japanese destroyer aggressively challenging other ships with economic torpedoes; a still-primitive Chinese junk weighted down with a billion increasingly unruly passengers; and the old Soviet battleship floundering uncertainly in the waters as its crew ignore the orders of its captain.

Darting among these larger ships will be a chaotic collection of smaller craft, many carrying such dangerous cargo as chemical weaponry, and captained by an assortment of despots, zealots and madmen. These waters also will be strewn with African and Latin life rafts bearing refugees from poverty and mismanagement and desperately seeking rescue from those on the larger, more luxurious liners.

In these dangerous waters the only way to avoid collisions will be for one of the large ships to send out strong enough signals to set a navigational pattern for the rest.

Statistics

The eminent British mathematician, physicist, and astronomer, Sir James Jeans, once suggested we "put three grains of sand inside a vast cathedral, and the cathedral will be more closely packed with sand than space with stars."

That sort of spatial analogy offers a clearer picture of vastness than all the huge numbers of bodies and light years than an astronomer might use with delight to befuddle us.

It is the sort of informational approach journalists should consider and even search for among story sources to give their readers a clearer understanding when statistics or the concepts they represent are complicated.

John McPhee, so effective a verbal clarifier, tells us in his book, *Basin and Range*: "With your arms spread wide again to represent all time on earth, look at one hand with its line of life. The Cambrian begins in the wrist, and the Permian Extinction is at the outer end of the palm. All of the Cenozoic is in a fingerprint, and in a single stroke with a medium grained nail file you could eradicate human history."

Universal and epochal matters, of course, entice the writer to find pictures in numbers. When William Kaufmann III dealt with neutron stars in an article for *Science Digest* (March 1983), he explained that these stellar corpses consist of neutron-rich matter so dense "that one teaspoonful brought to earth would weigh one hundred million tons. That's roughly equal," he or someone estimated, "to the combined weight of all the people — four billion of them — alive today."

My first reaction might be: how did someone figure that out, and is the teaspoon a heaping one? But my more considered, follow-up reaction is, "That's heavy. That's dense."

Of course, there's the more direct approach, as effectively employed by Walter Sullivan in his *New York Times* (September 14, 1982) discussion of the very durable proton. He wrote, "The time in which half of any given number of protons will decay must exceed . . . one thousand billion billion billion years."

Hmm.

But then Sullivan added: "Still, that is less than forever."

Statistics, in other words, must be given meaning, significance, relevance.

And some good rules to start with are:

1. Don't distort, lest you mislead your reader.
2. Don't overuse, lest you tire him.
3. Don't underuse, lest you confuse him.
4. Be accurate.
5. Be clear.
6. Be selective.
7. Be creative, whenever that's desirable or appropriate.

"In the fifteen minutes that it takes to read these two pages," said staff writer Timothy Aeppel in *The Christian Science Monitor* (July 6, 1987), "more than 2,200 people will be added to the world's population. Each week we add the equivalent of another Houston; each year, another Mexico." And so he goes on to discuss "5 Billion and Counting," a graphic story about the planet's explosive population.

Note, please, Aeppel in 1987 wrote of five billion. Kaufmann, you'll recall, in 1983 had written of four.

Enormity is both reduced and magnified, all at once. The technique clarifies a concept, identifies a problem, isolates information.

We're told by environmentalists, for instance, that every minute of every day fifty-three acres of the world's tropical rain forests are cleared. That, I figure, is more than twenty-six times my two-acre homestead in Bloomington, Indiana, and that, to me, is an awful lot, awful in the environmental sense of the word, too. But do some multiplying. Those fifty-three acres every minute multiply into more than forty-three thousand square miles every year — an area equivalent to Tennessee or Ohio. Frightening.

Statistics like that have meaning. Statistics like that are interesting. Statistics, properly used, can shed light or heat. They also can prompt both a writer (to explore a facet of a subject) and a reader (to ponder, to wonder, to worry, to laugh). Statistics, properly used, are neither dry nor lifeless.

But be reminded of the story about carrots.

Carrots are eaten by nearly all sick people (you can make up percentages—like 99 percent), by nearly all who die of today's incurable or hard to cure diseases, who serve in our military, who serve in the numerous military forces of the world, who die in train, plane, and car crashes. Juvenile delinquents, we're reminded, come from homes in which carrots are served. And 100 percent of those who were born in 1850 and ate carrots are now dead. So carrots obviously lead to disease, war, crime, and death.

Yes, indeed, a writer can do anything with statistics.

"Statistics create an aura of certainty and neutrality," according to economist Robert Samuelson. "They're supposed to convey truth, settle debates, and make it easier to control our environment. Up to a point, they do. But they can also be manipulated or misunderstood and, thereby, distort reality."

Samuelson pointed to the *Statistical Abstract of the United States: 1987*. In 1985, the *Abstract* told him, "48 percent of Americans over the age of fourteen reported they did volunteer work. That caused my calculator to self-destruct. Granting all the Little League coaches, Scout leaders, PTA officials and church choir singers, does every other person do volunteer work? It's not me and not (I think) half my friends. Are all the nonvolunteers on the East Coast offset by the fact that everyone in Illinois, Iowa and Idaho volunteers?" Statistics, he's reminding us, need a reason for being, need a point to illustrate, need a validity.

Janet Norwood, while commissioner of the U.S. Bureau of Labor Statistics, said, "Increasingly, this country is becoming a country which is actually run by the numbers," numbers collected by her people and countless other government agencies, by scientists and money people and so forth, numbers that determine public policy, numbers that are passed along by journalists to the various interested publics out there.

She cited a 10 percent unemployment figure, a level at which certain benefits are made available by law. Those benefits are not activated at 9.9 percent, but only kick in at 10 percent. Yet, statistically, she says, 9.9 percent and 10.1 are not significantly different. If her bureau played games with such statistical insignificance, it could at 9.9 percent save the government millions of dollars while creating additional hardships for many victims of the economy, or it could at 10 or 10.1 percent cost the government a bundle while helping those same unemployed. And would we as journalists know enough to point out the problem? Would we question closely enough to discover it?

What do statistics mean?

If you use them, be sure to find out and pass along the meaning. What rigidity of meaning comes with statistics?

If you use them, be sure you know before you attempt to make numerical truth out of what may be merely numerical fact.

These cautions should not, however, dissuade you from using statistics if they serve you and your story and your reader.

Take, for example, the figure one billion. Add the word seconds to it, and you can tell your reader that one billion seconds ago Dwight Eisenhower was in the first term of his Presidency and Earl Warren was chief justice of the Supreme Court. Then change seconds to minutes, and tell your reader that one billion minutes ago Nero had just burned down Rome and Jesus had died on the cross fifty years earlier. Then change minutes to hours, and tell your reader that one billion hours ago people lived in caves and the first written language lay one hundred thousand years in the future. Then change hours to dollars, and tell your reader that in terms of government expenditures, one billion dollars has been spent just since last night.

Apples and oranges, the purists will say. Yet those statistics take on a meaning more powerfully than other collectible facts – if the purpose of your article is to point out how swiftly (for better or worse) our government uses funds.

You can, with numbers, make an editorial point. Peter Navarro, a researcher at Harvard, did so with another, still more astronomical figure – the trillion dollars that the Federal government, by estimate, spent on military affairs between 1986 and 1990. Navarro told us that one trillion dollars in thousand dollar bills would stretch to the moon and back several times. So what, you might respond. But more tellingly, he advised in an article for *USA Today*, the cost of one trillion dollars is:

- One thousand new hospitals, 500,000 new schools, and – not or – 500,000 new factories.
- Or, it's a free college education for every U.S. child, a new car for every eligible driver, or a year's worth of groceries for every U.S. family.
- Or, it's enough to completely rebuild our bridge and highway system, provide free mass transit for a year to every major city, or put an additional $4,000 in every person's pocket to do with as he or she pleases.

Use numbers with purpose. Use them honestly, too.

Hugh Sidey in his syndicated newspaper column praised Tennessee Sen. Howard Baker's stamina and good sense for deciding to drop out of the race for the Republican Presidential nomination: "He gave it a whirl and a good one. One of the nice young ladies in his staff figured out that the senator had been through forty-three states, 347 counties, 155½ Holiday Inns, three of Arthur Adler's best suits, 197 chicken wings, and 1,324 Rolaids. There is a story around this city that after the Massachusetts primary, Baker sat down and figured out that he had drunk more cans of Tab while campaigning than he had gotten votes. He got the message — from his alimentary canal if from no other place." That's an effective use of statistics.

So is Larry Keith's, in his March 3, 1979 *Sports Illustrated* article, "Not Only a Game of Inches." Keith writes about a peewee shortstop for the Chicago White Sox:

> In a world where bigger is presumed to be better, shortness has never had much of a following. Shortcomings are failures, short circuits cut off the electricity and short odds do not pay big money. Consider the undesirability of being short-lived, short-tempered, shortsighted and shorthanded. Who wants to be sold short, shortchanged, short of breath or waited on shortly? Indeed, who among us wants to be short?
>
> Well, Harry Chappas does. He has been short all his life, though *how* short is now under dispute, and as far as Chappas is concerned, it's no big deal. In his twenty-one years, Chappas has heard all the jokes, endured all the insults and, along the way, converted nearly all the skeptics.
>
> Chappas is a switch-hitting rookie shortstop with the Chicago White Sox. As this year's rookie crop is judged, Chappas is something less than a phenom but something more than a prospect. The White Sox are giving Chappas a long — not short — look because last season he hit .302 and stole sixty bases for their Class A affiliate in Appleton, Wisconsin, and then hit .267 and handled ninety-two chances without an error in twenty games with Chicago in September.
>
> White Sox President Bill Veeck feels that Chappas has many of the qualities — defense, speed, a high on-base percentage at the top of the batting order and ticket-selling pizzazz — that the team so obviously lacked in 1978. Chappas could be particularly appealing to Chicago's large Greek community: both his mother Valli (five feet) and the parents of his father Perry (5'7") were born in Sparta. If it all works out, Comiskey Park may become Parthenon West, and souvlaki will be a big seller for the concessionaires.
>
> The promotional value of a very short shortstop has not been lost on Veeck (6'½"), who is to baseball what P.T. Barnum (6'2") was to the circus. Barnum had Tom Thumb (3'4"), and Veeck had Eddie Gaedel (3'7"), the midget who pinch-hit for Veeck's St. Louis Browns twenty-eight years ago. Gaedel's career began and ended with a walk. The wily Veeck imagines a lot of walks for Chappas — and a lot of customers looking on.

For the remainder of the article, every time a person is mentioned, so — in parentheses — is his height. The author makes clever use of a device. Not only that, but his compilation of commonly shared beliefs about shortness adds gusto to the story.

Always take statistics seriously. But sometimes don't take them too seriously. In "Fear of Fattening," Jim Krohe, writing in the *John Deere Journal* (December 1981), said:

> It is hard to get a handle on America's fat problem. If it is true (as some surveys indicate) that eighty-eight million Americans are overweight, and if

one assumes that each of them tips the scales an average of fifteen pounds over his ideal weight, then the amount of excess weight in the U.S. totals 1.32 billion pounds. That's really a gross national product. It's been estimated, perhaps unreliably, that if all the excess weight in the U.S. could be burned, it could light the cities of Chicago, Boston, San Francisco, and Washington, D.C. So far the Department of Energy has not figured out how to do this, but OPEC is a little nervous, just in case they do.

Look for the unusual, as journalists are supposed to. So, when you see a list circulating in Washington that says . . .

Lord's Prayer: 56 words.
Twenty-third Psalm: 118 words.
Gettysburg Address: 226 words.
Ten Commandments: 297 words.
United States Department of Agriculture order on the price of cabbage: 15,629 words.

. . . then know you have a story. And it's all in the numbers.

DON'T BE EASILY SATISFIED

Be creative in your exposition. That's the challenge. That's what editors look for, along with accuracy, brevity, and clarity—those journalistic A-B-Cs. Be creative, as when James Trefil, professor of physics at George Mason University, introduced his *Smithsonian* article, "Quantum Physics' World: Now You See it, Now You Don't." He wrote:

Some people have it easy. When their kids ask them what they do at work, they can give a simple, direct answer: "I put out fires" or "I fix sick people" or "I do arbitrage." As a theoretical physicist, I never had this luxury. Society has come to expect many things from physicists. It used to be that we only had to discover the basic laws that govern the world and supply the technical breakthroughs that would fuel the next Silicon Valley. With these expectations we were fairly comfortable: they involve the sorts of things we think we know how to do. What bothers us—and what makes it hard for us to tell our kids what we're up to—is that in this century we have become, albeit unwillingly, gurus on philosophical questions such as "What is the nature of Reality?"

We now deal with a whole new class of problems. We ask how the Universe began and what is the ultimate nature of matter. The answers we are coming up with just do not lend themselves to simple explanations.

In the good old days we could explain Sir Isaac Newton's clockwork Universe by making analogies with things familiar to everyone. And if the math got a little complicated, that was all right: it gave a certain panache to the whole enterprise. But those days are gone forever. How is a physicist supposed to find a simple way of explaining that some of his colleagues think our familiar world is actually embedded in an eleven-dimensional Universe? Or that space itself is curved and expanding? The math is still there; the theories are as coherent as they ever were. What's missing is the link between those theories and things that "make sense" — things the average person can picture. This leads to a situation where it's easy for anyone to ask questions that can't be answered without recourse to mathematics, such as my all-time least favorite: "Well, if the Universe is really expanding, what is it expanding *into*?"

Trefil understood his readers, mostly intelligent nonscientists, and because he understood, those readers undoubtedly began to understand what quantum physics is all about.

Matters of science and medicine, of economics and legal theory require exposition that makes complex concepts and facts assimilable. The editors of *Popular Science*, in their guide to writing articles for the publication, offer excellent advice:

A properly done *Popular Science* article is intensely journalistic. Occasionally a writer makes the mistake of assuming that since we deal with technical subjects, we publish articles similar to those in technical and trade journals. *We do not.* Our articles are journalism; they exist to inform the reader and thus must present material in a clear, logical way so that it is easily accessible. *But they must also do it in such an interesting way that the reader is drawn into the story and feels compelled to keep reading.*

Think about it from this point of view. When you as a writer go out to see someone working on a project or doing research, you will find that he is usually very excited about what he is doing and interested in telling you about it. Generally, you will become intrigued, fascinated, and excited yourself. It's your job to convey that sense of excitement to the reader. You must report not only the basic information about the project and what has been accomplished, but something of the sense of excitement that you experienced as well. Your job is to take the reader on a vicarious trip with you and let him see and feel and touch and smell the things you did. Remember, the reader may never have been in a laboratory, or at least not the one you are visiting. It's a new and different world for him, and he should experience it the way you did. *Show* him, do not *tell* him, what you saw. Do not explain what is going on. Describe it. Use narrative to report what happened. If, for example, there was an interesting demonstration, tell about it in narrative form with plenty of description and quotes. Give him a word picture. Remember, you are taking the reader on a journey with you. Use first-person reaction freely. Record what you did, what you saw, and your reaction to it. That helps make it come alive for the reader.

Richard Rhodes, a prominent writer about matters scientific, says: "You assume, in writing a magazine article, that the reader doesn't know. You explain, describe, list, draw analogies. By itself that would or could be boring — certainly the writing of it is boring — but that's just one layer, and it's required. Another layer is drama: plot, character, action, surprise, reversal, climax, end. The beginning of the story is almost always drama more than information, the middle is information more than drama, the end is drama again."

Let's end this chapter with an expository example. John Poppy, a health columnist for *Esquire*, authored "The Chemistry of Love" (May 1989). As a sidebar, he analyzed what drugs do to the body. Complicated material. Poppy has considered his audience and written to it, perhaps a little up to it, but certainly not down to it. "The Drug Trap" is effective.

When you're living a good life, your body is exquisitely balanced, producing the right amount of specific chemical substances at the right time to arouse you, relax you, reduce pain, produce feelings of pleasure, or fortify the immune system. Drugs can do some of the same things, but only temporarily — and only by laying a nasty trap.

The opiates, for example. Those you produce inside, the endorphins, soothe you and please you. So do opiates you get from outside, such as the morphine in heroin. The difference is that external opiates are not always available to you, whereas internal ones are — until you mess with the system. Under normal conditions, your body produces a steady supply of endorphins that are stored in nerve cells, against the times when they're needed to balance the chemicals of arousal that make you jumpy and tense — adrenaline and cortisol, for instance. The minute you stick an opiate in from outside, you signal your body to slack off the production of opiates inside. Meanwhile, it keeps on producing flight-or-fight chemicals. The result: just to keep things in balance, you depend on ever-increasing amounts of a drug from outside.

Simply put, when you take in a drug from outside, your brain attempts to *adapt* to it. A drug molecule either mimics the effects of a molecule that the body makes itself or blocks its effects. It does so by occupying a "receptor" site on the surface of a brain cell, much as a key fits into a lock. The receptor is a complicated molecule itself that can be an on-off valve. Slightly different molecules may compete for the same receptor. One may turn things on (an *agonist*) and the other may turn them off (an *antagonist*). When the one that fits most tightly bumps the other one off, its effect is the one you feel.

Caffeine, nicotine, and other external stimulants play the flip side of the opiates. Caffeine is suspected of speeding up the release of adrenaline. When adrenaline kicks in, the brain normally buffers it with other substances, particularly one called adenosine, that promote tranquillity and relaxation. Caffeine has a second effect, though: it is a potent antagonist to adenosine. A short-term result of too much coffee can be a jag of anxiety, even panic. A long-run result seems to be that the adrenal glands get lazy, the adenosine is still waiting in the wings, and you need repeated jolts of caffeine (or nicotine, or last-minute deadlines, or whatever upper you use) to feel normal.

Similarly, Valium, which is not an opiate, seems to do its work mainly as an antagonist, by blocking a naturally occurring peptide, diazepam-binding inhibitor (DBI), which makes you alert and nervous. Snatch the block out of receptors that have been clogged with it for a long time, and the resulting rush of DBI can make you crazy.

Whatever happens, the brain tries to keep things stable. It works for homeostasis. A drug coming in from outside can trick it into signaling a cut in production of your body's own form of that drug; or a boost of its antagonist; or both. Either way, the brain is doing its best to tamp down the effects of the drug and restore stability. Everything in the brain is interlinked, so one reaction affects others, cascading across entire systems in a profusion of yin-yang effects, with peaks on one side and valleys on the other. When you push your brain and body past their ability to match peaks with valleys, you run the risk of addiction, and possibly death. As with any trap, you're better off not putting your foot in it.

10

Additional Techniques — Compression and Fictionalization

JANUARY 1940

Swift had pains in his head.
Johnson dying in bed
Tapped the dropsy himself.
Blake saw a flea and an elf.
. . . .
Donne, alive in his shroud,
Shakespeare, in the coil of a cloud,
Saw death very well as he
Came crab-wise, dark and massy.
I envy not only their talents
And fertile lack of balance
But the appearance of choice
In their sad and fatal voice.

— Roy Fuller

What a collection Roy Fuller pieced together to make a point about envy and about greatness in eccentricity in "January 1940" (in shortened form here). He has compressed information. He has carefully lumped his poets. Into a small space Fuller has gathered a heavy dosage of material, and all to leave one thought with the reader.

Such clustering of information — as you develop exposition — offers a way to impress the reader with the scope of a subject. *National Geographic*'s extended article about Chicago included this paragraph, an excellent example of the technique:

> This is the city that has given you everything from the first self-sustaining nuclear chain reaction . . . to Sara Lee cakes; from the Encyclopedia Britannica, the Great Books of the Western World, and World Book to *Playboy* and *Ebony*; from the McCormick reaper and the Pullman car to the zipper and the modern lie detector; from the prototype skyscraper and the first cafeteria to the great mail-order catalog firms (Sears, Montgomery Ward, Spiegel);

from Schwinn bicycles to Zenith TV's and Motorola radios to Wrigley's gum, Quaker Oats, International Harvester, Household Finance, Hart Schaffner and Marx, and—amid a plethora of other American household phrases—McDonald's hamburgers.

If you know and love Chicago, you may react negatively. You may say that this particular lumping overstates the materialistic and underestimates the spiritual and cultural aspects of a complex metropolis. Agreed, but then this is but a single paragraph in an article of considerable length. Other sections give proper attention to the city's other strengths. What this paragraph does is to introduce commerce, and to do so impressively.

Such a compressed verbal picture requires that the author have thorough knowledge of the subject, in this case Chicago. Otherwise, the material selected might distort through overplay or underplay.

Fred Ferretti, feature writer for *The New York Times* (October 28, 1983), used lumping to reeducate his readers about a borough of the city of New York:

> For many New Yorkers, Queens is a place to go through to get somewhere else, like the airport, for instance, to go to another country. But in this, the country's 300th anniversary year, Queens would like you to know that not only is it home to the Mets and Jets, but also to the only Dravidian-style Hindu temple in North America, perhaps the best Greek cooking outside of Athens, the birthplace of Quakerism in America, a scale model of New York City that includes 835,000 buildings and every street in the five boroughs, a collection of Chinese art in the only Peking-style building in the city, the heart of the city's growing Korean community, Civil War fortifications, a weeping beech tree that is an official city landmark, a protected wildlife preserve filled with herons, geese and migrating ducks, sixteen thousand acres of parkland and a major museum, not to mention Governor Cuomo's brick house.
>
> Queens is a large and irregular borough, stretching between Brooklyn and the Nassau County border, and it encompasses one-third of the city's total land area, two million of its people, what many people believe to be the best pastrami sandwich in the city, the city's only race track, one of the largest motion-picture sound stages in the world (where Francis Ford Coppola happens to be working now), some reasonably good Chinese restaurants and more beachfront than you can walk in a day.

How much that tells us about Queens. Ferretti collected facts: stray yet fitting, far-ranging and yet unifying.

Charles Lockwood and Christopher Leinberger took notice that "Los Angeles Comes of Age" in an article of depth for *The Atlantic Monthly* (January 1988). They used compression to begin their piece, blending mythology and reality in their gathered facts:

> Los Angeles conjures up a myriad of images: a city dominated by show business, where businessmen take meetings beside swimming pools and

don't wear ties to the office; a palm-shaded city where blond young men surf their days away at the beach; a city of transplanted midwesterners who ignore the threat of the next earthquake; an intellectually and culturally vapid city where many residents worship rampant materialism while others pursue various forms of self-realization with equally intense preoccupation; a city with no downtown — a sprawling amoeba of unending stretches of suburban tract houses, connected by more freeways than exist anywhere else in America.

Whatever their suitability for jokes on late-night talk shows, these images of Los Angeles no longer tell anything like the whole story. Within the past decade greater Los Angeles has undergone economic, social, political, and cultural upheavals deeper and broader than those experienced by any other large American city during the same period.

Once a prosperous but provincial regional metropolis, greater Los Angeles has become America's true "second city" — second only to New York in economical power and cultural influence. And Los Angeles rivals New York in attracting ambitious people who want to make it, in almost every professional endeavor and field of business. If present trends continue, and if certain nagging problems don't overwhelm the metropolitan area, Los Angeles might even emerge as the Western Hemisphere's leading city in the early twenty-first century.

Again, we get a picture, one we're asked to see as the writers saw the city. This compression is their interpretation of Los Angeles. It certainly prepares us for what comes next, an exploration of the growth, problems, trend setting, and likely future of this sprawling urban area.

What works for a place like Chicago or Queens or Los Angeles can work for people and periods of time. In *Vanity Fair* (June 1989), Stephen Schiff acquaints us with "The Secret Life of John Le Carré," master of the spy story. In a masterful bit of compression, Schiff brings the reader close to contact with the novelist:

He is at once a confirmed recluse and a social dazzler, a serious artist and a reliable manufacturer of best-sellers, a punctilious puritan and a twinkle-eyed swiller of numberless midday vodkas, none of which ever causes the slightest slur or stumble. He is, in short, dual, paradoxical, a double agent bristling with secrets and surprise. He even has two names: David Cornwell, the one he was born with and still goes by, and John Le Carré, the one he invented to grace the covers of his novels, among them *The Spy Who Came In from the Cold; Tinker, Tailor, Soldier, Spy; Smiley's People; The Little Drummer Girl;* and *A Perfect Spy*. What does one do with such a bundle of contradictions?

Mostly, one walks.

For Roger Rosenblatt of *Time*, it was a period of human history that mattered. The publication was celebrating sixty years of covering the world scene (1983, Special 60th Anniversary Issue). Rosenblatt's compression made one realize afresh the import of those decades:

At least one may say with confidence that it has been quite a time. Ride through these sixty years as through an amusement park tunnel. They're playing Gershwin, Stravinsky, *I Want to Hold Your Hand*. From hidden cabinets in the dark lurch Stalin. Nixon. De Gaulle. Ben-Gurion. Mao. Initials cover the walls: W.P.A., P.L.O., F.D.R., I.R.A., NATO, O.A.S., L.S.M.F.T. Observe the tableaux: Gandhi on his salt march. Einstein in his study, the bodies in Auschwitz, the bodies in Biafra. James Joyce complaining that World War II will interfere with the reception of *Finnegans Wake*. John Kennedy riding in an open car. "The only thing we have to fear is fear itself." "We shall fight on the beaches." "We shall overcome." Lucky Lindy. The Lindbergh Law. Guernica is bombed. Guernica is painted. Cuba si. Yanqui no. Ladies and gentlemen. Mr. Charles Chaplin. Dr. Jonas Salk. Mr. Joe McCarthy. Mr. Al Capone. Oppenheimer staring at the desert. "One giant leap for mankind." "Oh, the humanity."

Half-forgotten names recur as at a class reunion. Nkrumah. Nguyen Cao Ky. Bulganin. I.G. Farben. Lord Beaverbrook. U Thant. Ben Bella. Cardinal Mindszenty. Do you recall that Patty Hearst was known as "Tania"? Does the name Sherry Finkbine mean anything to you? Frank Wills? It is hard to believe that we danced till we dropped, perched on flagpoles, swallowed all those goldfish, streaked, twisted, marched, sat in, dropped out, rioted, fought, wept. The places we have been: Woodstock. Suez. Dresden. My Lai. Beirut. Johannesburg. Keep cool with Coolidge. I like Ike. Brother, can you spare a dime?

This picture of parts reveals a truth larger than those parts. And that is your opportunity with such visionary and vista-widening compression.

Fictionalization is another technique you can make use of. Writers turn to the method sometimes in an effort either to universalize a subject or to heighten impact. Let's imagine we're doing an article about cabdrivers. For information gathering we'd order cabs and ride in them. We'd talk to cabbies young and old, thin and not so, crabby and cheerful, men and women, native born and foreign born, ear-benders and silent cusses. We'd attempt to find out what they think, what their days are like, how they live, what their families think, what they do after the long driving hours, whether they take busmen's holidays, how they care for their vehicles, what heavy traffic does to their tempers.

We'd then look through all this material. And we'd decide perhaps to build our story around a typical cabdriver, bringing in along the way the comments of others, the problems of the many, the peculiar approach toward work of a few. Our notes we find helpful; they're full of morsels. Still, we discern no one fellow or woman who fits as our subject within a subject. So, instead, we decide to make up a cabdriver, a fictional character. We build him based on personalities and comments and actions of our real cabbies. As we sit down to write, we make sure that somehow the article indicates that this is fiction, and yet not so. Although it's a make-believe cabbie, he is made of fleshy-bloody-head-unbowed-despite-the-rigors-of-the-day cabbies.

If that's clear to the reader, and if a taxi driver who later reads the story can react with, "That's the way it is," then fine. Fictionalization is a legitimate, if potentially dangerous, technique. It should be used rarely, and only if other methods don't work as well, and only if you, as writer, know how to handle it.

Malcolm Brown used fictionalization as a way of introducing us to the problem of computer trespassing. Written for *Discover* (November 1983), "Locking Out the Hackers" begins with fiction signifying fact:

> *It is night, and the scene is a teenager's cluttered bedroom. For hours its occupant has been dialing telephone numbers and listening for the high-pitched tone that tells him he has reached the automatic answering device of some distant computer. Finally, one responds in a way that seems interesting. With his own desktop computer connected to the telephone line, the boy stares at his video monitor as he taps letters, numbers, and symbols on his keyboard. Dissatisfied with the result, he tries again and again, until . . .*
>
> *A thousand miles away, a computer system tucked inside a guarded building answers the student's keyboard doodling. Within seconds, the computer opens the floodgates of more than twenty Tennessee Valley Authority dams scattered over an area nearly the size of England, and walls of water come roaring down over farms, roads, and towns.*

That particular nightmare galvanized TVA officials a decade ago, after a systems expert told them that their computers system was dangerously vulnerable to penetration by outsiders. The TVA quickly closed its loophole, but in the years since then, troublesome, expensive, and dangerous breaches of computer security have spread across the land.

Note how Brown and the editors have set off the pieces of fiction. It's set in italics. And immediately after its conclusion Brown said, "That particular nightmare . . . ." Fiction must be clearly identified as fiction. Then you're on safe ground.

Charles Smith, a technology writer for *TWA Ambassador*, discussed "Microchip Medicine" (April 1986), revealing its potential in an article-opening piece of fiction:

> A mother is awakened in the middle of the night by the cry of her baby boy. When she goes to comfort the infant, he is flushed and fiery. She fetches a thermometer to take his temperature, and at the same time switches on her personal computer and activates a medical-care program. The family has kept computerized records of the baby's medical background, so there is quite a supply of information immediately at hand to help them assess the significance of tonight's fever — information concerning the child's history of allergies, medications, and recurring conditions requiring specific treatment.
>
> When the mother enters the temperature data, certain diagnostic questions appear on the screen. Is the infant teething? Coughing? Breaking out in a rash? Is there any vomiting or diarrhea? Has the child been feeding normally? Does he have a runny nose or discharge from the eyes? Given the mother's answers, the computer determines the nature and severity of the

baby's sickness and recommends what action to take, typically one of three things: call the child's doctor, bundle up the child and head for the hospital, or give the child an over-the-counter fever-reducing medicine and re-evaluate the situation in the morning. The mother types in a query asking if she should give the child aspirin. Immediately a warning flashes on the screen. In this situation, aspirin could have dangerous side effects; better use some other medication.

A half-hour later mother and child are sleeping peacefully. Without calling the family physician, without making a middle-of-the-night dash to the nearest emergency room, without even cracking a copy of Dr. Spock, the mother has received helpful medical consultation that has enabled her to ease the child's discomfort and prevent a bad situation from becoming worse.

The scenario is imaginary, but one day it may well be real. Computer use in diagnosis and treatment has already become routine at many hospitals, and the home market for high-tech medical advice is bound to be developed before long.

Here the word "scenario" serves as label.

If you enhance reality or if, as in the above, you deal with a likely future, fictionalization can be useful.

Ernest Lehman, a columnist for *American Film*, used fiction differently. After watching all those Academy Award shows, he spun a yarn that compresses the feelings that every winner must have experienced. None of this happened, and yet all of it has happened. Lehman achieves truth through fiction in this "Lehman at Large" column entitled "And the Winner Is . . ."

It's too nerve-racking.

You start writing acceptance speeches in your head the day they announce the nomination.

Who should I thank?

Why should I thank *him*? Why should I thank *her*? The *hell* with them, they should thank *me*. If it hadn't been for *me*, there wouldn't have even been a *picture*. I'll be damned if I'm going to give *them* credit for *anything*. Let them win their *own* Oscars. And if they do, they better thank *me*. They better, or they'll be marked lousy in this town. I'll see to that.

Who should I thank?

Better thank *everybody*. Don't leave *anyone* out. The more people you thank, the better you look. Isn't he marvelous? What humility. What generosity. *Listen* to him. None of that "I did it all myself" crap. Thank everybody. They'll love you for it. They'll respect you for it. Remember this: The Oscar isn't important. Winning isn't everything. It's the *acceptance* speech that counts.

God, I'm so pale. I'll look awful on television. Better use makeup. Makeup? What'll people think? What people? The people sitting next to you in the theater. They'll see *makeup* on your face. Look at *him*, they'll say. He's wearing *makeup*. OK, so I *won't* wear makeup. I'm not going to have people *staring* at me all night for one lousy Oscar. I'll go to *Palm Springs* for a week, that should do it. A week in Palm Springs. A beautiful tan. I'll look great up there.

But how can I get away for a week? I can't drop everything just like that. I can't leave everyone high and dry just because I'm going to win an Oscar. But I'm so pale. What'll I do? Those lights are deadly. Those cameras are merciless. I can't go up there looking *sick*. *Look* at him, they'll say. He must be *very ill*. I'll buy a sunlamp. In *California*? You're gonna use a sunlamp in *California*? Well, what *else* can I do? It's the *rainy* season. I'll buy an expensive sunlamp and I'll go up there looking terrific. It's worth it. It's *worth* the five hundred.

What'll I wear?

What do you *mean*, what'll you wear? You'll wear your tuxedo, that's what you'll wear. You'll wear the black velvet jacket and the black worsted trousers and the Turnbull & Asser shirt and the black velvet tie and the patent leather shoes with the silk bows on them. But I wore that *last* year. So what? Are you supposed to throw a thousand dollars' worth of evening clothes away every time you wear them? No, but *I* can't go up there in *old clothes*. What'll people think?

They won't even *know*. They're too busy worrying about how *they* look. You think they're gonna say, Look at him, he's wearing the same thing he wore last year? Yes, that's *exactly* what they're gonna say. And they're gonna say he's in trouble. Oscar or no Oscar *he's in trouble*. Who needs *that*? You know this town. No one wants to go *near* anyone who smells like he's in trouble. You'd have to be *crazy* to go up there and *advertise* that you're too broke or too cheap to buy a new tuxedo.

So *buy* one then, and stop all the inner turmoil. You haven't done any work in two weeks now just *thinking* about it.

I *haven't* been thinking about it for two weeks.

Well then what *have* you been thinking about?

I've been thinking about my *car*.

Your *car*? What's wrong with your *car*? It's beautiful. It drives like a dream. It looks brand-new.

Yeah? Well it *isn't* brand-new. It's three years old.

So what?

I can't drive up to the grandstand in front of the theater and have all those cheering people see me step out of a *three-year-old car*.

What do *you* care? Those people are just fans. They're just the *public*. After going to the movies every week, they probably can't afford a *bus* ride. You think they'll know your car is three years old?

You're damn right they will. And so will Rona Barrett when she comes up to me with her microphone. The first thing she'll say to me is, When did you start collecting old cars? *I* know *her*. And when I drive up to the Governors' Ball after the awards, I can see the paparazzi positively *blinding* me with their flashbulbs and climbing all over each other to get a shot of this guy with the sunlamp tan in the old tuxedo getting out of an old car with a brand-new Oscar in his hands, and all the tourists and film buffs and autograph hounds *crushing* the police to get a closer look at this *strange apparition* which is *me*. No sirree, *I'm* gonna hire a chauffeur-driven limousine for the evening. *I* know they're all gone by now, but there's a black-market outfit where you can get one for only seventy-five dollars an hour provided you take it for a minimum of ten hours, and it's *worth* it. It's worth *anything* to feel confident and secure, to *know* that when you pull up in front of the cheering crowds in the bleachers, and Rona Barrett comes up to you with her microphone, the first thing she'll say is, When did you start collecting old limousines?

The table. Who am I gonna have at my table? Why does it have to be *my* table? Why can't I be at someone *else's* table? Why do I have to spend a thousand dollars, or is it *ten* thousand dollars, just because I'm in the Oscar derby? Well, if the nominees and winners didn't buy tables, who *would*? It's your *responsibility. I* didn't ask for this responsibility. *I* didn't ask to be nominated. Well, you *voted* for yourself, didn't you? Yes, but what's *one* vote? Why can't the *studio* heads buy all the tables? They're not *that* busy packing.

You're avoiding the question. *Who* are you going to have at your table? The question is, Who do I want to *be* with? Not my close friends, *that's* for sure. They all voted against me. Acquaintances? Why should I spend a thousand dollars, or is it *ten* thousand, on *them*? How about your enemies? Never, I can't afford that many tales. So *wander* all night. Wander from table to table accepting congratulations from old friends and acquaintances, and no one will ever know that you didn't even have a place to sit.

Oh, yes, she will. Rona Barrett will know. The very next morning, she'll ask me, right at the beginning of her broadcast, When did you start collecting old friends and acquaintances?

One thing I know for sure, I'm not going to take a *single ad* in the trades. *Nobody* is going to be able to say I *bought* the Oscar. Not *me*. Sure, everyone *else* will. Especially in my category. It's absolutely disgusting. They'll spend a fortune blowing their own horns, not giving a damn *what* the voters will think of them. They'll think: Say, they must be *good* if they're willing to spend that kind of money on themselves. *Me*? I know what they'll think. They'll think: He must be in trouble, he can't even afford one lousy ad, he'll probably show up at the awards in an old tuxedo and a three-year-old car, *that's* what they'll think. You better take an ad. But how can I word it so it doesn't look like my ad? You could ask a close friend to do it *for* you. A close *who*? The hell with ads. They don't do any good anyway. Your best hope is that your competitors have more close friends than you do.

Suppose I forget my speech?

You haven't even written it yet, how can you forget it?

Well, suppose I finally figure out who to thank and who not to thank and how to say something so goddamn clever that they'll remember the speech long after the picture is forgotten, even longer than Eva Marie's "I may have the baby right here," suppose I do all that and then I go up there and forget the whole thing?

So you'll say thank you and get off, like you should.

Thank you? That's *all*? *Thank you*? Can you *picture* the seething, burning, bitter resentment that night when they return home from the Governor's Ball and start undoing their ties and corsets and gowns and cummerbunds? Did you hear him? Did you *hear* him? Can you *believe* it? After all I did for him. He doesn't even *mention* me. *Thank* you, he says. The son of a bitch. I'll get him.

Don't listen to all this talk about an Oscar boosting your career. Just memorize your acceptance speech or write it on the back of your hand and remember to thank *everybody* because today's propman is tomorrow's chairman of the board, and it won't hurt you a bit if you trip on the stairs going up to the stage and fall flat on your face because *that* they'll remember long after they've forgotten your next five flops.

But it's too nerve-racking.

Thank God I'm not up for anything this year.

Dammit.

11

Behind Some Words Essential Concepts Throb—How to Add Thrust and Depth to Your Work

Time is
Too Slow for those who Wait,
Too Swift for those who Fear,
Too Long for those who Grieve,
Too Short for those who Rejoice,
*   But for those who Love*
*   Time is not.*

—Henry Van Dyke

These I Have Loved:
White plates and cups, clean-gleaming,
ringed with blue lines; and feathery, faery dust;
Wet roofs, beneath the lamp-light; the strong crust
Of friendly bread; and many-tasting food;
Rainbows; and the blue bitter smoke of wood;
And radiant raindrops couching in cool flowers;
And flowers themselves, that sway through sunny hours,
Dreaming of moths that drink them under the moon;
Then, the cool kindliness of sheets, that soon
Smooth away trouble; and the rough male kiss
Of blankets; grainy wood; live hair that is
Shining and free; blue-massing clouds; the keen
Unpassioned beauty of a great machine;
The benison of hot water; furs to touch;
The good smell of old clothes; and other such—
The comfortable smell of friendly fingers,
Hair's fragrance, and the musty reek that lingers
About dead leaves and last year's ferns.

—Rupert Brooke

Van Dyke's words freshen a truth: that we view from within; we react as individuals; we bring to any scene or situation our own perspective.

Brooke's beloved lines are so because his chosen images reflect on our own experiences; the words reverberate; they resonate.

SOME MAGIC WORDS

Perspective and resonance are two words you, as a writer, should remember, not merely as words but as representations of possibilities and practices which can enhance your work. So are anticipation, context, and zoom. Let's take them alphabetically.

Anticipation

Magazine journalism is anticipatory journalism. Editors work ahead. They bring their staffs together for annual planning sessions to determine content, particularly of major articles, as far ahead as possible. That's to give writers and photographers and artists more lead time. That's to assure that primary issues and events and personalities will be covered and included.

That's also to get a story ready for when the reader will be most interested in its content. An article about an ice hockey star should run when the season opens, a travel piece when readers are most likely to plan their vacations.

Editors work at becoming seers, not always easy or even possible in our fast-changing era. But it's their job, and the more successful they are at it, the more satisfied the magazine's readers will be.

If you would market your articles, you need to gain that sense of the developing future, too. You must strive to be timely or, at least, timeless. So teach yourself to be sensitive to what's ahead, to what will be on the reader's mind six or eight months from now, to what people will be doing or talking about when the article is published. Anticipate.

Context

The context is the background or environment. The dictionary considers context to be "the parts of a discourse that surround a word or passage and can throw light on its meaning," and also "the interrelated conditions in which something exists or occurs."

Context suggests the import of content, or at least gives it meaning. Supply context. Editors consider context a form of depth coverage. In magazines readers expect that extra dimension.

A Nicholas Lemann commentary for *The Washington Post National Weekly* (May 24, 1984) offers context through two carefully selected quotes. There's a hint of message in the title, "Up and Out: The Underclass Is Not New, and Not Hopeless," and in the deck that follows: "Blacks are just the latest turn in the cycle of urban ethnic poverty." Lemann seeks to cement the notion with contextual quotes:

> *The Irish, crowding into the cities, posed problems in housing, police and schools; they meant higher taxes and heavier burdens in the support of poorhouses and private charitable institutions. Moreover, the Irish did not seem to practice thrift, self-denial and other virtues desirable in the "worthy, laboring poor." They seemed drunken, dissolute, permanently sunk in poverty.*
> —William V. Shannon, "The American Irish," 1966

> *Hardly less aggressive than the Italian, the Russian and Polish Jew . . . is filling the tenements of the old Seventh Ward to the river front, and disputing with the Italians every foot of available space in the back alleys of Mulberry Street. The two races, differing hopelessly in much, have this in common: They carry their slums with them wherever they go, if allowed to do it . . . . The Italian and the poor Jew rise only by compulsion.*
> —Jacob Riis, "How the Other Half Lives," 1890

The present always imputes a degree of innocence to the past. One of many possible examples is our attitude toward the underclass, which is, essentially, that no similar social problem has ever existed in urban America—and that therefore the problem can't be solved. An ethnic group living in isolated slums in the very heart of our prosperous cities; fatal disease spreading as a result of irresponsibly licentious behavior; rampant welfare dependence; out-of-control violent crime; abuse of lethal intoxicants; rampaging youth gangs; rich, swaggering criminals who sit atop the society of the slum; a breakdown of family values; a barely disguised feeling among the prosperous classes that perhaps the poor are inherently not up to being fully functioning Americans—the whole picture has been around, intermittently, in this country since about 1850.

We may not agree with Lemann's view of history, but context permits us to understand what he's trying to say.

When *Newsweek* planned its twenty-years-after look at "The Summer of 1969," staffers decided readers would need to be reminded of that season's significance. Method? Context:

> It was a summer for grown-ups and for growing up. America reached its technological zenith by putting men on the moon. And began coming to terms with its earthly power by starting to retreat from Vietnam. The youth culture was ending. Woodstock was a blast, or so those not there recalled, but Haight-Ashbury had already gone to ruin. The excesses of the time led to death: The maniac Charles Manson, by his own hand, became exhibit X. Ted Kennedy behaved like a spoiled rich kid who knew Daddy could repair anything. The love that dared not speak its name came out of hiding and gave birth to a movement. And on the field of dreams, a baseball team eased our pain.

Here context has prepared the reader for what follows.

Guest columnist Evelyn Klein filled the "Seems to Me" page of

American Way (October 1984) with some anti-nostalgia. "Nostalgia buffs would have us believe," she wrote, that "once upon a time *it* was easy and now *it* is tough. Whatever *it* is." What followed is context (as well as perspective, which is next on our list of words).

> What if electricity wasn't around?
> Awake at dawn and asleep at twilight is boring. A candelabra in the window needs a caretaker, and oil lamps must have wicks trimmed and chimneys cleaned. No listening to stereos, no watching television, no reading in bed.
> I don't want to wait for the iceman to cometh; I much prefer pushing a button for cubes . . .
> Remember the time the milkman came after everyone had gone to the beach, and you came home to quarts of curds and whey?
> Don't forget. The honey wagon was part of the exalted past. There was no ignoring its stench or the infestation of flies. I give daily homage to the garbage disposal . . .

Molecular engineering, Eric Drexler's subject in "Mightier Machines from Tiny Atoms May Someday Grow" for *Smithsonian* (November 1982), has a past we need to know about before we can comprehend what's now and, even more so, what's to come:

> Coal and diamond, cancer and healthy tissue: Throughout history, the arrangement of atoms has distinguished the cheap from the cherished, disease from health. Arranged one way, atoms make soil, air and water; arranged another, they make ripe strawberries. Arranged one way, atoms make air and steel fenders; arranged another, they make rusty scrap.
> We have come far in our atom arranging, from chipping flint for arrows to machining aluminum for spaceships. We take pride in our technology, with its gleaming metal and desk-top computers. Yet for all our progress in arranging atoms, we still use primitive methods: we handle them not as individuals, but as unruly herds. Like it or not, the greatest technological revolution in history still lurks in the future.
> Today's technology builds on an ancient tradition.

Chip Brown won a National Magazine Award for his January 1988 *Esquire* piece, "The Transformation of Johnny Spain." He attempted to find out "how . . . a boy can be born white and innocent, then spend his life imprisoned as a black revolutionary." Brown investigated. He also contemplated. He investigated every facet of Spain's troubled life. He contemplated what sort of information the reader needed to be ready for Brown's verbal unspooling of that life. This is what he decided to supply:

> Long before the killings, the trials, the fantasies of revolution, Johnny Spain was a six-year-old boy who lived in a small bungalow on the south side of Jackson, Mississippi. His father, Fred, drove a beer truck; his mother, Ann, manufactured TV cabinets. He had an older brother, Charlie, a younger

sister, Lissie, a baby brother, Ray. That summer of 1955 his name was Larry Armstrong and he looked pretty much like anybody else's kid except for his hair — "nigger hair," people called it. The children in Choctaw Village liked to put their hands in it, but no barber in Jackson's white parlors would touch it.

Johnny Spain remembers a little from those days, but not much: the time Charlie, his steadfast defender, called him a nigger; the times he hid under the bed when Fred came home; when he heard his father slap his mother and holler, "Take the nigger baby and get out!" He would have entered first grade that fall were it not for his hair, and the talk and all. Even the superintendent of Jackson's public schools knew about him. Nearly twenty years would pass before children with hair like his would sit in class with whites.

Of what happened next, he recalls virtually nothing. His mother broke the news that he was going to live with a family in California, where he could attend school out of harm's way. She packed his clothes, and then the three of them, Fred and Ann and the boy, piled in the car and eventually he found himself on a train with an elderly woman. He thought his parents would turn up and take him home at any moment, but the sun went down, and morning broke over new country, and the train was streaking west. It was three days to Los Angeles. He would never forget the trestle bridges that traversed the canyons, nor the woman riding with him, but it would be years before he could understand the impact of that journey. This was the child who grew up to be Johnny Spain, the onetime Black Panther, protégé of George Jackson, and sole member of the San Quentin Six convicted of murder. And this is the central fact of his life: A long time ago he boarded a train in Mississippi as a little white boy; when he got off in California, he was black.

Context. We are given background, the origins to the tragedy that Spain's life becomes.

Perspective

Perspective is a point of view. It's a way to help a reader understand what something really means or what you, as a writer, want that something to really mean. Perspective invites the reader into your head so that two people become one in the mental and emotional approach taken toward a subject.

I think of Chief Seattle of the Puget Sound Indians when he said: "The white man must treat the beast of this land as his brothers. I am savage and do not understand any other way. I have seen a thousand rotting buffaloes on the prairie, left by the white man who shot them from a passing train. I am savage and do not understand how the smoking iron horse can be more important than the buffalo that we kill only to stay alive. What is man without the beasts? If all the beasts were gone, man would die from a great loneliness of spirit. For whatever happens to the beasts, soon happens to man. All things are connected."

That's perspective.

So is astronomer Sir Fred Hoyle's comment: "Space isn't remote at all. It's only an hour's drive away if your car could go straight upwards."

Such a quote can bring reader, writer, and subject together. In an article on heart transplants by William Boly which helped *Hippocrates* (May/June 1988) win a National Magazine Award, a recipient says "Marvelous! Astonishing!" Here's how Boly used those and other words of the man to provide perspective:

> "Marvelous! Astonishing!" declares sixty-six-year-old heart transplant recipient John Smith. "Instead of being a bunch of ashes in a vase on the mantle, here I am!" He gestures around at the family's new home near Houston, the recent snapshots of himself in a sailboat on Galveston Bay. For the irrepressible Smith, a retired officer of Army intelligence in Japan who used to moonlight by dubbing Godzilla movies into English, each day is a little miracle. A year and a half ago, his diseased heart was so weak he barely survived the flight back to the United States. Now he visits hospitals to put on magic shows for sick kids. "It's like dying and going to heaven," he says of the transplant he had at nearby Methodist Hospital. "I feel better now than I have in years. I'm desperately pleased and grateful."

Gail Regier wrote about "Users, Like Me," his memoir for *Harper's* (May 1989). It is an article approached from a particular perspective, one he wants me, the reader, to understand. Me, the nonuser. But probably a reader who uses, too.

> Profiles of typical drug users, in the newspapers and on TV, obscure the fact that many users aren't typical. I used to do coke with a violinist who was the most sheltered woman I've ever known. My mushroom connection was a fifty-year-old school-bus driver. And one of my highschool buddies, who moved $1,000 worth of drugs a day in and out of his girlfriend's tattoo shop, would always extend credit to transients and welfare moms — debts he'd let slide after a while when they weren't paid.
>
> It's easy to start thinking all users are media stereotypes: ghetto trash, neurotic child stars, mutinous suburban adolescents. Users, the media imagine, can't hold jobs or take care of their kids. Users rob liquor stores.
>
> Real users, for all their chilly scorn of the straight world, buy into the same myths, but turn them inside out. The condescension becomes a kind of snobbery: we are different from the straight people, we are special, we are more free. We are spiritual adventurers. When I was twenty-four, which was not that long ago, my friends and I thought nothing was more hip than drugs, nothing more depraved, nothing more elemental. When we were messed up, we seemed to become exactly who we were, and what could be more dangerous and splendid? Other vices made our lives more complicated. Drugs made everything simple and pure.
>
> Anyone who hangs around drugs learns not to think too much about all this, learns to watch the bent spoon in the water glass.
>
> Some of the users I knew were people with nothing left to lose. The rest of us were in it only a little for the money, more than a lot for the nights we would drive to one place after another, in and out of people's parties, looking

for a connection. It was a kind of social life, and we weren't in any hurry. What we had in common was drugs. Getting high bound us together against outsiders, gathered us into a common purpose. No one else understood us and we understood each other so well.

Russell Baker, Pulitzer Prize winning columnist for *The New York Times*, thrives on perspective. While we were busy celebrating the 100th anniversary of the Statue of Liberty, he thought about all the to-do, then penned a column (May 31, 1986) with these paragraphs included:

. . . To be frank about it, I think France has given us many things better than the Statue of Liberty.

To name just a few: ice cream, perfume, the wines of Bordeaux, pasteurization, Molière, the Impressionist painters, Balzac, Edith Piáf and most of the United States from the Mississippi River to the Rocky Mountains, also known as the Louisiana Purchase.

The Statue of Liberty is nice enough, but is it really in a class with Molière, Château Margaux or New Orleans, St. Louis, Kansas City, Des Moines, Omaha and Denver combined? As a statue, is it even in a class with the work of Rodin?

True, it was there after 1886 to welcome immigrants to New York in the era when they arrived by ship, but this can mean little to descendants of those who arrived at Boston, Philadelphia, Baltimore, New Orleans, Galveston or the Pacific Coastal ports.

And how about all those immigrants who had been arriving, some at slave ports, during the 250 years before the statue went up? To many of their white descendants Miss Liberty's words of welcome to the earth's poor and wretched could only have meant "There goes the neighborhood."

This is the cry that still goes up against the poor and wretched immigrants, like today's Haitians, despite the sentimental self-congratulation for our own tolerance that is now being generated about the forthcoming Statue of Liberty rites.

Perspective adds spice, the spice of personality. It also lets the reader know from whence you come, in terms of opinion and angle. You might be satisfied to simply offer the perspective of one or more of your informational sources, letting your reader know where they stand. But you can create your own perspective on a subject and that way lead your reader toward the sharing of a point of view.

Resonance

A quality of richness or variety, the dictionary says. "The intensification and enriching of a musical tone by supplementary vibration," the dictionary adds. Words that supplement, that vibrate, that intensify, that enrich, that bring variety to the flow of words in a publication. That's what resonance means. It's writing that jars the reader's sensibilities. Gently. Violently. It means writing that readers are likely to remember.

Fragrant writing. Evocative writing. Writing that transports the reader back or away or ahead. Writing with a feel to it.

Broadcast newsman and essayist Charles Kuralt described his vacation (quoted in *Express*, November 1981):

> I saw a moose. I saw a blue heron. I saw a bald eagle catch a fish in the Snake River. I caught a fish myself in the Snake River and held him in my hand — a rainbow in my hand — and let him go into the dark water. I saw a sunset that had in it all the same colors of the trout, let it go too in the dark.

The most elementary of narratives. It is simple. It is undecorated. It resonates.

"Smell is perhaps the strangest and most unique of all the senses," Alexander Theroux concluded in the September 1984 issue of *New Age Journal*. The novelist and travel writer had turned to the sense of smell for his subject in "The Name of the Nose." And we learn:

> You can't describe smell. It is the only one of the five senses one cannot imagine, and yet it is among them all the most evocative of the past.
>
> I think the five best smells on earth are oranges, chocolate, pipe tobacco, freshly ground coffee, and a baby's head. But there are so many — rosewater, burnt matches, Christmas trees, suntan lotion, wet sassafras chips, the hot nails and wood of houses being built, rootbeer extract, and, among the sweetest of flowers, lilacs, roses, peonies, phlox, hyacinths, and honeysuckle. Then there is the smell of someone you love. I once asked John Updike his favorite. He said "Pencil shavings."
>
> There are so many memories attached to specific smells. Marcel Proust's narrator in *Remembrance of Things Past*, dipping a madeleine into a cup of tea, caught an elusive scent of geraniums and orange blossoms and saw again his whole youth. I remember vividly the wonderful smell of my first-grade desk. When I was a boy my father used to sit me on his lap and read me the comic strips; the biscuity smell of those newspapers took my entire attention. I remember the smell of my mother ironing shirts. At school, there was the smell of sweet paste, the musk of oiled floors, the tank of books issued on the first day.

Just a list. But what a list. It evokes individual memories. Resonance.

Quiet resonance in Theroux's piece. Tom Wolfe gets noisy, as in his essay on Las Vegas reprinted in *Esquire* (from his book, *The Kandy-Kolored Tangerine-Flake Streamline Baby*, Farrer, Stuart & Geroux 1965):

> Las Vegas is the only town in the world whose skyline is made up neither of buildings, like New York, nor of trees, like Wilbraham, Massachusetts, but signs. One can look at Las Vegas from a mile away on Route 91 and see no buildings, no trees, only signs. But such signs! They tower. They revolve, they oscillate, they soar in shapes before which the existing vocabulary of art history is helpless. I can only attempt to supply names — Boomerang Modern, Palette Curvilinear, Flash Gordon Ming-Alert Spiral, McDonald's Hamburger Parabola, Mint Casino Elliptical, Miami Beach Kidney. Las Ve-

gas sign makers work so far out beyond the frontiers of conventional studio art that they have no names themselves for the forms they create. Vaughan Cannon, one of those tall, blond Westerners, the builders of places like Las Vegas and Los Angeles, whose eyes seem to have been bleached by the sun, is in the back shop of the Young Electric Sign Company out on East Charleston Boulevard with Herman Boernge, one of his designers, looking at the model they have prepared for the Lucky Strike Casino sign, and Cannon points to where the sign's two great curving faces meet to form a narrow vertical face and says:

"Well, here we are again—what do we call that?"

"I don't know," says Boernge. "It's sort of a nose effect. Call it a nose."

Okay, a nose, but it rises sixteen stories high above a two-story building. In Las Vegas no farseeing entrepreneur buys a sign to fit a building he owns. He rebuilds the building to support the biggest sign he can get up the money for and, if necessary, changes the name.

Such writing may be admired or despised, but it's hard to forget. It reverberates, vibrates, resonates.

Zoom

To zoom is "to move toward (or away from) an object rapidly so that the image appears to come closer to (or move away from) the observer; to keep the subject in focus while so doing."

Well, the writer can zoom, too. Zooming out can sometimes serve a purpose, but zooming in is usually more effective. Zooming in is your way of quickly bringing readers close to a subject, by dipping them or enveloping them in a situation or scene. The result should be to make the subject become immediately clear. Because of zoom readers should grasp what the article is about almost instantaneously.

Call it revelation.

Let's take a scene that's history as you read it, some years after the event. The characters are (1) Elie Wiesel, the previously quoted author dedicated to keeping alive the memory of the World War II holocaust which consumed six million Jews, and (2) President Ronald Reagan, whose decision to visit a German cemetery had turned from commemorative to politically troubling. A writer for *Newsweek* (April 29, 1985) used the zoom factor to begin his article. In one paragraph he condensed or collapsed or reformed the entire dilemma that a President faced at a particular moment:

His tone was respectful and gentle, but Elie Wiesel's words were devasta-ting—and Ronald Reagan, sitting just a few feet from the sad-eyed chronicler of the Holocaust, had little choice but to listen. Speaking softly and passion-ately, Wiesel delivered a moving peroration to Nazism's murdered Jews and gave thanks for the American Army's liberation of his fellow inmates at Buchenwald forty years before. He praised Reagan as a friend of Judaism and of Israel, and said he was convinced the president had not known of the presence of SS graves in the German military cemetery at Bitburg, where Reagan is scheduled to lay a memorial wreath next month. But then Wiesel, who had almost boycotted the ceremony in his honor, came to the point, sending a tremor through the White House audience and a look of anguish to Reagan's face. Now, he said, "we are all aware" of the SS graves. His voice quavering with emotion, he implored Reagan "to find another way" to commemorate Germany's suffering in the war. "That place, Mr. President, is not your place" Wiesel said. "Your place is with the victims of the SS."

In a way, nothing more need be said. The whole situation is revealed in that paragraph. But because of its power, a reader would be tempted to read on. Zoom. Instant recognition. Instant command of a President's problem.

Patricia Morrisroe had less weighty matters to deal with:

The customers are lined up on the street, waiting to get into the newest Italian restaurant on Third Avenue. Those fortunate enough to reach the bar drink Bellinis, a concoction of champagne and peach juice, and exhale cigarette smoke onto the plates of pasta on the table below. Those lucky enough to be sitting down ignore the smoke and concentrate on the aesthetics of their pumpkin-filled tortelloni in tomato cream sauce.

They can't hear one another because the restaurant's hard edges pump up the noise level. They can't move because there isn't any room—the place is the size of a Laundromat. They eat under the blinding glare of an overhead light. After forty-five minutes of waiting and fifty-five minutes of dining, they hand over eighty-five dollars and walk out the door.

"What's it like?" asks a woman who has been waiting in line outside.

"The Lexington IRT," a customer replies.

"Thanks," the woman says, elbowing her way through the door.

New Yorkers are in the grip of restaurant madness. Never before have so many people spent so much money on eating out. Popular places are jammed and *everybody* is talking about food. A New York telephone operator was recently asked the number of the Yellow Rose Cafe. "It's 595-8760," he said. "Order the pork chops."

The article, for *New York* (November 26, 1984), is titled "Sex, Exercise, and Apartment Hunting Can't Match Restaurant Madness." It's all there in that nugget. Morrisroe has zoomed in. We become privy to a slice of the big city or are reminded how we can fall victim to trends.

Candace Stewart, one of my Indiana University graduate students, shared a recipe in an article of hers:

Ingredients:

525 grams Quaker cornmeal
(about two 5-lb. boxes)
622.5 milliliters dark molasses
(about two 12-oz. bottles)
75 grams yeast

(about eleven packages)
7,500 milliliters water
(about two gallons)
45 grams Agar
90 milliliters of 95% pure alcohol
mixed with 9 grams methyl p-Hydroxybenzoate

Mix in big cooking pot and stir. Bring to full boil. Let sit for five minutes. Serves fifteen thousand

Zoom, she then explains:

There you have it—Drosophila's Delight, a feast for the flies. Common, ordinary fruit flies have to make do with overripe bananas and shriveled grapes, but the Drosophila fruit flies housed on the fifth floor of Indiana University's Jordan Hall sup on sumptuous slop prepared especially for them. While most people abhor the pests that dive bomb their fruit bowls, scientists at the Drosophila Stock Center nurture them. They breed mutant strains of the insects for genetic research.

There's drama to zoom. But there's education also. You can heighten both interest and knowledge.

Anticipation. Context. Perspective. Resonance. Zoom. Five words that can help you deepen the subject and heighten the contentment of an editor. Employed in your articles, they give readers reasons to consume your work and reasons to remember it.

12

A Couple of Case Studies

Blot out, correct, insert, refine,
Enlarge, diminish, interline;
Be mindful, when invention fails,
To scratch your head, and bite your nails.

—Jonathan Swift

The path from idea to publication can be arduous to traverse. At least part of the journey is a joint one involving both the writer and the editor. Sometimes writer and editor travel harmoniously. At other times not so.

But interaction there must be between writer and editor. Whether a writer has offered and sold a story idea to an editor or an editor has come to a writer with an assignment, the project that ensues will succeed only if writer and editor collaborate.

SITUATION ONE

We turn the spotlight first on writer James McKinley and Walter Lowe, at the time an editor at *Playboy*. The two collaborated on an investigative piece, an exposé on arson. The problem had assumed critical scope in some metropolitan areas. The project began with a phone conversation: Lowe and McKinley talking arson. That was followed by Lowe's discussion of the idea with his bosses who agreed on a go-ahead. Lowe wrote McKinley a letter of assignment. He enclosed clippings from *Playboy* files and specifics about length and payment. Then he said, and please note the guidance from a skilled editor:

> Your first task will be to do some preliminary investigation and then get back to me with a letter outlining what you see as the possible directions the story might take. The three things we don't want are an article that tries to cover the entire country arson-wise; a story that presents so many overview facts that we wind up with a repeat of a lot of previously published information; or a piece that focuses on California arson (California is due to burn up for one reason or another anyway).
> I think the story *should* include these factors:
>
> 1. A classic real-life example of the chain of collusion that goes into a big

torch job for insurance (insurance company investigators, lawyers, businessmen, criminal contacts, the torch who does the job, etc.)

2. A sense of the human misery caused by arson—the loss of life, homes, businesses (in cases where arson is used as the last resort of extortionists), and the fear that grips communities when a rampage of arson breaks out.

3. The arson business from the view of the torch—his techniques, contacts, experiences, etc. This could also be a sidebar to the main article.

4. The implication of the arson boom: What it means in terms of our attitudes toward property; its use as an urban renewal technique; the reasons for its increasing popularity as a method of obtaining quick big money; how the insurance pay-offs are used, particularly in cases where it's strictly a profit-making venture, rather than a way for a staggering businessman to recoup losses.

Above all, there should be a human, visceral feel to the article. We need to smell the smoke, see the flames shooting into the night air.

Ideally, you can dig up the kind of information that leads to indictments and investigations by law enforcement agencies.

I think the story should have a certain sense of urgency, just as if one's own house was burning down (which it one day might be).

McKinley went to work. Some particulars of his reporting activities are detailed in Chapter Thirteen. He calls investigative reporting "a painstaking process as old as journalism—a laborious, vexing but vital process of sniffing out and disclosing wrongdoings that menace society." By deadline, he turned in his copy: a long, main article accompanied by two sidebars, one based on an interview with an arsonist or "torch," the other enunciating the difficulties of probing arson. McKinley hoped, he says, the copy submitted had "the dross driven out and the materials sculpted so that the face of arson emerged clean and sharp," adding that "Clear, forceful, interesting writing helps do that since it is the concomitant of clear, forceful, interesting thinking. I tried for that kind of prose," he says, "and with 'Fire for Hire' the organizational talents of a fine editor helped achieve whatever success the article had as writing."

McKinley is a gifted writer and strong reporter who had immersed himself in a complex subject about which he obviously cared. He submitted material worthy of him and the subject, a main article and a sidebar written from the perspective of an arsonist. In so doing, he knew, of course, that the project was far from finished, that the sensitive task of editing, of refining, sharpening, targeting lay ahead. Rarely is that period of editing without bumps and bruises. Writers, quite naturally, have strong views about work they've accomplished. Editors also have strong, and frequently differing, views. Somehow, an editor must bring writer realization and editor expectation together.

The waiting editors at *Playboy* read McKinley's manuscript and reacted, having the benefit of detachment. They judged parts of the manuscript as rambling and too difficult for a reader to get through. Theories and suppositions needed to be tied down, they decided. "After the opening scene with the charred bodies, we live in an abstract limbo of copy accusations," said one.

McKinley had begun his article this way:

Well if your house catches fire
and there ain't no one around, Well if
your house catches fire, and there
ain't no water 'round, put your suitcase
by the window, better pull that shade
on down . . .

—Ian and Sylvia

The mother lies beneath the burglar-barred window leading to the fire escape. She cradles an infant in each arm. The three are charred, stiff-fired like stoneware in the last rictus of death by flame. One baby's mouth presses his mother's black breast. The other's mouth is open, caught in mid-scream. One small tooth gleams. Six feet away under the kitchen table's skeleton, are a boy and a girl, about eight and ten, hiding there they thought, and reaching for one another. Their charcoal hands now touch in last communication. Three feet farther on, three smaller children make a clump, their basted bodies fused like amber wax. Their seared skin flakes off when the firefighters, hiding their pain in gallows humor, call them Krispy Critters, and averting their eyes, put them in the body bags.

Twenty-one died in this fire in Hoboken, New Jersey. They were murdered by an arsonist. At 4:00 a.m. someone splashed gasoline in a first-floor hallway and tossed a match. Someone as yet unknown. With an unknown motive. The arsonist could have been seeking revenge on some of the twelve-in-a-room East Guyanese and Latino tenants. It's estimated at least half this nation's 200,000-plus arson-fires are set to avenge a real or imagined wrong. It could have been a pyromaniac or other twisted sort. About one in ten arsons are. Maybe a kid did it fevered by a street-punk glory, or perhaps it was someone lashing out at landlords in ghetto desperation. Vandals probably set 20 percent of the fires. But if, as is likely, this murderous blaze was part of arson's recent wildfire growth, the building's owner, or his torch, set the fire to collect insurance. Six tenements like this one went up in northern New Jersey within a month, killing over fifty people. All were insured, and if national trends hold, the owners will collect their claims, since fewer than 20 percent of the claims are rejected, arson or not. Only about 2 percent of arson incidents result in a conviction because, unlike other crimes, to prove arson you must prove both the crime (the set fire) and the criminal, the arsonist either as hired agent or owner of the structure. Even fewer convictions are returned in arson-for-profit cases, where the link between crime and criminal must be totally taut . . . .

McKinley's sidebar—about an arsonist—unfolded this way:

No article on arson would be complete without a word from the torch's mouth. Reporter McKinley found one, as he details below:

He had worked in this nice mid-American town for several years, I'd been told. He was firmly allied with the city's ruling Mafia clan, doing odd jobs for them, paper scams mostly, like running their bookmaking operation. He'd been suspected of heavier crimes, too, including arson. But although the police, FBI, Department of Justice, insurance investigators and prosecutors were sure he'd burned things, he'd never been convicted. Until recently, his official business had been running a disco, and that's where I met the man we'll call Lenny Ajax (he's more Italian than that), one morning just after closing.

Stale smoke, booze fumes, body odor and perfume hung in the air. A slick place it was, with fancy furnishings and high overhead, the sort of place that burns when business falls away, as this joint had a few months before. I told Mr. Ajax I just wanted information, not to put anybody in jail. He laughed. A federal indictment for bank fraud had landed on him three weeks before. Now he sat in the gloomish vapors silhouetted by the red fire-exit sign. About mid-thirties, dark disco-frizzed hair, stocky and strong-looking but the clean sort, altogether pleasant, like one of Hogarth's bluff and hearty villains come to life. Except that Mr. Ajax's eyes narrowed when you asked questions so that his head looked like a bunker.

"How many fires have you set," I asked.

"Who said I set fires?"

"I heard it, and I wouldn't tell you where just like I wouldn't tell anyone who you are." This is called covering your ass.

"About twenty," he said.

"Tell me about some."

What follows is what I remember, because Mr. Ajax had a horror of tape recorders, and was not a big admirer of pencils and pads. A hulking friend patted me down to make sure I wasn't wired. When Ajax spoke, it was cordial, like anyone talking about his business. I wondered, is he really a bad-ass burner, or just someone blowing smoke?

"The biggest was a warehouse down by the river. Guy wanted the insurance and to get new stock so we burned it. It was simple, just some gas in leaking jugs, and a candle. Lots of trailers. He got the money."

"How about you?"

"I got some, too. I've also burned things for nothing, as a favor."

Etcetera.

It became Walter Lowe's task to make changes that would satisfy everyone. First of all, he says, "the opening paragraphs, a description of burned children in a New Jersey tenement arson, were so jarring and depressing that it didn't draw the reader further into the article." Second, "The purpose and intent of the article—where it would take the reader—was over-explained by McKinley, who also adopted a somewhat stiff manner of presenting his facts, making for slow reading." Information about the state of the fire insurance industry was scattered, he says. Arson cases were introduced too early, before readers were made fully aware of the mechanics of fire insurance. And the ending "wasn't quite right. It lacked the punch that characterizes a good closing paragraph." As Lowe worked and deliberated with fellow editors, considerable rewriting occurred. Someone suggested a consolidation of sidebar and main piece with the sidebar material used as lead. Someone decided on an italicized beginning based on the "torch" talking, with a shift then to McKinley's original lead of the victims in a three-dimensional death portrait. For a kicker ending, the editors decided to set more copy in italics, once again material from the incorporated sidebar. Considerable editing went into the many inches of copy between start and finish. It's a complicated process, getting an article ready, involving writing and editing talents (not even to speak of artists who then must fashion appropriate visuals and design). It's ego bruising work frequently. But the soothings come when the article is complete and published.

Here is the beginning of McKinley's article as run in the September 1979 issue of *Playboy*:

He had worked in this nice mid-American town for several years, I'd been told. He was firmly allied with the city's ruling Mafia clan, doing odd jobs — paper scams, mostly — such as running the bookmaking operations. He'd been suspected of heavier crimes, too, including arson. But although the police, the FBI, the Department of Justice, insurance investigators and prosecutors were sure he'd burned things, he'd never been convicted. Until recently, his official business had been running a disco, and that's where I met the man I'll call Lenny Ajax one morning just after closing.

Stale smoke, booze fumes, body odor and perfume hung in the air. It was a slick place, with fancy furnishings and high overhead, the sort of place that burns when business falls away, as this joint had a few months before. I told Ajax I just wanted information; I didn't want to put anybody in jail. He laughed. A Federal indictment for bank fraud had landed on him three weeks before. Now he sat in the gloomy vapors silhouetted by the red fire-exit sign. In his mid-thirties, stocky and muscular, with dark disco-frizzed hair, he seemed like one of Hogarth's bluff and hearty villains come to life. Except that when you asked questions, Ajax's eyes narrowed so that his head looked like a bunker.

"How many fires have you set?" I asked.

"Who said I set fires?"

"I heard it, but I wouldn't tell you where, just as I wouldn't tell anyone who you are." This is called covering your ass.

"About twenty," he said.

"Tell me about some."

"The biggest was a warehouse, down by the river. Guy wanted the insurance and to get new stock, so we burned it. It was simple — just some gas in leaking jugs and a candle. He got the money."

"How about you?"

"I got some, too. I've also burned things for nothing, as a favor."

"What kind of things? For whom?"

"Houses. If a friend wants a new house or needs money, I'll burn something for him."

"Such as?"

"A restaurant. A bar. You don't have to take 'em down. Do it right and you'll cause enough damage to get the money and then you rebuild. Or get a new partner."

"Did your fires ever hurt anybody?"

"No. Killing people's dumb. You want to burn when nobody's around."

"What do you feel when you see something burning that you've set?"

"I don't see it. I'm long gone. In Vegas or somewhere."

"You don't feel anything?"

"What's to feel? It's just a piece of brick. Arson don't hurt anybody except insurance companies. And who, your average citizen, doesn't like to fuck insurance companies?"

* * *

The young mother lies beneath the burglar-barred window leading to the fire escape. She cradles an infant in each arm. The three are charred, stiff—fired like stoneware in the last rictus of death by flame. One baby's mouth presses his mother's blackened breast. The other child's is open, caught in mid-scream. One small tooth gleams. Six feet away, under the kitchen table's skeleton, are a boy and a girl, about eleven and twelve, hiding there, they thought, and reaching for each other. Their charcoal hands now touch in last communication. Three feet farther on, three smaller children make a clump, their basted bodies fused like amber wax. The seared skin flakes off when the fire fighters, hiding their pain in gallows humor, call them crispy critters and, averting their eyes, put the charred remains into the body bags.

Twenty-one died in that fire in Hoboken, New Jersey. They were murdered by an arsonist. At 3:30 a.m., someone splashed gasoline in a first-floor hallway and tossed a match. Someone as yet unknown. With an unknown motive. The arsonist could have been seeking revenge on some of the twelve-in-a-room East Guyanese and *latino* tenants; it's estimated that at least half this nation's yearly 200,000-plus arson fires are set to avenge a real or imagined wrong. It could have been a pyromaniac or other twisted sort: About one in ten arsons is. Maybe the arsonist was a kid fevered by street-punk glory, or perhaps he was someone lashing out at a landlord in ghetto desperation: Vandals set 20 percent of the nation's arson fires.

But if this murderous blaze was part of arson's fastest-growing category, then the building's owner—or his hired torch—set the fire. To collect insurance.

Five tenements like that one went up in northern New Jersey within three months, killing more than fifty people. All were insured, and if national trends hold, the owners will have collected their claims, since fewer than 20 percent of the claims are rejected, arson or not. Only about 2 percent of arson incidents result in a conviction because, unlike other crimes, to prove arson, you must prove both the crime (the set fire) and the criminal—the arsonist as either hired agent or owner of the structure.

Thomas E. Kotoske, attorney in charge of the organized Crime Strike Force in San Francisco and a fierce arson investigator, flatly says that "arson is the toughest case to prosecute." As a result, in many locales, the greenest or most lackadaisical prosecutors are assigned to arson cases, because, as one arson investigator put it, "Arson cases are hell on your won-lost record." Even fewer convictions are returned in arson-for-profit cases, in which the link between crime and criminal must be completely taut.

Unfortunately, several other factors usually make the linkage loose. Among them:

- An insurance system inviting fraud.
- Undermanned, underfinanced, undertrained arson-investigation agencies.
- The difficulty of detecting arson, especially when torches use sophisticated techniques such as time devices to remove themselves from the scene of the crime, or other methods to conceal the fire's origin.
- A public whose attitude toward arson has been, "So what? It's only property." Until Congress recently acted, arson wasn't even the same category of crime as auto theft, despite the fact that it kills about one thousand people per year.
- Shrewd, resourceful criminals determined to take advantage of all such weaknesses.

Little wonder that arson for profit is, according to the insurance industry and law-enforcement officials, one of the country's hottest growth industries, a nearly risk-free crime that lets bodies and buildings fall where they may. How big is this racket? How costly? How does it work? Who's doing the burning? And what, if anything, is being done, or can be done, to stop it?

McKinley goes on to explore at length the problem of arson and the efforts of legislators and prosecutors and all sorts of officials to solve it. With the ending, McKinley and editor Lowe summarize the current status and then return to the humanized example used to get the article underway. The article's end:

Much of this program can be implemented without new laws. The Senate's Permanent Subcommittee on Investigations has been holding hearings on the arson problem, but the minority's chief investigator, Jonathan Cottin, believes that no new statutes are needed. "We have the laws," he says. "The fact is, we've all been lax and apathetic. The public, the insurers, the FBI, LEAA, other agencies, everybody. Arsonists had to rub our noses in it for us to move."

* * *

Lenny Ajax looked as if he wanted to end the interview. I wasn't reluctant, especially since I'd heard that he wasn't averse to cracking heads.

"You admit you're an arsonist, then?"

"I've burned things."

"The cops would like to put you away, you know that?"

"Sure. But let 'em prove I set any fire. You know, fires can just happen.

"To anybody. Remember that."

Because McKinley was in Spain during part of the editing period, the process of communicating recommendations and acceptances was more difficult than the usual writer-editor interchange. But McKinley and Lowe are thorough professionals and managed the task, ending up with a thrusting and hard-hitting article, one of *Playboy*'s best.

SITUATION TWO

Toni Lydecker, then senior editor and later managing editor of *Restaurants & Institutions*, wrote an article on high labor turnover in that industry for the January 22, 1988 issue. It won a certificate of merit in the Jesse H. Neal editorial competition from the American Business Press.

"The subject is one we deal with all the time," she says. "We put an article on 'labor' into our editorial schedule, our yearly plan. Just in general terms, mind you. Our competition sees our schedule as we do theirs, so we don't get too specific." But Lydecker and Jeff Weinstein, the staff's labor specialist, and editor Michael Bartlett began to think about their "labor" piece. "We needed to find a focus," says Lydecker. "Turnover is a major problem. We discuss it constantly. But our challenge was to find a different way of looking at it. And when I heard a Burger King executive address an industry conference on the subject, I knew we had our focus. He argued that too much emphasis in the food service industry is put on recruitment and too little on retention."

The staff, at Lydecker's prompting, "kicked the idea around." During the discussion Audrey Garvey, the executive editor, a "turner of phrases," according to Lydecker, remarked: "How to stop the revolving door."

"We had it," says Lydecker. "We had our organizing principle. We had our title." But the limits of the story had not yet been determined. The original plan was to cover turnover in the entire restaurant-hotel-institution industry. Bartlett thought in terms of limits. He pointed out that the problem was worst at the fast food and full-service restaurant chains. Lydecker researched and wrote the story. Weinstein contributed to the information gathering.

Lydecker prepared a "Story Proposal for *R&I*: Labor Turnover." It read:

Head: How to Stop the Revolving Door

I. Two pages—outline, analyze the turnover issue. The problem is a classic supply/demand dilemma: To expand, companies need more employees, but traditional labor pool (teens) is shrinking. Companies are resorting to ingenious strategies to find warm bodies (TV and radio ads, bounties, etc.) and targeting alternative groups such as seniors, handicapped, etc. Recruitment won't help much, however, if employees leave within months, and that's what happens much of the time. For hourly employees, turnover of 100 percent/year in fast food is considered moderate; some companies have turnover of 200-400 percent. Conservative estimate of cost of replacing hourly employee (recruitment, training of someone new) is four hundred dollars.

II. Six pages — strategies to retain employees. Burger King will be one example. Company has lowered turnover of hourly workers from 250 percent annually to 175 percent by making retention a company-wide priority; bonuses are awarded, in part, on basis of how well manager controls turnover. Goal is to "turn the worst job in the neighborhood into the best job in the neighborhood." To figure out how to slow down turnover, company used market model: Just as would research how to market product to customer, researched how to sell work to employee. Changes included uniforms that bolster self-esteem, job ladder, college tuition contribution as new benefit (interestingly, didn't increase wages).

Will also include examples from parts of industry that have better record than fast food in retaining employees; namely, institutions and full-service restaurants. Identify elements of employee satisfaction that are transferable to rest of industry.

Wings [Sidebars]: Interview real foodservice workers to find out what they like/don't like about their jobs; ask them what employers could do to make foodservice jobs have long-term appeal.

Graphics: Opening graphic will be concept shot of foodservice worker entering and leaving revolving door . . . Other shots would be of restaurant help-wanted signs, managers training employees, long lines at counter (consequence of not having enough employees).

"One doesn't usually start with a title," says Lydecker, "but in this case it helped my angle, my approach." Title and idea became one. Limits of breadth were set.

The information gathering had started at the conference where she heard the speaker from Burger King. That speech for members of the Council of Hotel and Restaurant Trainers became fodder for Lydecker's lead. She also interviewed the speaker, who in the process mentioned other possible contacts at other companies. Lydecker and Weinstein knew that executives at Golden Corral, another chain, treated their employees well. "One thing, one source led to another. The information wasn't difficult to get. But we wanted to get information from various companies so that the reader would see depth in the broadness of our search."

She looked at previous issues of the magazine and the competition. She hunted through the *Wall Street Journal* and *The New York Times* for background. She made her list of experts to talk to. "My preparation for the interviews came mostly from experience, from prior knowledge." But she did pose a short list of questions to each source: What's your turnover rate? Have you noticed improvements? What strategies are you following? Have you a model that other companies might use? The questions, she says, were defined by the subject. They all had to do with "how companies were trying to slow the revolving door."

The article became a collection of case studies. "Aside from some labor statistics and brief clippings from here and there, we had little to go on. This story was ours to do. Those in the field became our story."

Information gathering took a couple of months, midway between idea refinement and go-ahead in August and publication in January. But Lydecker had additional duties along the way: other writing to do, other editing, other staff work. Only on rare occasions does a trade publication staffer get the privilege to lavish full-time attention on one project.

Sources were cooperative, says Lydecker, "so cooperative that I couldn't use them all. I tend to over-research anyway. I tend to have more sources than I need. I had more sources here, so I dropped the less productive ones."

The writing took four days, in part or full. "I read through my notes several times, thought about what to lead with, then followed my outline. It worked. Not always is the writing so easy. This time, however, the information just led me through. I began with the story that gave me the idea, that employee training at fast food chains is the worst job in the neighborhood. I began with Burger King because the company had dramatically reduced turnover. It seemed a simple way of giving the reader a quick notion of where the article was going."

She found that the information "just fell into place, based on the different approaches being used by the chains. Everything was straight-forward. It was the kind of article that turned out to be the way I thought of it versus some where research takes the writer in new directions. One has to be flexible and be ready to shift. But in this case, I didn't have to shift."

Bartlett and Lydecker knew that their magazine's readers are passionately interested in the subject. "They're always looking for anything they can use," says Lydecker. "My job was to deliver the goods."

On a major article at *Restaurants & Institutions*, editor Bartlett reads carefully. He gets involved with the manuscript. He makes recommendations. He and the executive editor and the managing editor all do substantive editing. But because most of the material at *Restaurants & Institutions* is staff written, editing seems to be less severe than it can be at a magazine like *Playboy* where geographical and mental distance often separates the editorial staff and the freelancers. "Planning reduces editing later," says Lydecker. On her turnover story, Bartlett did little editing. "This one he liked," she says. This one contest judges from the American Business Press also liked.

The flow of the article, you'll find, is smooth, a natural extension of the idea and the gathered information. It breaks down into something akin to the reinforcement structure, with lead, thesis, proof of thesis, conclusion.

Lydecker gets the story under way with the Burger King example. She cuts away to provide needed background, then returns to her example. The example gets intense treatment; the reader learns of the various steps the chain has taken to mend the employee drain, and of results. From Burger King we move to Rax and Hardee's and Godfather's Pizza. Professionals at each firm share ideas with the professionals who will read the article.

The author then expands on those ideas, presenting the reader with a string of answers: improved wages and benefits, psychological rewards, training, raising self-esteem, and more sensitive management. For each she provides more examples. She ends with the thought that the industry faces a nagging and long-term problem that requires a change of priorities at top management levels. A strong quote sends the reader off into his own field of struggle.

Three sidebars approach the subject from the employee's point of view, important to Lydecker and colleagues because "we think food service employees are, in general, not treated well." The employee comments didn't fit comfortably into the main story. As sidebars, they made informational exclamation points.

"Even the main graphic worked out," says Lydecker. "We happened to find twins, two aspiring models working in a hotel restaurant. They agreed to be photographed. We put them into a revolving door and had our visual key for the whole project."

Lydecker's article is solid. It covers the angles and the sources. It holds a logic in its construction. Its language is always clear. The author's work is at all times appropriate for the reader, a practitioner in the restaurant and food institutions industry.

How to Stop the Revolving Door

Turn the worst job in the neighborhood into one of the best.

That was Glenn Jeffrey's mission, as he set out to halve Burger King's 300 percent turnover rate for hourly employees, increasing the average tenure from four to eight months. He started with the premise that "the restaurant industry doesn't have an image problem. It has a reality problem. The jobs we offer are entry level and low status, and the rewards are all in the future—we tell employees that if they're lucky, they can go into management someday."

Other restaurant chains, both fast food and full service, are equally alarmed about high turnover; 400 percent annually is not uncommon. The traditional solution—to find more warm bodies—no longer works. Inexorably, the youthful labor pool is shrinking, and alternative labor sources are no panacea. Despite such endeavors as McDonald's much-touted McMaster's program, the proportion of seniors in foodservice actually dropped by 10 percent between 1980 and 1986, according to the U.S. Labor Department.

More adults between the ages of twenty and thirty-four are taking foodservice jobs, but this raises other problems. Won't they want good wages, health insurance, child-care benefits, flexible scheduling and more respect from management? One industry observer thinks the answer is yes. "We're going to have to stop treating the equipment better than the employees."

In light of this situation, many chains have decided that keeping the workers they already have beats running the recruitment machine faster. Unless a worker goes into management, it's probably not practical to keep him or her on the job ten years or even five. But adding even three months to the average tenure of a fast-food worker could make a dramatic difference.

Often the pressure for stopping (or, at least, slowing down) the revolving door comes from the bottom, as unit managers discover what the labor crisis means to them: understaffed crews, help-wanted ads that draw a woefully small response, poor morale among existing staff. Country Kitchens International, based in Minneapolis, is focusing on retention because "our franchisee advisory committee told us they wouldn't make it through '88 unless we did," says Barbara Weinstein, director of training and personnel.

Equally worried about the labor situation, Jerrico has organized a Labor Availability Task Force. "We're already having trouble hiring and retaining employees in some markets," says Doug Higdon, vice president for training. "Where that's the case, we're willing to try extreme measures."

[Sidebar] What's Wrong: Working Conditions
I used to work for fast-food places. The managers slave you, make you work like a dog. Now I'm a waitress in a hotel restaurant. They pay more and you get benefits. And the clientele is nicer—they treat you with respect.

The hardest part about the job is being on your feet all day long. Everyone is on the clock. People need things done in a certain amount of time, so you're running to the kitchen, to the register, to the other side of the dining room.

You can't lose your cool. A customer left a penny tip for a girlfriend of mine, so she followed him out the door and threw it at him. She lost her job. I'm good at what I do because I'm more patient and understand other people's needs.

Having the right co-workers is more important than the right manager. Sometimes the busboys don't think you're passing on enough of the tip, so they won't give your customers ice water. And last week I had a fight with the cook—when I gave him an order for a fruit plate, he said, "I don't have time to make it." The manager was gone, so I had to go to the hotel's personnel director to straighten it out.

—twenty-year-old female

Burger King's Battle

Glenn Jeffrey's first move in the battle to improve Burger King's retention rate was to grab the attention of the Miami-based chain's top management. Not an easy task, as his audience at a conference of the Council of Hotel and Restaurant Trainers well knew; human resources often play second fiddle to profit-generating aspects of a business.

A savvy executive who has since become Pillsbury's vice president for executive and organization development, Jeffrey decided that to sell the idea of making retention a priority, "marketing was the horse to ride." That is, employees would correspond to customers, jobs to products, employee relations to customer relations, and turnover to customer rejection.

Rejection of jobs by hourly employees was costing Burger King a bundle—

that much was clear. Jeffrey calculated the cost of replacing a trained employee at $1,100. Convinced that the upper echelons would think he was exaggerating, however, he used a "more credible" figure of $400. Even based on the lower figure, turnover cost a mind-blowing $120 million, a number that definitely caught management's attention.

Next came a fact-finding phase. Just as it might survey customers to find out why they rejected a product, the company polled employees to find out why so many were leaving their jobs. The results were sobering; employees rated the company as "poor" in the areas of income, job skill training and self-esteem, and "fair" for social needs.

Company leaders thought they could raise those scores to "fair" for income and "good" for the other categories. As a prerequisite, they made one sweeping change in company-owned stores: 25 percent of top managers' bonuses would be based on performance in developing and retaining personnel.

Marketing Model Works

Following the marketing model, investment in improving the labor force was comparable to investment in development. So the company put some money into that endeavor.

A formal career ladder gave hourly employees more potential to progress, for example, from food handler to training coordinator. An educational assistance program was started and more emphasis was placed on teaching lifetime job skills, such as punctuality—moves that pleased parents of teenage workers as much as the workers themselves. Uniforms were redesigned to please employees.

These actions trimmed turnover from 300 percent to 175 percent. In some locales, the results were even more dramatic. After two Detroit-area Burger Kings began offering college tuition aid, turn-over dropped from 300 percent to 40 percent.

[Sidebar] What's Right: The Money

In the four months I've been working at Burger King, the money ($3.65 an hour) has been the best part. I'm saving for a BMX bicycle. I like the hours, too. I work about fifteen hours a week and only once during the weekend. I feel proud when my friends come and see me working, and my parents are glad I'm not running around as much.

There really isn't much I don't like about my job. It does get a little greasy and I wish my manager would trust me more. He is always looking over my shoulder, waiting for me to make a mistake.

As long as they give me the raise they promised in January, I guess I'll stay at the job for another year or until my dad lets me go to work for him.
—*sixteen-year-old-male*

Company-Wide Priority

What's most significant about Burger King's approach is not the specific programs, but the decision to make retention a companywide priority, for which managers are partially responsible.

Similarly, Rax of Indiana (Rax Restaurants Inc.'s largest franchisee) is trying to make the turnover problem more "top of mind" by requiring districts to document it, just as they would food costs. "Once you start tracking data, you see consistent trends developing. You can dig in and see why one operator is losing more employees than another," says Personnel Director Mike Landram.

Although making managers accountable is important, the state of the company itself greatly affects retention. Companies have a much better chance of keeping employees if they're on a roll, if profits are soaring and new products are a hit. It's no accident that Hardee's most financially successful year in a twenty-six-year history coincides with its highest volume of job applications. "People want to join a winning team. When the company's doing well, the enthusiasm filters down," says spokesman Jerry Singer.

Moreover, the corporate culture must be people-oriented. "From the top of the company on down, there has to be an evangelical spirit, an attitude that employees are the company's most important asset," says Spencer Wiggins, vice president of human resources for Godfather's Pizza. "You're sunk if the person at the top is a people killer, determined to get bottom-line results at all costs," echoes Donald Smith, professor of hotel and restaurant administration, Washington State University, Pullman, Washington.

Companies that do have their houses in order are ready for a major assault on the problem. Retention programs try to make employees happier in three crucial areas: tangible rewards, job and personal growth, and self-esteem.

Rewards You Can Touch

Wages and benefits are the tangible rewards that come first to mind. Letting the market drive wage levels, most companies simply pay the going rate for a specific kind of job. "If other restaurants are paying $5.00, you don't necessarily have to pay $5.50 — as long as yours is a better place to work," says Country Kitchens' Weinstein.

White Castle attributes its relatively low turnover of 100 percent to a generous array of benefits. The package, which is highly unusual for a fast-food chain, includes profit sharing, an annual Christmas bonus, pension, and life and health insurance. And the company promotes only from within.

More typical is Godfather's, which has cautiously expanded the groups eligible for benefits. Hourly shift supervisors recently gained access to dental and medical insurance, a step that has improved their job satisfaction. Jerrico, based in Lexington, Kentucky, is thinking of extending benefits to part-timers.

Godfather's is also putting together a crew incentive program. "We've always rewarded managers. Now, we have to get everyone else into the loop," says Wiggins. Based on their length of service and the quality/service/cleanliness rating of their store, crew members will earn certificates to be redeemed for prizes: radios, watches, jackets, bicycles and jewelry.

A Richer Job Experience

Often the monetary reward attached to a promotion is less important than the psychological reward that goes with it — the recognition that a worker has done a good job. Greater attention to the quality of employees' job experiences can help them develop good lifetime work habits as well as technical skills.

New Hardee's employees are evaluated after three months and, if the report is good, they get a raise; they're then evaluated at least once every six months. Many Hardee's stores have adapted a "fast-track" program originally developed for managers to motivate top-notch hourly workers. A performance-plus test measures such leadership qualities as decisiveness, judgment and teamwork. Crew members who are performing well on the job and score high on the test are earmarked for promotion to crew leader or assistant manager.

Just introduced by Hardee's is a new retention program, Serve with Pride, which trains hourly workers in a broad spectrum of skills and encourages pride in performing those tasks. One of the rallies kicking off the program was attended by about six hundred people from thirty Hardee's units in the Harrisburg, Pennsylvania area. Crew members from each restaurant performed skits with a QSC theme, and prizes such as watches and "boogie boxes" were awarded for the best of those. Everyone left with T-shirts, mugs and visors proclaiming the Serve with Pride message.

But the guts of the program is cross-training back in the individual units. At a minimum, all workers must be certified in hospitality. Beyond that, they have the opportunity to become proficient in six other work stations.

Once they've passed a test, workers receive a stick-on decal showing, for example, a spatula for knowing how to work the grill. "It becomes a big deal—customers and the rest of the crew notice the decals. The kids end up wanting all seven," comments Singer.

The rare manager who might think this is all too much trouble is gently prodded by the requirement to post proficiencies of crew members on the bulletin board. A visiting district manager who notices that few workers are trained in more than one station will pressure the unit manager to make time for more cross-training.

Rax of Indiana runs a similar cross-training enterprise called All-Star Employee. Once workers have mastered two-thirds of the stations, the All-Star insignia goes on their nametag, and an extra twenty-five dollars goes in their paycheck.

Raising Self-Esteem

To a young person, a retail job carries more prestige than one in a restaurant, and one of the reasons is the freedom to wear regular clothing. Like Burger King, Rax of Indiana has created a "more stylish uniform" that makes employees feel better about themselves.

Recognizing the achievements of employees also raises self-esteem. Golden Corral, based in Raleigh, North Carolina, has created "clubs" to recognize employees who know the names of customers. To earn the first button, an employee must sit down with the manager and write out the names and some bit of information about one hundred customers. After mastering the names of two hundred customers, the worker gets another button, and so on; about a dozen Golden Corral employees belong to the One Thousand Club.

The clubs make both customers and employees feel special. More importantly, knowing names is "part of taking ownership" of the restaurant, says Dan Corsgaard, partner and manager of a Georgetown, Kentucky operation.

By that, he means that employees gain a feeling of commitment to the restaurant and its goals. Another visible sign of excellence is a star pin Golden Corral headquarters executives on tour can award when they spot hourly employees giving exemplary service.

Why Managers Count

Whether these retention programs make a dent in the labor problem depends largely on how they're carried out. "You have to make people feel they belong, and the key player is the unit manager who delivers the program," says Landram.

[Sidebar] What's Wrong: Manager's Attitude

I worked the counter at McDonald's one summer while I was in college. It was an easy job to get and, although the pay wasn't super, it was about what I could expect to get anywhere else.

You're always busy, and that makes the time go by. Even when there weren't many customers, we'd wipe the counter or wash the floors. I didn't realize how important it is not to be bored until I worked for a photo shop the following year and had very little to do.

The manager knew I'd be leaving at the end of the summer and that's how he treated me. He'd let regular employees revise their schedule, but with someone like me, there was no flexibility. It was, "This is the way it's going to be." Students who had to be in school early the next day sometimes had to close the store at 1 a.m., and I thought that was bad.

I think managers should change their attitude and treat everyone as if they're worthwhile, even if they're going to be there only a short time. They could encourage people to have career plans, even if they're working as a counter clerk at the moment.

— twenty-five-year-old female

To make sure they're landing enthusiastic, motivated managers, many chains are taking more care in hiring. Golden Corral uses a prestructured interview to look for people with a gift for interpersonal relations.

The company's looking for more managers like Dan Corsgaard. Rather than learning the principles of good management in a classroom, Corsgaard mastered some basic concepts while working in a fast-food restaurant as a teenager. "I was treated like someone with a minimum-wage mentality. Nobody gave me responsibility or spent time with me. I vowed then that if I were ever in a position to be in charge, I'd treat people the way I want to be treated."

In a tough environment where unemployment is often less than 1 percent, Corsgaard rarely has to put an ad in the newspaper, because his restaurant has a reputation for being a good place to work. One of the reasons is that Corsgaard spends time talking to employees — small talk, problems, career goals, whatever happens to be on their minds. Because he doesn't like to be called into the store on his day off, he tries to avoid doing that to a co-worker. Schedules are readily altered to allow working students to attend homecoming or prepare for a test.

But Corsgaard is far from a pushover. Like a good parent, he tells workers what he expects and chastises them when they don't deliver. He says this is important not only in running the restaurant, but to show employees he cares. Citing an experience from his own adolescence, he says, "Once I decided not to empty the trash. When I came in the next morning, no one said a word. I was relieved but also disappointed, because I knew I deserved to get my butt kicked."

As a manager, Corsgaard makes a point of noticing such details. He is quick to praise workers when they do tasks well, and someone who performs with valor on a busy Saturday night is likely to get an extra twenty dollars at the end of the shift. Knowing what his hot buttons are—such as leaving a dishrag on the grill—employees aren't surprised to be chewed out when they violate one.

Teaching Tough Love

"Tough love" is Donald Smith's term for good management. "The more you listen to and care about employees, the tougher you can get in making them hold to high standards," he says.

The kind of abilities Corsgaard comes by naturally can be taught, to some extent, and that's what several chains are doing. Guides currently in preparation by Country Kitchens will help managers become more sensitive to people and more creative and flexible in managing personnel. "We're trying to get rid of the horror stories—managers hiring someone who wanted part-time work and then schedulingthe person for forty-five hours a week," says Weinstein. "They have to learn that it's better to have someone for sixteen hours a week than not at all."

Country Kitchens is encouraging managers to talk more to employees, both individually and in a group setting such as a weekly meeting. The training materials will urge them to conduct exit interviews to find out why people are leaving.

Still Not the Best Job

Although controlling turnover has become a priority of many chains, the struggle is far from over. So far relatively few are changing basic structures such as wages and benefits. Changing the conditions of the jobs themselves—the long hours and physical discomforts—is another area that's ripe for change. And even though more young adults are taking hourly jobs, many retention programs are still oriented to teenagers.

Despite Burger King's progress in curbing turnover, Glenn Jeffrey says, "As far as offering the best job around, we're still not there. The way you can tell the problem's licked is when you can send your own son or daughter to work in any of the company's operations, knowing he or she will have a good work experience."

13

In Expansion—The Essay and Other Hybrids

ON HEARING A SYMPHONY OF BEETHOVEN

Sweet sounds, oh, beautiful music, do not cease!
Reject me not into the world again.
With you alone is excellence and peace,
Mankind made plausible, his purpose plain.
Enchanted in your air benign and shrewd,
With limbs a-sprawl and empty faces pale,
The spiteful and the stingy and the rude
Sleep like the scullions in the fairy-tale.
This moment is the best the world can give:
The tranquil blossom on the tortured stem.
Reject me not, sweet sounds! Oh, let me live,
Till Doom espy my towers and scatter them.
A city spell-bound under the aging sun,
Music my rampart, and my only one.

—Edna St. Vincent Millay

Poems like Millay's are bursts of personal expression. They're essays. Your prose article could be an essay. Magazine editors scatter them about. They're changes of pace from news-oriented and how-to pieces. They're thought-generators. They give a certain depth and scope and variety to a publication in that they're more personal in approach, more visionary in goal.

Virginia Woolf said a "good essay must have this permanent quality about it; it must draw its curtain round us, but it must be a curtain that shuts us in, not out." That sense of the permanent. That feel of quality. That presence of a curtain opening to let us in on a show of reflective words.

THE ESSENTIAL ESSAY

An essay can give a magazine class. It's a lesson that grips, angers, uplifts, beguiles. It may aim to explain or hypothesize or interpret. For a writer it's an opportunity to fuse experience and philosophy. For a reader it's an agreeable way to learn and empathize.

Here are six essays, entire or in part, each with a different purpose or approach. They were selected because they're well written and because they're meant to serve different purposes.

The Essay as Exploration

Richard Majors remembered "Playing It Cool" as he grew up in New York City. He instructs and questions in his essay for *American Visions* (April 1987):

> "Cool" is a fortress that black males have built against white American society. But like most walls, just as it keeps outsiders out, it keeps insiders in.
>
> The trademark cool poses of black males are both a survival mechanism and — to borrow a phrase from sociologists' jargon — an "expressive lifestyle." The messages of these poses go something like this: "See me, touch me, hear me, white man, but you can't copy me. You may control everything about me, but you can't control my pride and dignity. That is mine and mine alone. Although you may have tried to hurt me time and time again, I can take it. And if I am hurting or weak, I'll never let you know."
>
> Cool poses are everywhere. In black athletes' stylish dunking of the basketball, the spontaneous dancing in the end zone. In shucking and jiving. In "high fives" and other special handshakes. And they keep changing. If mainstream society takes on some of the phrases and mannerisms, black males move on — perhaps to rap talking or break dancing.
>
> It is possible to trace this survival technique a long way back, to a time when it had a different function. Among the Yorubas of western Nigeria, cool was integrated into the social fabric of the community. A young man's cool was part of the way he carried himself among his peers and impressed his elders during initiation rituals. Coolness helped to build character and pride among the young men of this society. Sociologists would categorize its use as cultural adaptation.
>
> With the advent of Western slave trade, coolness became the survival mechanism that it remains today — not a cultural adaptation so much as a way of remaining aloof from a social order not of blacks' making. A way of saying, "I'll express myself as a person, as a distinctive member of a distinctive group, in ways that you can never quite get hold of. It certainly hasn't worked very well to adopt and adapt to white society's norms. At least these protective devices will give me some inner confidence, an identity."
>
> But cool is not without its price. The very behaviors and attitudes that have enabled blacks to survive, in a society in which the game has always been rigged against their winning, are detrimental when indiscriminately applied. Conditioned to keep up their guard, black men often won't allow themselves to express or show weakness or fear in any form. It's as if they were telling themselves that if they never show that they are vulnerable, then they can shield themselves against the risks of humiliation. This facade of strength helps keep racial barriers in place. And, equally important, it often

prevents the forming of lasting attachments in their personal lives — a phenomenon to which many black women will attest.

Few social or psychological factors have so shaped, directed and controlled the black male. Yet coolness has received almost no serious study. The question that calls for exploration is this: Is coolness — which figures in the personality and behavior of most black males — useful in today's American society? More precisely, is it useful enough to be cultivated at the sacrifice of other possibilities?

The Majors style is straightforward. It speaks of pride and concern. The essay contains the touch of a scholar and, indeed, the subject of "cool" served to fulfill Majors' thesis obligations at the University of Illinois. He obviously wanted the subject to reach beyond the dusty dissertation shelves of a university library. The essay gave him the way.

The Essay as Dream

Quite a different purpose is sought and achieved in the dreamy, imagination-inspired lines of "a young woman we know" in *The New Yorker*'s November 19, 1979 "Talk of the Town." She sought merely to amuse. Merely? Amusement is a welcome gift for readers. They get too little caprice in their reading.

This morning, I was listening to the radio — I mean, I was ironing my shirt and the radio was on — and the disc jockey said that the Beatles were getting back together, that they were going to give a benefit concert for some important cause or other, and how great that would be. He said, "Can you imagine the Beatles back and playing together?" I imagined that, and while I was at it I imagined a number of other things. I imagined that I was in love with the man who discovered the principle of hydrogen bonding and that he was in love with me, too, and that it was all almost wonderful; I imagined that my favorite color was red and that my favorite words were "vivid," astonishing," "enigmatic," "ennui," and "ululating;" I imagined that even though I hadn't died I was in Heaven; I imagined that all the people I didn't like were gathered up in one big barrel and rolled down from a high mountain into a deep, deep part of the sea; I imagined that all the books on my shelf had long legs and wore flesh-colored panty hose and that their long legs in the flesh-colored panty hose dangled from the bookshelf; I imagined that the trains in the subway had all the comforts of a private DC-9, I imagined that I had the most beautiful face in the whole world and that some men would faint after they got a good, close look at it; I imagined that I had different-colored underwear for every day of the year; I imagined that it was a real pleasure to be with me, because I was so much fun and always knew the right thing needed to be said; I imagined that I knew by heart all the poems of William Wordsworth; I imagined that it rained only at night, starting just before I fell asleep, so that the sound of the rain would lull me to sleep, and that it stopped raining just before I woke up every morning; I imagined that I could run my tongue across the windowpane and not pick up, perhaps, some deadly germ; I imagined that all the people in the world were colored and that they all liked it a whole lot, because they could wear outlandish colors and not feel ridiculous; and then I again imagined the Beatles back and playing together. None of it did a thing for me.

So there. Do your own fantasizing.

The Essay as Lesson

There's no fantasizing in A.M Rosenthal's emotional distillation of reaction to a visit. "No News from Auschwitz" appeared in *The New York Times Magazine* (August 31, 1958). The essay is appropriately elegiac and yet outlines an undercurrent of anger and sorrow. Never again, it seems to say.

The most terrible thing of all, somehow, was that at Brzezinka the sun was bright and warm, the rows of graceful poplars were lovely to look upon and on the grass near the gates children played.

It all seemed frighteningly wrong, as in a nightmare, that at Brzezinka the sun should ever shine or that there should be light and greenness and the sound of young laughter. It would be fitting if at Brzezinka the sun never shone and the grass withered, because this is a place of unutterable terror.

And yet, every day, from all over the world, people come to Brzezinka, quite possibly the most grisly tourist center on earth. They come for a variety of reasons – to see if it could really have been true, to remind themselves not to forget, to pay homage to the dead by the simple act of looking upon their place of suffering.

Brzezinka is a couple of miles from the better-known southern Polish town of Oswiecim. Oswiecim has about twelve thouasnd inhabitants, is situated about 171 miles from Warsaw and lies in a damp, marshy area at the eastern end of the pass they called the Moravian Gate. Brzezkina and Oswiecim together formed part of that minutely organized factory of torture and death that the Nazis called Konzentrationslager Auschwitz.

By now, fourteen years after the last batch of prisoners was herded naked into the gas chambers by dogs and guards, the story of Auschwitz has been told a great many times. Some of the inmates have written of those events of which sane men cannot conceive. Rudolf Franz Ferdinand Hoess, the superintendent of the camp, before he was executed wrote his detailed memoirs of mass exterminations and the experiments on living bodies. Four million people died there, the Poles say.

And so there is no news to report about Auschwitz. There is merely the compulsion to write something about it, a compulsion that grows out of a restless feeling that to have visited Auschwitz and then turned away without having said or written anything would be a most grievous act of discourtesy to those who died there.

Brzezinka and Oswiecim are very quiet places now; the screams can no longer be heard. The tourist walks silently, quickly at first to get it over with and then, as his mind peoples the barracks and the chambers and the dungeons and the flogging posts, he walks draggingly. The guide does not say much either, because there is nothing much for him to say after he has pointed.

For every visitor, there is one particular bit of horror that he knows he will never forget. For some it is seeing the rebuilt gas chamber at Oswiecim and being told that this is the "small one." For others it is the fact that at Brzezinka, in the ruins of the gas chambers and the crematoria the Germans blew up when they retreated, there are daisies growing.

There are visitors who gaze blankly at the gas chambers and the furnaces because their minds simply cannot encompass them, but stand shivering before the great mounds of human hair behind the plate glass window or the piles of babies' shoes or the brick cells where men sentenced to death by suffocation were walled up.

One visitor opened his mouth in a silent scream simply at the sight of boxes—great stretches of three-tiered wooden boxes in the women's barracks. They were about six feet wide, about three feet high, and into them from five to ten prisoners were shoved for the night. The guide walks quickly through the barracks. Nothing more to see here.

A brick building where sterilization experiments were carried out on women prisoners. The guide tries the door—it's locked. The visitor is grateful that he does not have to go in, and then flushes with shame.

A long corridor where rows of faces stare from the walls. Thousands of pictures, the photographs of prisoners. They are all dead now, the men and women who stood before the cameras, and they all knew they were to die.

They all stare blank-faced, but one picture, in the middle of a row, seizes the eye and wrenches the mind. A girl, twenty-two years old, plumply pretty, blonde. She is smiling gently, as at a sweet, treasured thought. What was the thought that passed through her young mind and is now her memorial on the wall of the dead at Auschwitz?

Into the suffocation dungeons the visitor is taken for a moment and feels himself strangling. Another visitor goes in, stumbles out and crosses herself. There is no place to pray at Auschwitz.

The visitors look pleadingly at each other and say to the guide, "Enough."

There is nothing new to report about Auschwitz. It was a sunny day and the trees were green and at the gates the children played.

Essays tend to be expressions that need to be uttered. "No News from Auschwitz" had to be written. It became an obligation, Rosenthal's compulsion, perhaps his release from guilt because so many died so he could live. One wonders, reading those words again, whether the distinguished newspaperman ever wrote another piece that meant so much to him.

The Essay as Shock Treatment

A need to write must certainly have been a factor in the evolution of an extended essay for the Spring 1989 issue of *Daedalus* by two physicians. Paul Farmer and Arthur Kleinman authored "AIDS as Human Suffering." Here is a section labeled "AIDS and Human Meanings."

Listen to the words of persons with AIDS and others affected by our society's reaction to the new syndrome:

- "I'm forty-two years old. I have AIDS. I have no job. I do get $300 a month from social security and the state. I will soon receive $64 a month in food stamps. I am severely depressed. I cannot live on $300 a month. After $120 a month for rent and $120 a month for therapy, I am left with $60 for food and vitamins and other doctors and maybe acupuncture treatments and my share of utilities and oil and wood for heat. I'm sure I've forgotten several expenses like a movie once in a while and a newspaper and a book."

- "I don't know what my life expectancy is going to be, but I certainly know the quality is improved. I know that not accepting the shame or the guilt or the stigma that people would throw on me has certainly extended my life expectancy. I know that being very up-front with my friends, and my family and coworkers, reduced a tremendous amount of stress, and I would encourage people to be very open with friends, and if they can't handle it, then that's their problem and they're going to have to cope with it."

- "Here we are at an international AIDS conference. Yesterday a woman came up to me and said, 'May I have two minutes of your time?' She said, 'I'm asking doctors how they feel about treating AIDS patients.' And I said, 'Well, actually I'm not a doctor. I'm an AIDS patient,' and as she was shaking hands, her hand whipped away, she took two steps backward, and the look of horror on her face was absolutely diabolical."

- "My wife and I have lived here [in the United States] for fifteen years, and we speak English well, and I do O.K. driving. But the hardest time I've had in all my life, harder than Haiti, was when people would refuse to get in my cab when they discovered I was from Haiti [and therefore in their minds, a potential carrier of HIV]. It got so we would pretend to be from somewhere else, which is the worst thing you can do, I think."

All illnesses are metaphors. They absorb and radiate the personalities and social conditions of those who experience symptoms and treatments. Only a few illnesses, however, carry such cultural salience that they become icons of the times. Like tuberculosis in *fin de siecle* Europe, like cancer in the first half of the American century, and like leprosy from Leviticus to the present, AIDS speaks of the menace and losses of the times. It marks the sick person, encasing the afflicted in an exoskeleton of peculiarly powerful meanings: the terror of a lingering and untimely death, the panic of contagion, the guilt of "self-earned" illness. There is the ironic meaning of a new incurable infection at a time when other infectious diseases seem to have been conquered — at least in the technologically advanced West — by a succession of magic bullets. There is the moral meaning of shame and humiliation imposed by the very commercialized culture that has made money from the images of sexuality and drugs: now these same images have been transformed, rationally but still hypocritically (since money is still to be made from the meanings), from desires into risks.

AIDS has offered a new idiom for old gripes. We have used it to blame others: gay men, drug addicts, inner-city ethnics, Haitians, Africans. And we in the United States have, in turn, been accused of spreading and even creating the virus that causes AIDS. The steady progression of persons with AIDS toward the grave, so often via the poor house, has assaulted the comforting idea that risk can be managed. The world turns out to be less controllable and more dangerous, life more fragile than our insurance and welfare models pretend. We have relegated the threat of having to endure irremediable pain and early death—indeed, the very image of suffering as the paramount reality of daily existence—to past periods in history and to other, poorer societies. Optimism has its place in the scale of American virtues; stoicism and resignation in the face of unremitting hardship—unnecessary character traits in a land of plenty—do not. Suffering had almost vanished from public and private images of our society.

Throughout history and across cultures, life-threatening disorders have provoked questions of control (What do we do?) and bafflement (Why me?). When bubonic plague depopulated fourteenth-century Europe by perhaps as many as half to three-fourths of the population, the black death was construed as a religious problem and a challenge to the moral authority as much or even more than as a public-health problem. Religious transcendence was its metaphor as much as medical crisis. In the late twentieth century, it is not surprising that great advances in scientific knowledge and technological intervention have created our chief responses to questions of control and bafflement. To be sure, the international community of researchers has learned an astonishing amount about the human immunodeficiency virus (HIV) in a very short time. We have the technological expertise to prolong the lives of many people with AIDS and to ameliorate some of the horrendous bodily effects of the virus. Yet bafflement is not driven away by the advance of scientific knowledge, for it points to another aspect of the experience of persons with AIDS that has not received the attention it warrants. It points to a concern that in other periods and in other cultures is at the very center of the societal reaction to dread disease, a concern that resonates with that which is most at stake in the human experience of AIDS even if it receives little attention in academic journals—namely, suffering.

A mortal disease forces questions of dread, of death, and of ultimate meaning to arise. Suffering is a culturally and personally distinctive form of affliction of the human spirit. If pain is distress of the body, suffering is distress of the person and of his or her family and friends. The affliction and death of persons with AIDS create master symbols of suffering; the ethical and emotional responses to AIDS are collective representations of how societies deal with suffering. The stories of sickness of people with AIDS are texts of suffering that we can scan for evidence of how cultures and communities and individuals elaborate the unique textures of personal experience out of the impersonal cellular invasion of viral RNA. Furthermore, these illness narratives point toward issues in the AIDS epidemic every bit as salient as control of the spread of infection and treatment of its biological effects.

Viewed from the perspective of suffering, AIDS must rank with smallpox, plague, and leprosy in its capacity to menace and hurt, to burden and spoil human experience, and to elicit questions about the nature of life and its significance. Suffering extends from those afflicted with AIDS to their families and intimates, to the practitioners and institutions who care for them, and to their neighborhoods and the rest of society, who feel threatened by perceived sources of the epidemic and who are thus affected profoundly yet differently by its consequences. Moreover, because this condition is a pandemic affecting populations throughout the world, the experience of AIDS is refracted through greatly varying cultural lenses and social conditions, so that the human consequences of the disease are as distinctive as are these cultures themselves. To get at the culturally distinctive human consequences of such a pandemic, we shall examine the experience of persons with AIDS in the United States and Haiti.

Our objective is to make the language of suffering more central to the academic and public-health discourse on AIDS. To discuss AIDS as suffering, we must make meanings and experience as salient to the problem of AIDS as are microbes and behavior; we need to make demoralization and threat and hope as legitimate to the public discourse on AIDS as are sexual practices, intravenous drug use, and HIV testing. If we minimize the significance of AIDS as human tragedy, we dehumanize people with AIDS as well as those engaged in the public-health and clincal response to the epidemic. Ultimately, we dehumanize us all.

Once again strong feelings are meant to be shared, to be passed along. These physicians were concerned about emotional pain brought on by people's fear and lack of knowledge. They compressed their thoughts and thereby magnified them. Consider also how strongly their essay is based on facts, on solid information.

The Essay as Personal Perspective

Not so tragic but wrenching nevertheless is an essay about reality and doubt that *Prairie Farmer* published in 1988. "Goodbye, Leaf River High School" won for Mike Wilson a best writing award from the American Agricultural Editors' Association. The essay is built on facts and events, but also on memory and emotion. The blend works. The words are neither too hard nor maudlin. We are reminded of a penalty that comes from change, from progress.

This spring they handed out the last high school diploma in my hometown of Leaf River, Illinois. After years of writing about school closings and talking to the folks who agonize over such decisions, I now know a little of how it feels. It's like getting your roots dug out from under you.

Leaf River is a village of about 650 souls, if you believe the signs at the city limits. A creek runs along the north edge of town, providing a namesake in 1880 when settlers noticed that trees would shed leaves into the passing waters.

Understand that few brain surgeons or pro baseball players or movie stars, that I know of, ever called this place home. Leaf River is a tiny thread in the fabric that makes up the tapestry of the prairie. Like the hundreds of other farm villages that dot the Illinois countryside, here people work and laugh and live and die in relative obscurity.

Yet, it is special because it is home, not only to me but to thousands of other sons and daughters of generations past and present.

For the past several years, as enrollment and funds have dwindled, the local folk agonized over consolidation or annexation, arguing the pros and foes of both sides with zeal. Living 175 miles away now, I had no part in this internal bleeding. But even now, as an outsider, it is easier to understand more about the emotional hysteria that fuels such soul searching.

Fewer Opportunities
When I learned of the decision to close the school, my reaction was pragmatic. Probably for the best, I figured. High school enrollment had dipped to around one hundred, with only twenty May graduates. Each dip in enrollment translates to fewer dollars from the state, which bases its aid on the number of warm bodies in class. Maybe the school had become too small to afford kids the opportunities they needed. Money was tight and debt was beginning to surge.

So the school board opted for annexation to nearby Forreston. This means that the only approval needed is from school board members of both districts. Annexation action is approved by a county board of school trustees at a hearing, where objectors can present their arguments. A consolidation would have required a vote from the masses.

Annexation also means that the one school district merely gobbles the other district whole, leaving nary a trace of the first school's shadow. Although Forreston will get the students and the tax money from Leaf River, there will be no mention of my hometown on the Forreston High School marquee, varsity lettermen's jackets, or anywhere else.

Adjustments will be made, as in any school reorganization. In Forreston, agriculture students are whisked away to nearby Polo for classes, and the vocational students head for Whiteside Vocational Center in Sterling. So the former Leaf River students who want vocational training will be bused the forty miles to Sterling, and those who want agriculture will hopscotch between home, Forreston, and Polo.

Meanwhile back in Leaf River, the old physical plant won't be put in mothballs. The village was one of the few school districts in the state with grades kindergarten through senior high all under one roof. Most of the high school building will now be used for kindergarten through sixth-grade classes. Part of it, the old brick structure with the date "1921" etched in stone above the entrance, will be closed for good, thanks to a nasty case of asbestos.

After all, a school building is just that: a building. They could bulldoze the place and it wouldn't erase the past.

On the other hand, it's also the heart of a community, the focal point of social activities, a galvanizing force in creating town pride.

Draped in School Colors
In a few years or so, the kids from Leaf River won't think twice about going to school in another town. They may even be grateful that they will have more classes to choose from. Perhaps they will have a better shot at college. I realize now that it's not the place that made high school special, it was the people. Kids going to the new school will meet new friends, and parents will still be there to cheer them on.

After all, quality education should be the top priority of any community.

Facing the decision to close a school takes courage. It's not easy to listen to your head when the heart would rather drape itself in the school colors.

But that urge to seize and hold on to those old school symbols, I have learned, is nearly irresistible. No matter how practical you feel about consolidation, a little piece of you dies when your high school ceases to exist. The emotional tuggings of days remain etched in the mind like sepia photographs.

My pictures include the cavernous gymnasium where concert bands stirred the hearts of spring; the football games where, on cool autumn nights, the cheerleaders were occasionally drowned out by a combine furiously harvesting a nearby cornfield; the stage where child actors sweated to memorize their lines, and where my father, then a school board member, handed me a high school diploma.

Now the locked doors are silent. In the ag shop, the musty odor of steel and wood no longer mingle. The old images remain frozen, neatly wrapped in your memory, now nothing more than bits and pieces of stories to be shared with future generations.

Only ghosts of students past walk these hallways now.

The writer understands. The writer doubts. "It's like getting your roots dug out from under you," he tells us. "Goodbye, Leaf River High School" had to be written, not to fulfill an assignment but to fulfill the writer's very being. He needed us to know how he felt. He needed us to think about what present realities sometimes do to revered history.

The Essay as Vision

Words can be few. David Greenfield proved that again in "Which Way Is Heaven?" He wrote it for himself and *Saturday Review* when humankind was poised to soar into space. The essay is both prophetic and questioning.

Heaven has always existed in the mind of man as the abode of spiritual beings and the ultimate destination of believers. Its location has always been "up." The devout either look skyward while saying prayers or bow their heads in deference to higher power. Hands are held palm to palm with fingers pointing toward the zenith. The great cathedrals are all vertically dimensioned with spire upon spire directed toward space above.

This upward reaching for guidance, through thousands of years among dozens of religions and scores of languages, long ago made height synonymous with godliness, therefore with virtue and goodness. If a man were a good man, respected by his community, he was described as having a *lofty* soul.

And now at last man is about to ascend physically into this heaven that he has identified with the wonderful, the beautiful, the desirable. He will travel bodily about the void of space overhead. Will his spiritual outlook be changed by a shock of disillusion?

Blackness will be all about him. The Sun will glow, but will fail utterly to brighten an ebon sky. There will be no birds to wake him in the morning, no forming of dew on the grass—for there will be no morning and there will be no grass. The glories of billowing clouds will be unknown to him, and the comforting patter of rain will not exist. Crickets will not chirp and brooks will not run. He will neither hear sound nor feel wind. His world will indeed be unpoetic, dreary, colorless. He will experience no motion. He will just be there in space, not knowing up from down.

Because of deadly radiations, he may not even be able to look out upon the blackness through a porthole. His sense of sight may orient him only at one remove, through a TV screen. On that screen Earth will be merely a blip of bluish light in the dark—one blip among millions, perhaps billions of blips. How many of these blips are home to other beings who live and dream and work and wonder? He will not know.

In that awful environment will he at first be able to care about the splendid wheeling of the solar system, the majestic procession of the brilliantly pinpointed silence of the universe about him? Or will he instead sink into deep nostalgia for the beauty and comfort he left behind? Will he watch the blip of light that is Earth and whisper, "Would that I once again could tread the fragrant soil and feel the scented zephyrs that carry hummingbirds from lilac to rose?"

And after that will he still believe in the pearly gates and the blinding light of scriptural heaven, the harplike music, the angels and the other beings of lofty regions? Or will he find a new faith in the profounder miracles of the very nature of things?

Which way will heaven be then?

Up?

Down?

Across?

Or far within?

The essay. The beliefs and thoughts of a writer constructed for sharing. Difficult to write, as you know or can imagine. But so rewarding.

HYBRID ARTICLE TYPES

In your passage through the pages of this book you've perused pieces and wholes of all sorts of articles about all sorts of topics. Let's pause before we finish to consider several for the first time or once again: the short, the inside story and the profile.

The Short

"Which Way Is Heaven?" is a short. It required artwork to complete one page of *Saturday Review*.

You can't call "Which Way Is Heaven?" a filler, although some short pieces are no more than that. They fill stray pages or bits of space. But they also can take the form of columns or sidebars or significant feature articles.

The short is a change of pace, snappy, reader-drawing. It provides the reader with quick pleasure, a convenient and satisfying way to use time.

Just because a short is short doesn't mean it's flimsy. Good shorts are instructive or entertaining, packed with information or experience. They leave the reader contented or gratified. The reader may want more but at the same time feel satisfied. Having enjoyed the reading experience, the reader is now ready to move on. That's how I reacted to Joseph Nocera's *Esquire* (April 1989) short, "Mid-life Sax."

Middle-aged married guy walks into a saxophone store. "Can I help you?" asks the proprietor. "This is a little embarrassing . . ." the guy begins, but before he can say any more, the proprietor cuts in. "Let me guess. You've just turned forty, and you've decided to take up the tenor sax." The guy blushes. "Actually," he replies finally, "I'm *about* to turn forty, and I was thinking more about an alto."

True story. Here's another one: Middle-aged married guy decides to hold a gala bash for his fortieth birthday. One of his middle-aged friends brings along his tenor sax, which he calls his "ax," and which, it turns out, he has been playing for all of a month. Despite this lack of—talent? experience? practice? all of the above?—he is planning on entertaining (subjecting? torturing?) this decidedly captive audience with his swinging rendition of "Happy Birthday." The moment he puts reed to lips, however, we in the audience realize that this is, quite simply, the most awful saxophone playing we will ever hear in our lives. Embarrassed looks are exchanged. There is a dramatic upswing in bathroom visits. Then—the topper—when he finally puts his "ax" away, the guy spends the rest of the evening pitifully fishing for compliments.

What's that, you say? You've got a few stories like this of your own? Yes, well, I'm not surprised. This business of middle-aged men dealing with their mid-life crises by taking up the saxophone has gotten completely out of hand.

You need not take my word for it. I offer, as confirmation, the experience of Sheldon Wax of Rayburn Musical Instruments in Boston—saxophone suppliers to the stars (Sonny Rollins, Archie Shepp, et cetera, et cetera). "Doctors, lawyers, brokers, they're all taking up the saxophone," he says gleefully. Mr. Wax does not see this as an ominous development. Unlike the rest of us, he gets paid to endure bad saxophone playing.

It is difficult to know what is in the air right now that has caused this pandemic of public saxophoning. Is it a form of cheap therapy? Does it speak to some peculiarly rich fantasy life of the average middle-aged guy, an attempt, perhaps, to retrace some road not taken long ago? Or maybe it is simply a sad, desperate plea for attention. (This is my own theory.) And why the *saxophone*, for God's sake? Why not some quieter instrument, like, oh, the flute, or something heavier, like the piano (which, among its many virtues, can't be lugged around to parties)?

I don't know. And, like most people who have been forced to put up with the honking and squeaking emanating from the proliferating number of saxophones held in hopelessly untutored hands, I don't much *care*. I just want it to stop.

Something needs to be said here, so I'm going to say it: Men, it's unseemly to play a musical instrument in public when you hardly know a sharp from a flat. It's embarrassing. It's painful. It's *dumb*. However much your friends may love you, they don't want to have to listen to you try to play an instrument you can't play. Really. They don't.

Sheldon Wax again: "I've got one guy who takes lessons from me. His wife couldn't stand listening to him. So finally, she converted a closet into a practice room, with a light, a seat, and a music stand. She had it completely soundproofed." This is what I call the Gene Hackman approach to saxophone playing (see *The Conversation* for further enlightenment). In the name of your friends and loved ones, I beg of you: go and do likewise. Otherwise, next time you pull out your ax, we're not going to be so nice.

Smile. A bit of reflection. I turn the page.

And what more need we know about Manny, "one tough G.I.," than *Time* (July 24, 1989) told us on an "American Notes" page:

> He talks. He walks. He does push-ups. He sweats. And he is almost inhumanly brave. Well, strike the almost. Manny is a robot, though with a body temperature of 98.6°F and a chest that heaves with each "breath," he is astonishingly lifelike. Come October, he will wade into clouds of nerve gas, which his owner, the U.S. Army, would never dare subject a real soldier to. Manny's mission, at the Army's Dugway Proving Ground in Utah, will be to test protective clothing—for example, to determine whether walking, bending or sweating might cause the clothing to leak and let gas through. Built for $2.35 million by Battelle's Pacific Northwest Laboratories and based largely on Disney technology, this is one expensive G.I.—but then the taxpayer needn't worry about feeding or paying him.

That short is short. But long enough.

Inside Story.

James McKinley, in the investigative "Fire for Hire" article we looked at in Chapter Twelve, laboriously pieced together information. It took him months. It involved good leads and dead ends and digging, digging, digging.

That's how some inside stories or investigative pieces get done. "Like going to the libraries and looking under 'arson,' and calling the Government Printing Office, the National Fire Association, the Underwriters Laboratory, any place where we could learn about arson," he explains. McKinley dug through books, reports, newspapers and magazines. He wrote letters to and called knowledgeable people, all this for background.

He then went to sources. "I talked with firemen in New Jersey and New York," he says, "with Treasury agents in Philadelphia, with Senate sleuths in Washington, with insurance men, fire marshalls, FBI agents, prosecutors, and other arson experts in Detroit, Rochester, Chicago, St. Louis, Kansas City, Houston, Seattle, Los Angeles, San Francisco, and San Diego. I went out on arson cases, smelled the burn and char, studied the 'sets.' I spent more than 150 hours on the telephone and about a month travelling—facts which emphasize that in large-scale investigative reporting today you need substantial financial backing." Such backing is hard to get unless you get an assignment from a publication with a plush budget (and there aren't many) or if you're a magazine staffer and your editor considers a topic a must.

McKinley went back to law enforcement officials, laid out what he knew, listened to them laying out what they could of their own investigations. He got names, to be used under the cloak of confidentiality. He gleaned other names from newspaper reports of arson indictments. He by then "knew people who knew people." And he began to make the more difficult and potentially more dangerous contacts. As he puts it: "Convicts and at-large sociopaths who knew or were arsonists, hit-men, leg-men, money-scammers and the like. The problem with extracting information from these sources," he points out, "is analogous to but different from talking with police, Congressional staff, and other legitimate sorts. Here the obligation was to assure anonymity. A firmly closed mouth becomes not obligatory but imperative. A judge might put you in jail for refusing to reveal sources. A mobster can put you in the ground for revealing one."

Finally, "if you're persistent and sincere, you'll connect," he says. "You tell the man, and mean it, that you don't want to put anybody in jail; you just want a few facts, a few true tales. And you get them, true or false, and present the next source with them, assess the contradictions and corroborations."

McKinley calls it all "white-knuckle, nightmare" activity. "There's nothing romantic about it. It's hard, harrowing work about which, I'll wager, Robert Redford knows nothing."

The staff of *Heavy Duty Trucking* won a Jesse Neal citation from the American Business Press for a package of articles on "Driver Schools: How Good?" Not very, was the magazine's answer. And as part of the proof, it published associate editor Eric Marchese's inside story. In "The Blacktop Blackboard" he told how "2,095 dollars and 125 hours got the editor a truck driving license." The license he received, but did that make him a trucker? Marchese investigated from within. His was much less a piecing together than a living through. As the editor of *Heavy Duty Trucking* explained in a note for the reader: Marchese's "article is based on his diary of experiences at Superior Training Services in southern California, and on followup reporting since his attendance." He began his article for the October 1987 issue:

Editor to trucker in three easy weeks? Not quite. It wasn't exactly easy, and I didn't become an instant trucker. But I was the logical choice for the assignment.

I'm twenty-seven and single—an ideal candidate for the "new career" which some of the schools talk about. I had never driven a truck before.

A good school candidate, we figured, was Superior Training Services, one of the largest truck driver schools in the U.S. with training facilities in seven cities. One is in Rialto, California, near enough for me to commute.

In summer of 1986, Superior was being investigated by state and federal authorities for, among other things, alleged false advertising and improper use of government-guaranteed student loans. Now, more than a year later, investigations center on use of loan funds and on the school's dealings with the California Department of Motor Vehicles.

And Superior was the subject of several investigative stories by a Los Angeles television station, which interviewed several former students who complained that the training they had received was inadequate.

The Recruiter
I called Superior's Garden Grove recruiting office in early June 1986 and talked to Dino Chevalier, a recruiter. He outlined the basics: The student completes a home study course of thirty-six lessons by mail before beginning resident training, which runs for eight hours a day, five days a week, for three weeks. This concludes with on-premises testing by a state DMV license examiner.

Dino said there were about twenty instructors per class of one hundred students. Job placement services are also available to graduates. He mailed me a sales brochure which showed a tractor-trailer and two pieces of heavy machinery on its cover. Inside were descriptions of the trucking industry in America and the "solid, secure future" and "earnings potential" that's "virtually unlimited" to those in truck driving.

I met Dino the next week in his store-front office. He didn't ask me about my background. He showed me a brief videotape which, like the brochure, described Superior's services, which it said has been teaching the truck-driving trade "for over a decade." The tape promised practice on a "skill course" and in actual driving with an instructor on "city streets and local highways."

The "basic course," Dino explained, was for those who paid cash: $2,095.

Later he takes us to school. He shows us, from the inside, what happens.

Steve Kirkpatrick, the location's director, ran a quick head count—there were thirty-four of us—and determined that the class would be too small to split into separate shifts. So he assigned us all to the early (5:00 a.m.) shift, and instructors spent the first morning on school paperwork.

Mike Searcey, the placement director, spent an hour explaining job placement services and claiming great success. One of his assistants outlined at length how to write a resume and cover letter for job-hunting. Several students fell asleep in the heat during this ninety-minute talk.

We were given a packet of study guides, including a detailed four-page vehicle pre-trip inspection checklist. A slide presentation on inspection techniques led to our first demonstration. During this, I asked if we would be taught to raise the tractor hood or tilt the cab to check fluid levels and componentry. An instructor said that, depending on time, we might be shown how to do this. We never received such training.

Class time included outdoor demonstrations of the sliding fifth wheel, sliding tandem on a trailer and "drop & hook," all over a period of one hour, twenty minutes. An instructor concluded the demo by announcing that the next day, students would be given the chance to "do this individually." We did: For a half-hour, I watched one student show another how to drop and hook up a trailer. That student, in turn, showed me. No instructor was present during the practice.

Two days were devoted to learning to properly complete driver logbooks, including a co-driver's log. Exercises alone and with a partner included logbook and summary sheet of hours of service, on which we were then tested. Passing the tests often involved repeating them once or twice until we got 'most everything right.

On the fourth day, we took the standard ninety-minute, sixty-six-question open-book exam on driving and related safety procedures as found in the Federal Motor Carrier Safety Regulations handbook. We'd been given a study guide listing the question number with the corresponding chapter/subsection containing the correct answer, but I didn't bother with it. My score: 95 percent.

Then comes road time. The author continues to use his personal experience to develop his "inside story."

The tenth school day, a Friday, we got our first day of what we'd come for: Road time. It's you, the truck, and the road—plus an instructor and two other students over your shoulder.

My classmates were Ian Austin and Chris Lange. Our instructor was Bob Williams, a man in his late sixties who said he'd been with Superior about three years.

After showing us how to check out our brake lights and marker lamps, Bob took the wheel and told us this would be the only time he'd be driving. After this, it was all us. We left the school grounds and headed toward a sparsely trafficked area near Cucamonga.

We quickly discovered that our tractor was in less than perfect working order. Its clutch brake didn't work, causing some extra gear clashing, and the steering pulled to the right.

My first turn came up after 2½ hours. Though my cabmates had driven straight trucks before, I hadn't even driven a manual transmission on an auto. Bob told me that a truck is so different from a car that it wouldn't matter.

The tractor bucked and jolted as I took my first crack—or "crunch"—at working a non-synchronized ten-speed transmission and double-clutching. The term describes the action of punching the clutch pedal twice: once to take the truck out of gear and again to shift into the new gear. Engaging the clutch between the two gearshift moves allows the engine to spin gears so they'll match.

While initially trying to coordinate this maneuver, I found that I was unconsciously single-clutching—pulling it out of gear, then upshifting without the clutch. Bob yelled, "You're floating the gears!" He said this technique was "terrible on the gears," and there wasn't a company around that would look favorably on this practice. (Not so, but at that point I didn't know any better.)

My major concern was keeping the truck moving and in gear, and it took me a couple more turns at the wheel to get comfortable and confident enough to keep track of everything. I never really felt fully in control of the truck, at least to the extent that I would want to take the rig out solo.

But the basics were all placed before me, and any willing pupil could catch on to them in just a handful of hours. My classmates seemed to be faring far better than I. They *had* to: They wanted to make it a career.

And then Marchese turned to what the school apparently considered instruction:

When we were finished on this first day, Bob noted my problems with shifting and told me to use the weekend to review the home study chapters on that subject. This was the first time in two weeks that any instructor had referred to the textbook materials.

Bob also showed us a photocopy of an instruction sheet he had typed up himself. It explained the basic motions of upshifting, and commanded us to "PRACTICE, PRACTICE, PRACTICE!" He insisted that I keep this one copy because I needed the information more than my cabmates. My total driving time on that first day was one hour, ten minutes.

The following Monday, our second road day, I tallied one hour, fifteen minutes of driving in the morning and about the same that afternoon—about what I'd get each day for the remainder of the course. I still had problems shifting, but I was catching on.

On Tuesday I was the first to drive, and everyone was surprised at how well I was handling the gears. Bob was convinced that I had gone home and "practiced." On what?

Marchese takes us step by step. We're inside with him. He is showing us, not just telling us. The problem he's stressing becomes much more graphic. The training included eleven hours of over-the-road driving time. Eleven. Marchese's school experience ended with commencement day:

Better known as "DMV Day," the entire time was devoted to the DMV testing for our Class I licenses. Students were carted a few at a time in the back of a pickup truck to the pad for one last chance to practice the ninety-degree alley docking.

From there we were driven to the school's front entrance, tested by DMV examiners, and returned to the classroom area. Those who failed the exam were told to wait for their names to be called again and for the process to be repeated—presumably until they passed.

I drew a Mr. Campbell as DMV examiner in my first shot at the test. He watched me dock the truck fairly well on the second or third try, then got in the cab and directed me out the gate and down a street. We drove around the roads nearest the school for about ten minutes, then came back. I was out of gear most of the time, losing my place while trying to shift.

Back at the school, Campbell wrote "F" at the top of the exam form. He said he didn't know whether I was nervous or just needed practice, but that I'd better work on my gears. My downshifts (which I struggled with for the past week) were smooth, but upshifting (which I thought I had a handle on) was bad.

I was brought back for a second try an hour later. This time I got another examiner, Ronald Miller, who watched me flub the alley dock three times (the maximum allowed). He told me to pull forward and said, "You know you've used up your three turns. Now I'm going to let you try it once more, so do it right this time."

I concentrated, put the truck in reverse and angled the trailer partly into the dock. Then I pulled up to straighten the rig, and backed it in well enough to pass.

Miller got into the cab and we took almost the same route as before. He noticed I lugged the engine in tenth gear as slow as 35 mph, but said nothing. I was using the gears as little as possible, but managed some smooth downshifts, as before. We returned to the school, and Miller said he knew why I "played it safe on the gears — because you flunked on gears the first time. Well, don't be afraid to use those gears. I think you'll get the hang of it with more practice."

He gave me a 75 out of a 100 — the minimum passing score. He completed the paperwork on my temporary license and told me how to obtain my permanent Class 1 at my home DMV office. I was now a fully licensed truck driver, and was carted back to the classroom.

Instructors then presented us with our graduation materials, including a Certificate of Completion, resembling a diploma; a yellow DMFV Certificate of Completion; a Road Test/Written Exam certificate; and a Resident Training Academic Achievement form.

My academic scores were impressive:

- 95 percent on the open-book DOT rules and regs.
- 95 percent on drivers' logs.
- A maximum 100 percent for pre- and post-trip inspections, though I'd forgotten several items.
- 100 percent for straight-line backing, when even on the last day I was still crooked.
- 90 percent for alley docking, although it took the help of three instructors during the pad phase.
- 100 percent for drop-and-hook (coupling/uncoupling) of tractor and trailer when I had screwed it up in several places.

The score sheet also indicated the 201 out of 250 on road driving by Bob Williams — the most honest grade of the course.

My total score out of a possible 850 points: 781. Comments: "Eric with experience will be a good driver." That could apply to anyone. I spent twenty minutes at the placement office, going through the motions of obtaining four local job leads.

Thus ended my student truck-driving career.

The author goes on to evaluate his training, not positively as one would suspect. His conclusion:

I have to admit, though, that in return for my (or my company's) $2,095, the people at Superior Training Services did fulfill at least one promise: They got me a Class 1 license. And, shaky training or not, many of my classmates have since made a go of it and are working as truckers.

As for me, I went back to editing and writing for *HDT* with a better knowledge and appreciation of equipment and what it takes to be a truck driver.

But does that make me a *trucker*? No way.

We've been on the inside with Marchese. Consequently, our understanding of what he learned and didn't learn, and what driving schools taught and didn't (and should have) is deepened and sharpened.

Profile

Cities can be profiled. So can streets. So can buildings. So can institutions. Mostly, however, we profile people. A profile recreates the subject, makes it come alive on paper, gives the subject shape and meaning, causes us as readers to meet and know that subject, that city, that institution, that person.

Let's start with an A-B-C-D combination.

A profile should be *authentic* — in facts, feel, and tone.

It should be a *bridge* from the little or nothing a reader knows about the person portrayed to an understanding; it also should be a bridge from the reader's life to lessons that can be learned through the life and work of the person being read about.

It should be a *challenge*, not answering every question or crossing every t; a part of the profile should remain enigma; the writer should leave some thinking room.

A profile should bring *discovery*.

Paul Murray Kendall profiled prominent figures of history during his career. He also wrote *The Art of Biography*, which subsequent generations of biographers have been reading for guidance. Kendall called biography "the simulation, not the ledger book, of an existence. The biographer," he continued, "cannot reproduce the actual concatenation of events. His subject may, over a period of months, be developing a dozen different themes of experience; if the biographer attempts to thread the tangle of details day by day out of which these experiences are being built, he will conjure up chaos. He must thrust into the reader's ears the noisy crosscurrents of man's passage through time; but if he is to make that passage intelligible, he must do violence to time; the clutter of events will be cut away, happenings scattered through years will be grouped in order to reveal underlying currents." Kendall wrote of "certain continuing sounds in the 'buzz and hum' of daily life — a hobby, an eccentricity of diet, a habitual inability to stay awake at lectures, a desultory friendship too important to omit but insufficiently substantial to be woven through — that will almost of necessity be grouped arbitrarily and brought into the narrative when the biographer's ear tells him that the moment has struck." Kendall separated biography from other literary arts. "They seek to evoke reality from illusion," he said. "Biography hopes to fasten illusion upon reality, to elicit, from the coldness of paper, the warmth of a life being lived."

Kendall wrote mostly book-length biographies. We in journalism write shorter ones. In so doing, we must select elements that make a man or woman stand out. More than that we probably cannot do. *Mother Jones* has run annually short profiles of ten heroes, described as "Verses for the unsung; regular, special people who build up, fight back, blow the whistle, and win the day." Jessie Deer-In-Water is such a person, and was featured in the January 1989 issue. Nancy Hanback Perreault sums up Deer-In-Water's life this way:

> My mom fights poison for a living," six-year-old Jay often tells his friends. Jay's mother is Jessie Deer-In-Water, a Cherokee woman and founder of Native Americans for a Clean Environment. She also happens to be a grandmother of two. And she is the driving force behind a campaign to convince government officials and Kerr-McGee's corporate executives to either operate a safe facility or shut down.
>
> Kerr-McGee's Sequoya nuclear facility in Gore, Oklahoma, is one of two in the nation that convert milled uranium into hexafloride, one step in the process of making nuclear reactor fuel and nuclear weapons materials. After much pressure and several NACE victories over the last four years, Kerr-McGee has given in to many of Deer-In-Water's safety demands, and although it hasn't shut down, it did recently sell out to G.A. Technologies, Inc.
>
> "We live in a wooded area, where we can't even see another house," says Deer-In-Water in her easy southern, Cherokee accent. "But we still don't feel isolated enough, because only ten air miles away is the Kerr-McGee facility."
>
> Deer-In-Water decided to take on Kerr-McGee the day in 1984 that she learned the facility had requested a license for a nuclear waste injection well on a spot flanked by two earthquake fault lines. She worried about leaks into nearby drinking wells: "We as Cherokees believe that water is alive. City water, with all its chemicals, is dead." Deer-In-Water helped to round up two hundred locals for a public meeting, where an increasingly frustrated health department official "started hollering at me, 'You can't stop this plant.' He made me so mad," remembers Deer-In-Water, "that I said, 'Well, I'll give it my best shot, buddy.' "
>
> She spearheaded citizen pressure until, a year later, Kerr-McGee withdrew its application for the injection well. Next she organized a widely publicized demonstration to spotlight the company's long record of safety violations

and illegal practices. And when Kerr-McGee wanted a permit for an on-site radioactive waste dump, Deer-In-Water's group helped block it. A Canadian epidemiologist is working with Deer-In-Water on a study of high human cancer rates and unexplained deaths and malformations of farm animals around Kerr-McGee, trying to discover if there is a link to the facility. The company's latest idea is to convert its nuclear waste into commercial fertilizer, which it has already spread over thousands of acres of Oklahoma farmland.

Meanwhile, Deer-In-Water attends college full-time to earn the law degree she sees as an essential tool. "I might as well become a lawyer," she says, "because it looks like I'm going to be in this business – 'fighting poisons,' as Jay says – for the rest of my life."

We get one aspect of the woman's life plus a bit of background. That's all. That's enough to serve the purpose of the article. It serves Jessie Deer-In-Water well, too.

We can but hint sometimes because to tell all would take more space than we have, far more space. So Lynn Norment condensed the insightful information about civil rights leader Coretta Scott King this way for *Ebony* (January 1990):

> At around 7:00 a.m. her day begins as the previous one ended: watching television news and reading the newspaper in the same bedroom she once shared with Dr. Martin Luther King Jr. After digesting the day's news, along with a cup of tea, she turns off the television set and in the early morning quietly meditates and prays – on world issues, on Atlanta, on social issues, on her day's schedule.
>
> At about 9:00 a.m., personal secretary Patricial Latimore arrives to assist Mrs. King with her correspondence and other personal business, as well as wardrobe selection for the day. At the same time, Mrs. King goes over the details of the day's schedule with special assistant Beni Ivey via a telephone line that links her directly to her office at The Martin Luther King Jr. Center for Nonviolent Social Change, of which she is founding president and chief executive officer.
>
> There will be an interview, a photography session, a lunch-time gathering with her children, meetings with her staff, a board meeting to coordinate, a visit to the King Center's early learning facility, and a pep talk to the student conference planning committee. The day is due to end about 11:00 p.m., after the final encore of *Stepping Into Tomorrow*, a theatrical production presented by daughter Yolanda King and Attollah Shabazz, co-directors of Nucleus Theatre Co.
>
> After going over her schedule, Mrs. King pulls on a jogging suit, crosses the hallway and exercises for thirty minutes . . . .

To profile is to select. In his introduction to *Best American Essays 1987*, journalist Gay Talese reminds us of that in discussing how he uses quotes. Rarely verbatim, he says:

> I was far less interested in the exact words that came out of people's mouths than in the essence of their meaning. More important than what people say

is what they think, even though the latter may initially be difficult for them to articulate and may require much pondering and reworking within the interviewee's mind—which is what I gently try to prod and stimulate as I query, interrelate, and identify with my subjects as I personally accompany them whenever possible, be it on their errands, their appointments, their aimless peregrinations before dinner or after work. Wherever it is, I try physically to be there in my role as a curious confidant, a trustworthy fellow traveler searching into their interior, seeking to discover, clarify, and finally to describe in words (my words) what they personify and how they think.

Occasionally, he adds, there is "a turn of phrase, a special word, a personal revelation conveyed in an inimitable style that should be put on paper at once lest part of it be forgotten."

Take this excerpt of quote and action from a story in the August 1, 1988 issue of *People* about Brazilian gold miners, most specifically about one prospector named Ismael Pereira. Ron Arias wrote the article:

> "That fist of gold is right here under my feet," says Pereira as a claim partner fills his sack. "If I work hard, I know I'll find the big one. God will reward me. We work like slaves, but every day we pray for the gold and the freedom it will bring."
>
> Amid the din of voices and a sputtering water-pump engine, Pereira hefts a load of ore onto his back, then jostles into the throng of mud-smeared bodies plodding toward one of the precarious wooden ladders used to reach the higher ledges. Muscles taut, sweat streaming down his face and body, he clambers up the slippery rungs until he reaches a terrace where he heaves his burden onto a waist-high stack of hundreds of similar sacks. Here, an official from the miners' cooperative carefully notes Pereira's first delivery of the day. Later, the gold-bearing ore will be hauled by truck to the cooperative's sluice works for processing.
>
> Pereira makes an average of forty hauls a day from his five-foot by five-foot claim to the drop-off site halfway up the giant pit. He knows that the more loads he hauls, the greater will be his tiny share of whatever gold dust or nuggets he and his eight partners find that day. "Years ago, I was a wild guy, drinking, smoking a lot and wasting my strength," he says with a swagger before an amused group of younger men. "But no more. I'm a grandfather. I just work and work, say my prayers at night and stay out of trouble. I guess now my only vice is hope."

There's a treasure of information in that passage. Pereira's own words turn a spotlight on his life and motivation.

The best profile work suggests closeness. Not interviews as much as observation, a being there. When newsman Harry Reasoner profiled jazzman Miles Davis, he sometimes drifted into the background. That was useful for observing. Reasoner's *60 Minutes* piece contained a scene in which the musician watched boxing on television, having forgotten the presence of the newsman who just sat quietly and watched his subject.

Observation. As in David Rubin's article for *Connoisseur:*

Young Uck Kim gently pulled away the red silk scarf concealing the charms of his celebrated Stradivarius violin. With radiant pleasure he pointed out the plum and yellow coloring, the flat belly, the graceful purfling, and the perfectly carved F-holes. "You can almost see its heart beat," he said. "You feel it's alive. It just radiates, even without playing. I have never seen anything so beautiful in my life."

Rubin's piece is less about the violinist than about the violin. It's a profile about Stradivarius violins. Young Uck Kim is a supporting player. But violin and violinist become one in that paragraph.

Observation. As in Whitney Balliett's profile for *The New Yorker* (September 19, 1988). Balliett has watched and listened carefully and caught his subject in the act—on paper:

Here is how the comedian Jackie Mason ended his one-man show at the Brooks Atkinson on a Saturday night in January, 1987. "I never thought I'd be a comedian," he said. "Who expected it when you come from a family of rabbis? I have three brothers who are rabbis to this day, and my father all his life was a rabbi. Everybody was a rabbi in the ancestry of my family. So when my father looked at me as his fourth son, naturally he waited for me to become a rabbi and I wanted to make him proud by following in his footsteps, and I started to deliver sermons, and as I was delivering the sermons I didn't feel honest, so I started to tell a few jokes here and there to make it more palatable for myself, and as the jokes were getting better and better I started to charge a cover and a minimum, and then, as the Gentiles in the area heard about me, more and more Gentiles came to see me. So many Gentiles came that before you knew it there was no room for the Jews. The Jews couldn't get in there. I became the only rabbi with a Gentile congregation." This classic Mason mixture of truth and hyperbole was delivered in his customary medium-heavy Yiddish accent, at high speed, yet conversationally, with a steady underlying chuckle (not always audible in the audience but visible in the half smiles that ducked continually across his face), and with a freshness that belied the twelve hours of monologue he had already delivered on Broadway that week.

We're there. We're there at a revealing moment.

Profiles shouldn't start with birth. Birth congeals a person with every other. The writer of a biography or profile or portrait must find that event or situation or feeling or relationship or trait that separates the subject from everyone else and makes him or her special.

It is midmorning, and Helen Frankenthaler, sixty-one, the grande dame of American painting is being interviewed in her Manhattan studio. Interviewed? Perhaps the term is a bit misleading. She's actually engaged in a mad, Monty Python-esque satire of an interview.

Deeply suspicious of the press, Frankenthaler has required that all questions be submitted in advance. As if that were not sufficient guarantee against the hazards of spontaneity, she has typed her responses on sheets of paper. She begins reading the questions and her answers, when suddenly she stops. Why should *she* have to do all the work, she demands of the reporter. At least *he* can read the questions. For the next few minutes, the artist and reporter hand the script back and forth, each reading his and her lines.

That telling moment published in *People* in 1989 exemplifies. We begin to know Frankenthaler.

A profile amounts to writing with multiple functions. Biography is story or narrative, impression or description, explanation or exposition, and opinion or argument. All of these—in varying degrees—depending on the purpose of your profile, the approach, and the depth. But the best biographical work combines, blends. It is a verbal portrait. It is a person placed in context so that he or she on paper becomes inseparable from the context because in real life he or she is inseparable from that context.

Remember, don't cover too much. Cover thoroughly those aspects or elements that make your case and color your portrait. Be selective. Be painstakingly comprehensive within those areas or parts of a person's life you've chosen to deal with. Being thorough doesn't necessarily mean long. Here's a complete piece from *People*, December 1989, "Well, Button My Lips if Dalton Stevens Hasn't Gone and Stuck 'Em on Every Ol' Thing."

If you ask fifty-nine-year-old Dalton Stevens of Bishopville, South Carolina, why he drives an old Chevy Chevette with more than 100,000 buttons plastered on it, he will gladly tell you: "Well, I reckon it's because I didn't want to irritate my wife, me climbing in and out of bed and all."

Uh, beg your pardon, sir?

"Well, I got insomnia," Stevens clarifies, more or less. "It was the middle of the night, and there I was, wide awake. The buttons, they were just lying there, so I started sewing."

Stevens stitched away on a pair of blue jeans night after sleepless night about four years ago until they were covered with buttons. Next he worked on a shirt, then a cap. He had put 15,333 buttons on the three pieces when "the weather got better, so I moved on outdoors and started on the Chevy." After attaching approximately 109,000 buttons to the inside and outside of his car with glue—"Needle and thread don't take too good to metal," he rightly notes—Stevens turned to his guitar (3,005 buttons).

Stevens didn't stop there. After the guitar he festooned his twenty-five-year-old banjo with buttons. Next he decorated a non-operating flush toilet with 26,000 buttons. Finally he adorned a casket that proclaimed him the Button King. Ripley's Believe It or Not Museum has offered to buy the coffin, Stevens claims, but he has refused, not only because he expects to take it with him but because he doesn't want to break up the set.

Stevens, you see, is a country music performer ("I don't play no tearjerkers") who works at small shopping malls near his home ("I don't entertain for free"). All those buttons are attention-getting parts of his act. Last month he and his wife, Ruby, who is "about fifty-seven," began a tour of the Land of the Rising Sun under the sponsorship of Japan's Iris Button Co., which claims it makes most of the buttons he buys. But what his visit will do to foster East-West understanding is still open to speculation.

E.M. Swift of *Sports Illustrated* had more space to portray skater Brian Boitano. But his article (in the January 27, 1988 issue) focused on pertinent moments, on training, on skating:

> It's 1:30 p.m. Boitano has been training since 7:45 — three hours of practicing figures, a few minutes' rest while the ice was resurfaced and then two more hours of freestyle skating. He's an uncomplaining worker, for he hasn't, even after all these years, lost his love of skating.
> The mist has lifted off the ice, and Boitano's blades are making short, quick, snicking noises as he picks up speed to attempt another quad. As he approaches the takeoff point, he thinks once more. Sit a little forward; push light; not too hyper on the turn. He pivots backward, coasting, his legs flexed. Then he sets his toe pick and *explodes*!
> You still can't follow the spin. Up and out he soars, an airborne top, some sort of impossible human gyroscope on skates. As he blurs before you, you are thinking, There will never be a quintuple toe loop; they will run a two-minute mile before a man can spin faster than this while in flight. And then — *crunkkkk!* — the moment is past. His blade hits, and he turns. He has nailed it. A perfectly executed quad. Leaver watches, a smile creasing her face, as Boitano makes a couple of perfunctory moves and then coasts past, hands on his hips, catching his breath. What was different about that one? he wonders.

That's how writer Swift ended his profile, with a pertinent moment. He preceded it with others to give some warmth and life to a gifted athlete on paper.

Of actor Michael Keaton much could have been written, too. Terri Minsky came to the subject when Keaton turned Batman. Her July 1989 *Premiere* article concentrated on that aspect of Keaton's life. His growing up, his maturation, his career development are not ignored, but Batman is the way back and the way ahead:

> Oh, man, this mask is the worst. Your neck feels like it's in a vise, you've got no peripheral vision, and you can't really hear — everything sounds like it's underwater. And the sweat — ten takes, eleven, twelve . . . . Check this out — if you want to go to the bathroom, you have to take the whole costume off, but you never need to, 'cause you're sweating so damn much. And the cape. Weighs a ton. Kills your shoulders every time you throw a punch. One thing is for sure, one thing is for *damn* sure: only a seriously strange person would put on this getup just to go beat up some bad guys.
> Michael Keaton, sitting in a canvas-back chair on the London set of *Batman*, is dressed for his title role — his Bat-glove wrapped around a Coke can, he is praying for somebody to call for a break so he can take off the Bat-mask and Bat-cape and loosen the corset ties of his Bat-suit. Nobody does. It's not as if he can remove the costume whenever he wants to; it's bolted together by two screws through the Bat-insignia on his chest. Meanwhile, Jack Nich-

olson is roaming around the cathedral-tower set, entertaining the crew with his banter; sure, why should he be cranky? As Batman's archenemy, the Joker, he's only got to endure white make-up, a lime green wig, and prosthetic cheekbones.

Today, Keaton and Nicholson are inching their way through the climactic confrontation between Batman and the Joker. At this rate, it could be a while before Keaton can don the more comfortable Armani suits favored by Batman's alter ego, millionaire Bruce Wayne. He'll be in the Bat-suit for the entire week. As it is, he's been in it for more than an hour — grabbing Nicholson by the back of his harlequin poker-dealer's outfit and hauling him head-first through some breakaway plywood. Grab, haul; grab, haul; grab, haul — with each new take, Keaton has to wait, swathed in full and torturous Bat-regalia, for the plywood to be reassembled and for a fresh burst of scenic fog.

Now he looks over and sees director Tim Burton in a clutch in the middle of the set, working out the blocking for the next shot. "Hey, Tim!" Keaton calls, his tone implying, *Haven't you forgotten something?* "Oh, uh, break, everyone," says Burton . . . .

One finds in each life . . . .

One finds in each life: that should be your guide.

It was mine in each of the little profiles I did on the great composers for *Highlights for Children* (April 1986). I shared two earlier: one in part, the other completely. And now, here's "Johann Strauss."

The little boy was only six. And there he was, sitting at the piano, picking out his own waltz tune. How pleased his mother was.

The boy's father also heard and listened. Carefully, for that father was Johann Strauss, the Elder. And he was the most-loved composer/conductor of waltz music in the world, music with a catchy *one*-two-three, *one*-two-three beat. He, too, was pleased.

But one day, when he discovered his son Johann, now thirteen, before a mirror doing a perfect imitation of his father playing and conducting with his violin, Papa was no longer pleased. Not because the boy wasn't good; he was. But the father knew painfully well the exhausting work and travel and financial worries of a musician. No, sir. His sons would become settled professional men.

Thank goodness for Mama Strauss. She insisted that Johann have a strong education in music. She cut corners in the family's food budget to pay for Johann's music lessons.

Of course she could not have known it, but her son would become a waltz composer more famous and more loved by far than her husband.

As Johann Strauss the Elder was called the Waltz King, so would Strauss the Younger be, and a greater one at that.

He must have thought about those moments of his childhood when, at age nineteen, he made his announcement with signs all around the city of Vienna. Young Johann would conduct his own orchestra in a concert of his own compositions.

He knew his father would be angry. But he didn't know that his father's friends were planning to disrupt the concert.

It was a lovely October evening—warm and clear. Thousands gathered both inside and outside a large restaurant/dance hall to hear the young Johann Strauss and his new orchestra.

Inside, it wasn't so lovely. Too many people were crowded in. It was hot and stuffy. The waiters gave up trying to serve food and wine. In one corner sat Mama Strauss praying.

Johann entered in a blue coat with silver buttons, gray pants—a fancy outfit he hadn't yet paid for. He'd grown a mustache to make him look older. So nervous was he that he almost ran out and away. But, instead, he raised his violin and set the orchestra into action.

The musicians played one of his new waltzes, a waltz with a haunting melody and a rhythm that made people want to dance.

When it was finished, boos could be heard from Father Strauss's friends. But there was more applause. And there were cheers. The applause and cheers wouldn't stop until Johann Strauss and his orchestra played the waltz again. And twice more.

Next, they played a Strauss polka. By then, even those who had come to boo began to cheer.

Another new waltz had to be played no fewer than nineteen times!

Obviously, the evening was a glorious success. The Viennese had a new musical king, one who ended his triumphant concert by playing one of his father's waltzes. It was his way of asking forgiveness.

By 1872 Johann Strauss the Younger was no longer so young. He was forty-seven. He was famous, too, with a long list of popular waltzes and polkas and marches to his credit.

And the Americans wanted him.

He had an invitation to perform in Boston and New York. At first he said a rousing "no." The truth was he feared the ocean crossing. But the Bostonians were so determined that they offered a hundred thousand dollars, an incredible sum in those days, so incredible that Strauss had to change his "no" to "yes."

It turned out that he loved the ocean voyage, all thirteen days of it. On stormy days, he was the only one in the dining room eating.

He didn't love his stay in the United States. He couldn't understand why reporters followed him everywhere and why people seemed to want to touch him. It frightened him, and he spent much of his time locked up in hotel rooms.

But the concerts were wild successes. Three of them in New York in a normal-sized theatre with a normal-sized orchestra of seventy. Fourteen in Boston, the biggest one in a wooden shed that held a hundred thousand people and was specially built for the event.

For that occasion Strauss had two thousand players plus a chorus of twenty thousand! Plus pieces of railroad track for chimes. Plus a bass drum eighteen feet across. Strauss stood atop a hundred-foot tower to give his directions to several dozen other conductors stationed around the huge space.

During rehearsals he became so disturbed that he again wanted to run away. But, as he said later, if he'd refused, it "would have cost me my life."

Somehow all those musicians performed his most famous of all waltzes, *The Blue Danube*, the waltz that had sold millions of copies of sheet music and that people everywhere were dancing to.

Strauss became even more of a hero. Women wanted locks of his hair. Well, they got locks – not of his black curly hair but from a Newfoundland dog that had to part with much of its coat.

In later years Strauss wrote a series of operettas which came to be as popular as his waltzes. Why not? They were filled with more waltz tunes.

His best-known operetta is *Die Fledermaus*, which in German means *The Bat*. It has a silly story about a man going to a party in the costume of a bat and all the foolish things that happen. The music is gorgeous.

The great composer Johannes Brahms once autographed a lady's fan with a phrase from Strauss's *The Blue Danube*. Under it he wrote "Unfortunately not by me."

But fortunately it was by Johann Strauss the Younger, who left us so much danceable and hummable music.

A scene from childhood. A follow-up from early career and first success. A visit to the United States. Some filler biographical material. As much as space would permit. Enough, I believe, to introduce a young reader to a distinctive individual.

Which brings me to "One Heart Warms Many Chilly Fingers" from *Time* (January 2, 1989), David Brand's profile of "a Samaritan of the streets" who on New York's Bowery "ministers to the old, the reticent and the shy." Brand, through selection of material, through approach, through purpose introduces us to a man whose life is completed within the life of others, who considers himself incomplete without those whose existence he sustains, even enriches, through his acts of kindness and caring. We are told, in brief, of his origin and his profession. But the focus of the profile is the Samaritan's street activity. That is what makes him singular. That is what made me want to learn about him.

The old man sits on a bench off the Bowery, glazed eyes staring into a void, sipping on a tall can of Bud enclosed in a brown paper bag. "Twelve dollars and fifty cents," he mutters. "Twelve dollars and fifty cents." It is the sum total of one man's life – the amount he says he has been trying to borrow from his family in Detroit to ensure his burial in potter's field, and to escape from the death beyond death: "They send you to medical school and cut you up into little pieces – that's not for me. No sir."

This observation on oblivion was prompted by something as mundane as a pair of gloves, which had been proffered tentatively by a short man wearing a cap and an aging leather jacket, with a faded green cotton bag slung over his shoulder like an Irish peddler. For the past twenty-four years, between Thanksgiving and Christmas, Michael Greenberg, sixty, has been taking his bag of gloves to Manhattan's Bowery, long the haunt of the down-and-outs and the lost-weekenders, and wandering the gritty neighborhood looking for "the old, the reticent and the shy." When he finds one, like the old man on the bench, he dangles a pair of gray or maroon woolen gloves and says, "Take them, please. They're free. They're a gift. No strings attached." Then he shakes a trembling hand. This simple act of communion, says Greenberg, "will almost invariably bring a smile of acknowledgment. You can tell the handshake is in earnest because they press your fingers."

It is hard work for this retired advertising account executive, handing out three hundred pairs of gloves every year on New York's infamous skid row, which runs from Chinatown a dozen or so blocks north to Cooper Square. "Oh, if I just wanted to stand here and give them away, I could get rid of one thousand in an hour. Easy. But I prefer to go looking for the people I want. The ones who avoid eye contact. It is not so much the gloves, but telling people they count."

Greenberg was shaped for his role of Samaritan of the streets by his memories of Depression hard times and by the charity of his father, Pinchus Joseph, who owned a Brooklyn bakery. "My father would often include a coffee cake or a sandwich in the bag without his customer's knowing," he says. "He would always tell us, 'Don't deprive yourself of the joy of giving.'" Money was short, and Michael has a searing recollection of losing a glove while helping bring supplies into the store on a bitterly cold morning. "I was never able to find it, and for years I went around without gloves. I never asked my father to replace them because I felt so guilty."

When his father died in November 1963, he searched for an appropriate memorial. "I remembered the incident of the lost glove, and it occurred to me that gloves are a powerful symbol because being warm is being well-off and being cold is being poor. At that time there weren't as many homeless people on the streets, and so I immediately thought of the Bowery, and I decided to put a pair of gloves on some poor fellow's hands just as my father had slipped free Danish rolls into customers' bags." Greenberg was then teaching sixth grade in a Brooklyn public school, and the following year, despite his modest salary, he bought seventy-two pairs of woolen gloves, took them to the Bowery, and handed them out (very timidly, he admits) to the destitute and the derelict. Why seventy-two? Because eighteen is the Hebrew symbol for life, and "four times life is seventy-two."

In 1966 Greenberg left teaching for the advertising business, and with a higher salary he could afford to buy gloves regularly; if they were on sale, he bought in bulk. For the next ten years the Bowery became his route every November and December. In 1976 he was in the subway, taking two bags containing $220 worth of newly purchased gloves back to his office, when someone grabbed the gloves and ran. He reported the theft to the police, the New York *Times* heard of the incident, and for the first time the world read about the "glove man."

As a result of that and many other television and newspaper stories, Greenberg has been inundated with gloves. A Girl Scout troop held a glove drive for him. A Colorado ski resort sent him its entire lost-and-found department. And when a story about him appeared in the *International Herald Tribune* four years ago, gloves flowed in, from Europe to India: leather gloves, driving gloves, fleece-lined gloves, children's gloves, even work gloves. Some people send pairs, but most often they send only rights or lefts (the rights outnumber the lefts by four to one, for some curious reason). Some also send cash, which is quickly returned "because I am not an organized charity."

Greenberg's tiny apartment in Greenwich Village is piled high with sixteen hundred mis-matched gloves, and he regularly has friends in for a glove-matching party because "I would never give out mismatched gloves. That's denigrating." The group sits around, drinking beer and matching gloves, "and the next day we discover there are not as many matched as we thought."

Greenberg has witnessed a parade of defeated humanity in his quarter-century of giving on skid row. He has offered gloves to his former professor at Brooklyn College and to a once famous baritone at the Metropolitan Opera, recognized by Greenberg from his days as a youthful walk-on at the Met. Most of the people he meets are confused, seemingly uncertain of where they are or what they are doing. The more frightened refuse the gloves, and he will follow them for several blocks, insisting, "They're a gift. I really want you to have them." One elderly man finally stopped, took the gloves, then asked, "Do you have them in blue?"

Major changes have swept down the Bowery since Greenberg first ventured out. Sad, abandoned men can still be found in the few remaining missions, and in hotels with names like the Prince and the Sunshine. But most of the eighty-two bars and dozens of flophouses that once served a floating population of aging, mostly white, casual laborers and alcoholics, have gone. Instead the area now boasts expensive apartments and chic restaurants. The newer homeless inhabitants of skid row are more likely to be young, unemployed men who clean car windows at intersections or mill in groups on street corners. Drugs have become a perennial problem on the Bowery. "It's a fearful place," says Greenberg. "The men are a lot younger, a lot tougher and a lot meaner."

But the man with the faded green bag continues to stalk the Bowery and its tributaries, staying clear of "the tough people, who have gloves anyway," and seeking out "the little old guy who is frightened of people." Sometimes he hands gloves to men who are muttering aimlessly over the rubble of their lives, barely aware of what they are clutching; some quickly trade them in for a pint of cheap wine. "It doesn't make any difference. When you give a gift, you let it go."

Occasionally, a star of hope radiates through all this gloom. Recently he was waiting for a train at Penn Station, when a well-dressed man asked him if he was "the glove guy." Says Greenberg: "He said that I had given him a pair of gloves on the Bowery five years previously and that now he was married with two children, and he wanted to give me twenty dollars to buy more gloves. I told him the same as I tell others who want to write me a check: no thank you. You spend the money on gloves, and you give them out."

14

Some Concluding Remarks — Providing Those Finishing Touches

Ah, what a death hath found thee, little one,
Poor little child.
Was it our ancient wall so savagely hath rent
Thy curls . . . here, where the bone-edge frayed
Grins white . . . Ah God, I will not see.
Ye tender arms . . . how from the shoulder loose
Ye drop. And dear proud lips, so full of hope
And closed forever. What false words ye said
At daybreak, when ye crept into my bed,
Called me kind names, and promised;
"Grandmother,
When thou art dead, I will cut close my hair,
And lead out all the captains to ride by
Thy tomb." . . . Tis I — old, homeless, childless,
That for thee must shed cold tears.

Those lines come from Euripides, during the final moments of his *Trojan Women*. Andromache's child has been thrown from the wall of Troy. The child's grandmother claims the little victim. She speaks to it.

The play is all pain and sorrow, weeping and torrents of tears. Euripides staged it in 416 B.C. to preach that war is cruel and pitiless and senseless, that it consumes the innocent.

Now read these words:

Delfonic McCray, thirteen, was big for his age, six feet tall. He liked basketball and girls, and kept love letters carefully folded in his Michael Jackson wallet. He and a friend were on their way to a Chicago Bulls basketball game and stopped at a housing project on the west side of Chicago to see a girlfriend. As they approached the back entrance of a graffiti-scarred tenement, a group of youths taunted them. Delfonic approached tentatively, then turned and ran. One of the youths casually drew a .22-cal. handgun and shot him. "We had a good kid coming along," said Delfonic's grandmother. Now that he was becoming a man, she had gone out and bought him a new suit. "I had no way of knowing he would be buried in it," she said.

Those lines come from *Time* (September 16, 1985). They highlight an urban tragedy, black-on-black violence. "When Brother Kills Brother" shows the problem in personal terms, the losses spreading to the innocent.

More than 2,400 years separate those two passages, and yet they represent one anguish, one expression, one line of thought. Fiction and nonfiction, and yet they blend, merge, express a continuity.

Euripides observed reality and weighed its consequence. So did the writers at *Time*. The serious writer, whether of fiction or nonfiction, gathers material from experience, gives it emotional and mental dimension, then uses technique — artistry, if you will — in adding words.

Artistry to captivate.

Artistry to compete with other material that will be read or watched or heard, to compete with other activities the reader could be engaged in.

Editors cannot forget the need to compete successfully. Nor can you as writer.

THE BEST AND THE BRIGHTEST

When judges judge what's best — those, for instance, who determine each year's prizes in the prestigious National Magazine Awards competition, sponsored by the American Society of Magazine Editors, and the Jesse H. Neal Awards of the Association of Business Publishers — they look for certain qualities that to them mark outstanding work. In a way, they're editors after the fact, evaluating accomplishments very much the way an editor might study your submission to that magazine.

The Neal competition takes three criteria into consideration. The first: how well does the entry serve the market; that is, how valuable is the subject covered to the reader? That's another way of saying that reader orientation is paramount. To repeat, for you this means: Know your audience.

Next, the ABP judges look for journalistic enterprise: the insight, initiative, imagination, originality, diligence, depth of reporting, and analysis exhibited by the story.

Finally, the judges look at editorial craftsmanship. That includes appropriateness of visual presentation (which shouldn't concern you) and effectiveness and clarity of writing (which should).

Those are useful guidelines for you. So, too, are similar qualitative measurements on the minds of judges of the annual National Magazine Awards. These acknowledgements honor editorial excellence and encourage editorial vitality. Judges are asked to consider superiority of performance in terms of the magazine's editorial objectives, innovative editorial techniques, journalistic enterprise, and how each entry demonstrates the strength and importance of magazines.

Take those guidelines to heart. They'll work for you as you try to market your efforts.

Rules to Write By

The editor of *The Mother Earth News* offers would-be writers fourteen legal-sized pages of guidance, single spaced. The last of twenty-seven points says:

NOW THAT YOU KNOW DAMN NEAR EVERYTHING WE DO, *WRITE BRIGHT!* I didn't *have* to tell you to "use every possible rule of civilized *word*fare" back in (8), you know. Nor did I *have* to talk about communicating "starbursts" of feeling. And maybe I shouldn't have.

Then again, I know of no law that requires an author to limit him- or herself to the same dull, dead, gray boilerplate that most of the rest of today's "writers" deal in. Have we all turned into IBM machines? Does no one now know how to sprinkle flecks of silver and gold into his or her copy? Are all the magical wordsmiths who once used nothing but paper and ink to conjure up misty moors, melodious chimes, and shimmering sunsets in the minds of their readers . . . all . . . . gone . . . . . ?

I think not. I hope not. I prefer to believe that such crafts men and women have only temporarily been forced to hide up in the cool, green hills . . . while the brutish mutants who identify everything by social security numbers and view the world through eighteen-inch screens and who lurch back and forth across the valley floor on clangorous trail bikes and snowmobiles and converse with such depthy expressions as "wow" and "you know" have their day. A short one.

And soon, those who value the texture and the color and the emotion and the feel and the nuances of the language will once again be able to practice and strengthen their craft. And today's stainless steel computerese will once again give way to living, breathing words that soothe and cradle grown people's hearts in the mysterious and marvelous worlds that language can create.

In the meantime, the least you can do is try to brighten and focus and intensify every part of every sentence you write for The Mother Earth News. I expect nothing less.

Expect, accept no less of yourself.

And take to heart a few left-over recommendations.

1. The word "many" means many, "consisting of or amounting to a large but indefinite number," according to Webster. "Three" is not "many." "Five" is not "many." Avoid use of this overused word. Use it only when "many" really means many.

2. Be careful about words like "feel," "believe," and "think." They're

overworked as well. They're often misused, too. How sure can you be that what a source has told you is what he or she actually feels or believes or thinks? You can say, "He expressed the view," or "She said she believes," or simply "She said." Those people you talk to may be thinking one view and talking another.

3. Watch out for "pretty," "little," "rather," and "very." They can trip you up in a different way. Stylist E.B. White called them "leeches that infest the pond of prose, sucking the blood of words." His proof: "We should all try to do a little better, we should all be very watchful of this rule, for it is a rather important one and we are pretty sure to violate it now and then."

4. Use the active voice whenever possible: noun *does* something— something isn't done to the noun.

5. More from E.B. White: "When you say something, make sure you have said it. The chances of your having said it are only fair."

6. Follow the counsel in this paragraph from George Orwell's 1946 essay, "Politics and the English Language":

A scrupulous writer, in every sentence that he writes, will ask himself at least four questions, thus: What am I trying to say? What words will express it? What image or idiom will make it clearer? Is this image fresh enough to have an effect? And he will probably ask himself two more: Could I put it more shortly? Have I said anything that is unavoidably ugly?

7. Obey White's partner (and former teacher) Will Strunk, in *The Elements of Style*.

Omit needless words. Vigorous writing is concise. A sentence should contain no unnecessary words, a paragraph no unnecessary sentences, for the same reason that a drawing should have no unnecessary lines and a machine no unnecessary parts. This requires not that the writer make all his sentences short, or that he avoid all detail and treat his subjects only in outline, but that every word tell.

And show, if possible.

8. Use the present tense if you and your subject feel comfortable with it, and if you think that by using it the reader will gain a sense of closeness or timeliness. If, for instance, you want your reader to gain a sense of immediacy or involvement while sharing a narrative, then you should consider using the present tense. It's designed to suggest things happening right now. If, for another instance, you want your reader to consider those thoughts collected from the nation's political and intellectual leaders about the state of tomorrow to seem contemporary, current, then write "says" versus "said." Those leaders would probably

say today and when the article is published what they said last week or last month. So use the present tense and make your piece more timely and timeless.

9. Try to raise the energy level of your article as you work your way through it. Because readership interest tends to wane, you must build in teasers. The short story writer builds toward climax. The nonfiction writer also can use climax, even a series of climaxes or sectional revver-uppers to keep the reader reading. Your task is to keep the reader expectant, wondering, "What's next?" and enthusiastically thinking, "I can't wait to find out."

10. Percival Hunt in his perceptive volume on writing, *The Gift of the Unicorn*, admonishes us to work for reality ("to tell an action or a picture so that it is raised to an experience"), spontaneity ("making life stop . . . impressing us with a moment"), and visibility ("seeing truly" in your writing).

The writer Henry Miller said the artist is one "who has antennae, who knows how to hook up to the currents which are in the atmosphere, in the cosmos; he merely has the facility for hooking on, as it were. Who is original? Everything that we are doing, everything that we think, exists already, and we are only intermediaries, that's all, who make use of what is in the air."

For the maker of articles, it is not enough to write. An article writer is expected to think. When a student of mine submitted an article to *The Chicago Tribune Magazine* some years ago, she received with the returned manuscript a rejection letter that addresses our complicated task. The article editor wrote:

> You have written a good newspaper feature on a good, current topic. It is informative, well-written, and to the point. Unfortunately (and I don't know how else I can say this; otherwise I would certainly try to be less blunt), it isn't a magazine article—or at least not the kind of article the *Tribune Magazine* is trying to print.
>
> The problem is that it is strictly a piece of reporting which is fine for general newspaper use, but in a magazine article the reporting is raw material, the starting point. What counts is where you go from there. A good magazine article gives the reader all the facts he wants to know, and then goes beyond that and tells him what to make of them. He tells him whether this is funny or sad, amazing or merely odd, good or bad. He doesn't do this in so many words, but rather by revealing his own attitudes and reactions toward the facts in the way he describes them and the relative importance he gives them. In short, he filters the facts through his own personality and tells the reader about them much as one friend tells another about something really fascinating he has just learned—full of snide remarks and little oddities and gee-whiz. The way it is written is very important—at least as important as the facts themselves.

Could I suggest this: Why not try taking this same article and writing it again, but doing it this time as if you were writing a letter about it to someone you know very well. Even do it in letter form, if you like. Make it chatty, unself-conscious, and . . .

A very good rejection letter that is — courteous, helpful, and bulging with instructive clues about what an article is and is not. Should you get such a letter, feel honored. Editors are frantically busy people. They tend to send form rejections. If you get more than that, frame the letter and definitely take it to heart. The editor considers you as a writer with potential.

The article should go beyond facts, as I have said. Maurice Zolotow once defined the "successful article" as "a work of art like the short story — a created whole, with a beginning, a middle, and an end, with climaxes, build-ups, tension, drama expressed in dialogue, and even sentiment and feeling." Zolotow compared the article to a short story. Of the short story, National Book Award winner Wallace Stegner has written: It is a work in which "one strives to put across the feel of things — this is what persuades us and moves us. To arrange a section of life in such a way that it acts its own meanings."

We've spoken of discipline. To do what Zolotow and Stegner seek, one must have discipline. The discipline of careful and thorough research, the discipline to select and organize, the discipline to sit down and write. Discipline is at the heart of a successful article, the discipline also to stick to the subject, to make every word, every sentence fit, and to leave out those words and sentences that do not. To leave out also those ideas, those pieces of information that prove nonessential, tangential. Our attitude as writers must be one of severe critical self-analysis. We must persistently question everything we do for and to and within the article. Poet and essayist John Ciardi, who for years enriched us with wisdom in his "Manner of Speaking" column for *Saturday Review* once said, "Everything in a good piece of writing must be *chosen into it.*" The italics were his or the editor's. They are appropriate.

And as you choose in, remember your market. Ask if the material you're using will be worth reading. People do not read without wanting. They look for reward. That reward may take the form of information to help them live their lives easier or better. It may be interpretation to help them grasp the meaning of something that perplexes. It may be entertainment to relax nerves or tickle pretension or expand horizon or unburden burden. Most likely what you do will be a combination. But it better be one or more.

The reader must consider what you've done important. The reader must feel a need or want. It is not enough for you to conceive, to gather, to plan, to write. Purpose must be present all along the way. The purpose should be to satisfy a want or need of readers and to do so by presenting your subject in a fresh way. The purpose should be to heighten a reader's awareness of something in this world (or another).

Litterateur Christopher Morley once noted: "When you sell a man a book, you don't sell him just twelve ounces of paper and ink and glue. You sell him a whole new life."

That, in shorter form, is what article writers do. They impart information which — executed with style and flair and verbal excitement — opens a reader to a whole new life. Or a new dimension. Or a new possibility.

Hard. Gratifying. Worthwhile.

Permissions

Page 1. "My Father's Shirt," Sharon Olds, *The Atlantic Monthly.* Used by permission of Sharon Olds.

Page 1. "Wearing My Son's Shirt," Patricia Hooper, *The New Criterion,* March 1989. Copyright © 1989, *The New Criterion.*

Page 5. "Talk of the Town," *The New Yorker,* September 1984. Reprinted by permission; copyright © 1984 The New Yorker Magazine, Inc.

Page 8. "Some Thoughts About a Magazine's Tremendous Audience of One," *Good Housekeeping.* Copyright © 1988 The Hearst Corporation.

Page 8. "Are Cats Smart? Yes, at Being Cats," Penny Ward Moser, *Discover,* 1987. Penny Ward Moser, copyright © 1987 Discover Publications.

Page 11. "The Best Words of All," Richard Lederer, *Writer's Digest,* May 1989. Used by permission of Richard Lederer.

Page 19. "The Bed," Wyatt Prunty, *Balance As Belief.* Prunty, Wyatt. *Balance As Belief* (page 29). The John Hopkins University Press, Baltimore, London, copyright © 1989.

Page 21. "What Every Child Should Know by Age Five," Paddy Yost, *Good Housekeeping,* September 1988. Reprinted with permission from Bank Street College of Education. Paddy Yost is an Associate Dean at Bank Street College of Education in New York City.

Page 23. "Under the Influence," Scott Russell Sanders, *Harper's,* November 1989. Copyright © 1989 by *Harper's* magazine. All rights reserved. Reprinted from the November issue by special permission.

Page 23. "Contemplating Suicide," Edward Hoagland, *Harper's,* November 1989. Copyright © 1988 by Edward Hoagland. Originally appeared in *Harper's.*

Page 30. Danish nursery rhyme, N.M. Bodecker, *It's Raining Said John Twaining.* Reprinted with permission of Margaret K. McElderry Books, an imprint of Macmillan Publishing Company from *It's Raining Said John Twaining* translated by N.M. Bodecker. Copyright © 1973 by N.M. Bodecker.

Page 31. "When Darkness Fell," *Time,* August 1989. Copyright © 1989 Time Inc. Magazine Company. Reprinted by permission.

Page 32. Article regarding anniversary of WWII, *U.S. News & World Report,* August 1989. Used by permission of *U.S. News & World Report.*

Page 32. "Radio Days," John McDonough, *Travel & Leisure,* April 1989. Reprinted with permission from *Travel & Leisure,* April 1989. Copyright © 1989 American Express Publishing Corporation. All rights reserved.

Page 33. Report on global warming, *Newsweek,* July 1988. From *Newsweek,* July 11, 1988. Copyright © 1988, Newsweek, Inc. All rights reserved. Reprinted by permission.

Page 34. Environmental article, *Not Man Apart,* July/August 1986, published by Friends of the Earth. Used by permission of Friends of the Earth.

Page 34. "Endless Summer—Living with the Greenhouse Effect," Andrew C. Revkin, *Discover,* October 1988. Andrew C. Revkin, copyright © 1988 Discover Publications.

Page 35. "Rediscovering Planet Earth," *U.S. News & World Report,* October 1988. Used by permission of *U.S. News & World Report.*

Page 37. "The Global Warming Panic," Warren Brookes, *Forbes,* December

1989. Used by permission of Warren Brookes. Warren Brookes is a nationally syndicated columnist for the Detroit News.

Page 39. "Fruitcake Is Forever," Russell Baker, *The New York Times Magazine,* January 1983. Copyright © 1983 by the New York Times Company. Reprinted by permission.

Page 42. Subway article, Paul Theroux, *The New York Times Magazine,* January 1982. Copyright © 1982 by the New York Times Company. Reprinted by permission.

Page 43. "Amphibian Rights: The Frog That Insisted on Being a Frog," James Gorman, *The Sciences,* May/June 1988. Copyright © 1988 by James Gorman. First published in *The Sciences.*

Page 47. "Tehran Summer," Robin Wright, *The New Yorker,* September 1988. Reprinted by permission; copyright © 1988 Robin Wright. Originally in *The New Yorker.*

Page 48. "In Search of the Source of AIDS," Alex Shoumatoff, *Vanity Fair,* July 1988. Copyright © 1988 by Alex Shoumatoff. This article was first published in *Vanity Fair* magazine July 1988.

Page 49. "A Walk on the Wild Side," John Heminway, *Condé Nast TRAVELER,* November 1988. Used by permission of John Heminway. First published in *Condé Nast TRAVELER.*

Page 53. Interview with Dolly Parton, *Playboy,* October 1978. Excerpted from the *Playboy* Interview: Dolly Parton, *Playboy* magazine, October 1978. Copyright © 1978 by *Playboy.* Reprinted with permission.

Page 54. "Alvin Toffler Predicts—The Shape of Future Meetings," David Ghitelman, *Meetings & Conventions,* September 1988. Reprinted from *Meetings & Conventions,* September 1988. Copyright © 1988 by Reed Travel Group.

Page 57. "On the Town," *American Heritage,* November 1988. Reprinted with permission from *American Heritage* Vol. 39, No. 7. Copyright © 1988 by American Heritage.

Page 59. "Mushrooms," John Cage, *Unmuzzled Ox.* Copyright © 1979, Michael Andre for the Unmuzzled Ox Foundation, Ltd.

Page 61. "Jon Bon Jovi's U.S.S.R. Diary," *US* magazine, October 1989. Used by permission of *US* magazine.

Page 67. "Andy Rooney, 24 Hours in the Life of an Essayist," John Grossmann, *TWA Ambassador.* Used by permission of John Grossmann. John Grossmann, a freelance writer based in Jamison, PA, has written for *Esquire, The New York Times, Audubon, Smithsonian* and other national magazines.

Page 68. "Bach," Peter Jocobi, *Highlights for Children.* Used by permission of *Highlights for Children* and Peter Jacobi.

Page 70. "The Supply Side Theory of Garbage," Begley and King, *Newsweek,* November 1989. From *Newsweek,* November 1989, copyright © 1989, Newsweek, Inc. All rights reserved. Reprinted with permission.

Page 73. "Her Infinite Variety" (covering the exhibit "Making their Mark . . ."), Sue Allison, *Life,* June 1989. Sue Allison, *Life* magazine, copyright © Time Warner. Reprinted with permission.

Page 74. "Contradictions: A Decade in Documents," Peter Kornbluh, *Mother Jones,* July/August 1989. Reprinted with permission from *Mother Jones* magazine, copyright © 1979, Foundation for National Progress.

Page 75. "Taffy Apples," Phillip Grant, *Chicago Magazine,* September 1989. Used by permission of Phillip Grant.

Page 78. "Money," Richard Armour, *Yours for the Asking.* Reprinted by permission of John Hawkins and Associates and Richard Armour.

Page 202. "No News From Auschwitz," A.M. Rosenthal, *The New York Times Magazine*, August 1958. Copyright © 1958 by the New York Times Company. Reprinted by permission.
Page 203. "Aids As Human Suffering," Paul Farmer & Arthur Kleinman, *Daedalus*, Spring 1989. Reprinted by permission of *Daedalus*, Journal of the American Academy of Arts & Sciences, spring 1989, Vol. 118, No. 2.
Page 206. "Goodbye, Leaf River High School," *Prairie Farmer*, 1988. Used by permission of *Prairie Farmer*.
Page 208. "Which Way Is Heaven?" David Greenfield, *Saturday Review*. Used by permission of *Saturday Review*, OMNI Publications International.
Page 210. "Mid-Life Sax," Joseph Nocera, *Esquire*, April 1989. Used by permission of Joseph Nocera.
Page 211. "Meet Manny, One Tough G.I.," *Time*, July 1989. Copyright 1989 The Time Inc. Magazine Company. Reprinted by permission.
Page 212. "Driver's Schools — How Good?" Eric Marchese, *Heavy Duty Trucking*, October 1987. Used by permission of *Heavy Duty Trucking* magazine.
Page 218. Jesse Deer-in-Water Profile, Nancy Hanback Perreault, *Mother Jones*, January 1989. Reprinted with permission from *Mother Jones* magazine, copyright © 1989, Foundation for National Progress.
Page 219. "Coretta Scott King: The Woman Behind the King Holiday," *Ebony*, January 1990. Reprinted by permission of *Ebony* magazine, copyright © 1989 Johnson Publishing Company, Inc.
Page 220. Article regarding Ismael Pereira, Ron Arias, *People*, August 1988. Excerpted from *People* Weekly's August 1, 1988 issue article on Ismael Pereira by special permission; copyright © 1988, Time, Inc.
Page 222. "Well, Button My Lips If Dalton Stevens Hasn't Gone and Stuck 'Em on Every Ol' Thing," *People*, December 1989. *People* Weekly, copyright © 1989 The Time Inc. Magazine Company. All rights reserved.
Page 223. "Double the Pleasure," E.M. Swift, *Sports Illustrated*, January 1988. This article was reprinted courtesy of *Sports Illustrated* from the January 27, 1988 issue. Copyright © 1988, Time Inc. E.M. Swift article. All rights reserved.
Page 223. Article regarding Michael Keaton, Terry Minsky, *Premiere*, July 1989. Used with permission of Terry Minsky and *Premiere* magazine.
Page 224. "Strauss," Peter Jacobi, *Highlights for Children*, April 1986. Used by permission of *Highlights for Children* and Peter Jacobi.
Page 226. "One Heart Warms Many Chilly Fingers," David Brand, *Time*, January 1989. Copyright © 1988 Time Inc. Reprinted by permission.
Page 229. "When Brother Kills Brother," *Time*, September 1985. Copyright © 1985 Time Inc. Reprinted by permission.

Index